Organization and Change
in Complex Systems

Organization and Change in Complex Systems

Edited by
Marcelo Alonso

An ICUS Book

PARAGON HOUSE
New York

Published in the United States by

Paragon House
90 Fifth Avenue
New York, NY 10011

An International Conference on the Unity of the
Sciences Book

Library of Congress Cataloging-in-Publication Data

Organization and Change in Complex Systems.

"An ICUS book."
Includes index.
1. System theory. 2. Science—Philosophy. 3. Complex-
ity (Philosophy) 4. Chaotic behavior in systems.
I. Alonso, Marcelo, 1921-
Q295.074   1988   003   87-8943
ISBN 0-89226-054-8

Manufactured in the United States of America

This book contains the papers presented at Committee I,
ICUS XIV.

Contents

Introduction

MARCELO ALONSO
Committee Chairman

We live in a world of extraordinary diversity as exemplified by the large number of biological systems on the Earth (plants, animals, humans), as well as the physical appearance of the Earth's crust and the heavenly bodies. The world is dynamic, with some changes, such as the succession of days and nights, occurring with amazing regularity, or others, such as chemical reactions and eclipses, with precise predictability. Other changes are more difficult to predict, or seem to be more erratic, such as the weather or human behavior. And other events are most unexpected and seemingly unpredictable, such as the timing of the explosion of a supernova, the time of disintegration of a radioactive nucleus or the flight of a butterfly. The first aim of the scientific endeavor is to try to understand this diverse world, how it functions and the laws that regulate its dynamics. A second, but no less important aim is to find some unity in this diversity.

In carrying out this analysis the scientist in general defines the "system" that is the subject of study, which normally is a part of the world, itself composed of subsystems or units, in some cases identical and in other cases different, interacting among themselves. A system may be, for example, an atom, a volume of gas, a crystal, a cell, a brain, a human being, a group of humans, a galaxy or a cluster of galaxies. A system may be "open" or "closed" depending on whether or not it exchanges matter, energy and momentum with its surroundings. This exchange of energy and matter is often structured or codified and we designate it a transfer of "information." In this broad sense information exchange is not necessarily limited to "intelligent" systems. Also in this context knowledge can be considered in a more restricted way as the amount of information required for properly describing a system, a process or an event, distinguishing it from the background. (See paper by Ayres in this volume for more elaboration on this point.)

The systems with which science deals differ in the amount of information required for their description. That is, they differ in "complexity." In this respect, one might question whether or not complexity is an objective concept which is an intrinsic property of the system being analyzed; i.e., whether complexity is an observer-independent property of the system. At the other extreme we may assume that complexity arises from the interaction of the system with its observer/regulator, or in other words, complexity depends on the amount of information the observer requires about a system. As J. Casti has said, in relation to this second interpretation, "complexity, like beauty, is as much a property of the beholder as of the object being described."

For the purpose of this book it is not critical whether we accept the first interpretation of complexity, which is more akin to Cartesian thinking, or the second interpretation, which perhaps is closer to the notions of quantum theory. Another view, perhaps the more correct, is that both interpretations of complexity are complementary rather than exclusive, so that we must distinguish between *intrinsic* complexity and *perceived* complexity. In fact our perception of the complexity of a system may change as we gain more knowledge about the structure of the system, but the intrinsic complexity remains the same. This, for example, has been the case with the cell, the atom and the nucleons.

Moreover, regardless of how we define complexity, what we observe in the universe is a continuous process of change by which new systems with different forms of order or of organization appear at the expense of previous ones, or systems evolve inexorably toward new levels of order or of organization (and thus of complexity). But all these highly ordered or organized systems appear to be immersed in a sea of equally highly disordered or disorganized systems—such as, for example, a crystal surrounded by molecules of air or galaxies immersed in cosmic dust and moving through the cosmic sea of photons and intergalactic plasma and gas.

At this point it is desirable to distinguish clearly between *order* and *organization* as well as between *chaos* and *disorganization*. *Order* refers to any space or time regularity exhibited by a system. The longer the range of the correlations among the components of a system, the more extended the order of the system. Of course order does not imply homogeneity, although the two properties are not mutually exclusive. A perfect crystal lattice is a highly ordered system, which may also be homogeneous (on a macroscopic scale). A liquid may show some short range molecular order resulting from short range intermolecular forces, but it does not possess long range molecular order. Thus a liquid is a less ordered system than a crystal although in general liquids are homogeneous (also on a macroscopic scale). Obviously a gas is a good example of a disordered system (even if it is very homogeneous). *Chaos* refers to the state of a system lacking any kind of correlations among its components except, perhaps, very short range ones. Chaotic systems may or not be homogeneous. It should be made clear that when referring to chaos the lack of correlations can be expressed in terms of space, time or other parameters.

For example, consider a system continuously emitting a signal $f(t)$ that may change in amplitude or some other characteristic. Suppose we compare the values of the signal at two instants separated a fixed interval τ, i.e., we compare $f(t)$ and $f(t + \tau)$. Then we define the correlation function $C(\tau)$ as

$$C(\tau) = \frac{1}{N} \left\{ \sum_{i=1}^{N} f(t_i) f(t_i + \tau) \right\} = <f(t)f(t + \tau)>$$

Of course for $\tau = 0$, $C(0)$ is a finite positive quantity, so that in general $C(\tau) < C(0)$. If $C(\tau)$ decreases monotonically as τ increases, and eventually goes to zero, the system of signals is chaotic.

Similarly, if we measure a property of a system at two points r and $r + \rho$, separated by a fixed distance, the correlation function is

$$C(\rho) = <f(r)f(r + \rho)>$$

If the order is maintained only over very short distances, with no long range correlation over position, then $C(\rho)$ is a monotonically decreasing function and the system is chaotic with respect to that property.

Another example is the distribution or spacing of energy levels in heavy nuclei, which appears to be random with a decreasing correlation function, a situation that is designated "quantum chaos."

On the other hand, the degree of *organization* of a system is measured by the functional correlations among the parts of the system. A crystal lattice, no matter how perfect or ordered it might be, has no functional correlations and thus cannot be considered an organized system. Cells and living systems cannot be considered ordered, but they exhibit clear functional correlations and thus each one is a system with a high level of organization. If we understand functional correlations in a broad sense, i.e. that the functioning of a part or component of a system is critically related to the functioning of the other parts, we may say that an atom, although it is not ordered, has organization in the sense that there is some degree of functional correlation between the nucleus and the electrons. Perhaps the same may be said of a nucleon, composed of three quarks. An army marching toward battle is an example of a system that has both order and organization, while people at a beach on a hot sunny day constitute a system that exhibits neither order nor organization except perhaps at very short ranges, among small groups of people. In general societies of either insects or humans or any other animal species always show some degree of order and of organization. When dealing with organization versus order in systems of increasing complexity, a rather important epistemological question arises as to whether a (complex) system is more than just the sum of its parts. This question is discussed in the paper by Jammer in this volume, where the "integrative" mode of thinking is discussed in a formal way.

To complete this brief conceptual analysis of complex systems we shall examine briefly the problem of statistical equilibrium. Consider a system composed of N interacting subsystems (where N is usually very large) which may be particles, molecules or even individuals. If the macroscopic parameters that describe the system, such as pressure, volume, temperature, density, internal energy, composition, velocity distribution, etc. are well defined and essentially time-independent, we say that the system is in *thermal equilibrium* both internally and with its surroundings and no changes occur in the system on a macroscopic scale. If the system is open and, due to external actions, some of the above parameters change at a vanishingly small rate, the system goes through a "quasistatic" process of change, and at each stage of the process the system deviates very little from equilibrium, that is, it is practically in equilibrium at all times. This is what in thermodynamics is normally called a reversible transformation. According to standard thermodynamics, if a system is closed, it eventually must reach a state of thermal equilibrium regardless of the initial conditions. Once it reaches a state of thermal equilibrium the system must remain in that state until it is subject to an external perturbation, i.e., the system becomes open.

It is important to recognize that in the case of open systems thermal equilibrium does not necessarily imply homogeneity of the system, but rather a steady-state regime. For example, a liquid between two plates at temperatures T_1 and T_2 eventually reaches a state of thermal equilibrium with the surroundings in which at each small volume of the liquid all the macroscopic parameters are well defined and constant although they may vary from one part of the liquid to another.

However, standard thermodynamics is only a macroscopic approximation (very good indeed!) to the actual situation. In a system composed of N subsystems the macroscopic parameters actually exhibit relative fluctuations. Typically these fluctuations are of the order of $N^{-1/2}$. Thus if N is very large, these fluctuations are negligible and produce no observable effects. But because of these fluctuations it is more appropriate to say that the system of N components is in a state of *statistical* equilibrium. Thermal equilibrium in the sense of phenomenological thermodynamics corresponds to the limiting situation in which N is extremely (infinitely) large.

If we divide the system into small cells, j, each with N_j subsystems large enough to be described using the methods of statistical thermodynamics, then it is natural to assume that the fluctuations in the thermodynamic parameters of each cell (i.e. local fluctuations) are all of the same order of magnitude although there is not necessarily any kind of correlation between the local fluctuations in different cells. Thus each cell may also be considered to be in *local* statistical equilibrium. As long as the system is described by linear relations (i.e. the thermodynamic fluxes depend linearly on the generalized thermodynamic forces), the statistical equilibrium of the system is preserved. It is also possible that for a non-equilibrium system, the cells show *local* equilibrium, although of course the conditions from one cell to another may vary appreciably.

A different situation occurs in non-linear systems. In these, a particular local fluctuation may be magnified considerably and propagated to other parts of the system. The consequence is that the system may spontaneously evolve to one of several possible equilibrium states (a process called "bifurcation" by Prigogine and his associates), resulting in a new type of order or of organization. It is conceivable that in this way some ordered states may even emerge from chaotic states. Of course if we start with a non-linear system that is not in equilibrium, the subsequent occurrence of bifurcations is all the more important, with the possible eventual emergence of order in the system out of that chaos. Similar considerations apply if the system is subject to external perturbations.

This is not the place to elaborate in more detail on these matters which may seem contrary to intuition and to standard equilibrium thermodynamics, but hopefully what has been said should be sufficient for a basic understanding of the evolution of the universe toward the diversity of order and organization that we observe from a general chaotic initial situation. However, an important consideration from the philosophical point of view is the intrinsic difficulty of predicting the future as well as of reconstructing the past in non-linear non-equilibrium systems because of unforeseeable fluctuations.

If we examine the universe from a historical or evolutionary (and obviously "earthly") perspective from its origin at the Big Bang about 15×10^9 years ago up to the present, we witness the appearance of three levels of order and of organization. The first level corresponds to order and organization in physical systems, which occurs all over the universe. The second level corresponds to order and organization in living systems, which, at least on Earth, is a more recent occurrence, dating from about 3×10^9 years ago, and which clearly is a more localized phenomenon in the universe because of the critical physical and chemical conditions required for life to be possible. The third level corresponds to social order and organization in living systems which is an even more local phenomenon that is characteristic of animals and that has reached an exceptional level of sophistication in human societies.

Was the Big Bang a highly chaotic far-from-equilibrium initial state of the universe or was it a strong local fluctuation in an otherwise chaotic state that, because of strong non-linearities, resulted in an extraordinary cosmic event? Most probably we shall never be able to find an answer to that question, because of, among other things, our total ignorance of the pre-Big Bang (or Before-the-Big-Bang, BBB) state of the system, or because perhaps the Big Bang is in itself the origin of spacetime. However, it has been possible to trace back with relative certitude the general trend of events that followed the Big Bang from about 10^{-11}s up to the present (10^{17}s). The story during the period from 10^{-44}s (the Planck time) up to 10^{-11}s is much more speculative. In particular it appears that at about 10^{-33}s a critical inflationary process (which might have been another fluctuation) took place which changed the size of the universe by a factor of about 10^{25} to 10^{50} resulting in a new state essentially independent of the initial conditions at the Big Bang. Since that time the evolution of the universe has been governed by two important factors: one is the matter-energy relation and the other is the universal expansion.

As the universe expanded the average energy of the particles rapidly decreased from about 10^{19}GeV (or 10^{32}K) at 10^{-44}s to 10^2GeV (or 10^{15}K) at 10^{-11}s, and to about 1 eV (10^3K) at 10^{13}s. Currently (10^{17}s) the background energy per particle of the photon sea in the universe is around 3×10^{-4} eV (or 2.7K). Using a terminology borrowed from thermodynamics we may say that as the universe expanded it cooled down. It is well known that as a gas is cooled it reaches a temperature (molecular energy), which depends on the external pressure, at which it suffers a transition into the liquid phase, and if it is cooled further a new phase transition occurs and the liquid becomes a solid. At even lower temperatures several solid phases may appear. For each substance these phase transitions depend on the strength and other features of the intermolecular forces. But one thing is obvious: the cooling (or de-energizing) process results in the appearance of structures exhibiting higher order and complexity and lower symmetry.

A similar sequence of phase transitions seems to have occurred in the universe as it expanded (and cooled down), except that to understand the process one must recognize that in quantum field theory the interactions between fermions are described as exchanges of bosons (X-bosons, gluons, $W^{\pm}$, Z^0, and photons). Thus the successive "phase transitions" occurred as the energy or temperature of the expanding universe passed through several critical values corresponding roughly to the masses of the bosons responsible for the different interactions (strong, weak, electromagnetic and maybe also gravitational). The higher the energy of the particles the less relevant their mass-energy and the smaller the difference between the different types of particles and their interactions, so that at extremely high energies all interactions are dynamically unified into one, and kinematically all particles appear essentially massless, resulting in what is called the "grand unification."

The first phase transition occurred perhaps during the inflationary process at 10^{-33}s, when the energy rapidly dropped to 10^{15}GeV (or 10^{28}K); at that energy the X-particles, the most massive of the bosons, disappeared because they either disintegrated or were captured in other processes and the collision energy of fermions was not sufficient to recreate them. At that stage the strong interaction became differentiated from the electroweak interaction. The next phase transition occurred at about 10^{-11}s when the particle energy was on the order of 10^2GeV (or 10^{15}K) at which the weak bosons $W^{\pm}$ and Z^0, whose mass-energy is of that order, disappeared as independent particles and a new symmetry-breaking took place with the weak interaction becoming distinct from the electromagnetic interaction. This can be explained by the fact that the electromagnetic bosons, the photons, have zero mass.

The world at that moment became a mixture of quarks, gluons, leptons and photons. Hitherto no ordered structures had appeared although the conditions for the eventual emergence of large structures, such as galaxies, were probably already present. The first ordering event in the universe, that essentially determined its future evolution, occurred between 10^{-6}s and 10^{-3}s when the particle energy reached 1 GeV (10^{13}K) and quarks and antiquarks were annihilated; concurrently the remaining quarks and gluons were frozen into hadrons (nucleons and mesons). From then on the pace of evolution of the universe slowed down appreciably under the influence of the residual strong interaction (nuclear force) and the electromagnetic interaction. Thus at about 10^2s or 10^5eV (10^9K) nucleogenesis began to occur with the formation of deuterons ($^2_1$H) and helions ($^4_2$He). Only much later, between 10^4s and 10^{13}s did atoms begin to appear, when the electromagnetic interaction was able to hold the electrons around nuclei without being disrupted through collisions. Since 10^{13}s (or 10^6 years) after the Big Bang the universe has not changed appreciably except for the emergence of large structures under the influence of the gravitational force: stars, galaxies, clusters and superclusters, though we are not sure of the order of their appearance. Although the background 3K radiation is very homogeneous and isotropic, the universe is presently neither totally homogeneous nor in thermal equilibrium, and there are strong variations in the particle energies from one region to another with a variety of processes, including nucleogenesis, depending on local conditions. However, one point that should be mentioned is that unless the average mass density in the universe is larger that about 10^{-29}g/cm^3, which would imply a future contraction of the universe and perhaps an eventual return to the conditions at the Big Bang (i.e. a Big Crunch), the evolutionary processes in the universe are irreversible although not totally predictable because of the effect of unforeseeable fluctuations and bifurcations.

The processes that have been described summarily are analyzed in detail in the papers by Sexl, Bekenstein and Fritzsch which appear in this volume. We may safely state that the appearance of order and organization in the physical universe as a result of the expansion and of the matter-energy relations is relatively well understood and that since 10^6 years after the Big Bang, when large structures emerged, no major fundamental change has taken place, or is expected to take place in the future, except for processes affecting large structures, such as collisions among and merging of galaxies.

A new level of order or organization appeared on the Earth about 3×10^9 years ago (or about 10^9 years after the Earth was formed): organized self-replicating systems, i.e., the first living organisms. It should be noted that the environmental conditions that allowed the formation of the basic biomolecules, i.e. a reducing atmosphere, were quite different from those needed for the flourishing of living systems, i.e. an oxidizing atmosphere. Living organisms on Earth increased in complexity and proliferated in an explosive way about 6×10^8 years ago. The development of higher forms of life such as mammals is a still more recent event, perhaps 10^8 years ago or less. The emergence of life on Earth poses several challenges. Can the origin and development of living systems be explained in terms of the physical laws? Was the emergence of the kind of organization associated with life an inevitable event? What kind of chemical precursors were needed for the emergence of life? Does life exist in other parts of the universe?

Living systems are extremely complex and far from equilibrium, but are in a steady dynamical state, with delicate organizations, and open in terms of matter and energy exchanges. On the other hand living systems are made of ordinary matter and therefore all the processes in these systems obey the physical laws. But they depend very critically on certain complex molecules, called *biomolecules* such as proteins, enzymes and nucleic acids, which are composed of a few elements, mostly hydrogen, carbon, oxygen, nitrogen and phosphorus. Nothing precludes, in principle, synthesizing the molecules of life in the laboratory, but that is not enough to make a living system. Life is more than matter; it requires a delicate functional organization characterized by four main features:

1. Metabolism (energy and matter processing)
2. Reproduction (propagation and genetic code)
3. Mutability (change in the genetic code)
4. Teleonomy (structured information transfer)

The evolution of organization in living systems must have begun with the formation of molecules of increasing complexity, where polymerization of rather simple molecules was an early step, given proper environmental conditions. Once molecules of amino acids and proteins were sufficiently abundant, the next giant step was the development of a genetic program or *genome,* composed of nucleic acids, specifically DNA. Although the genome is in this instance the structure responsible for the characteristics of living systems, the genome may also change or evolve, increasing its complexity and thus giving rise to new forms of life. Here one must recognize the importance of the time factor, 10^9 years, necessary to account for the development of this natural evolutionary process on Earth, and perhaps elsewhere in the Universe. (According to C. Ponnamperuna the formation and linking of life's building blocks—aminoacids and nucleotides—may have been all but inevitable, given the starting chemistry of earth's primordial soup. The conclusion is that wherever in the universe the conditions for the formation of such biomolecules exist, the probability of the emergence of living systems is very high. Some of these molecules have been observed recently in meteorites and in the tails of comets, suggesting that the genetic code as we see it operating on Earth may be repeated elsewhere in the universe wherever conditions are appropriate.)

The next step toward organization and complexity was the appearance of cells, i.e. well-structured biological units with new well-defined functions, including replication, in which the genome constitutes the central functional part. (However, it appears that some primitive unicellular systems probably did not need the genome at all.) The final step was that of cell differentiation and their functional association forming even more complex organisms (plants, animals, etc.). But still, the key issue goes back to the coding of genetic information in some particular types of molecules. Although atoms in biomolecules are held together by electromagnetic forces in accordance with the rules of quantum mechanics, as are atoms in other molecules, we still face formidable difficulties in understanding how these molecules are programmed to make a genome, a cell or a multicellular organism. The aspects related to organization and change in complex living systems are examined in the papers by Atalay, Pincheira and Villee in this volume.

In the process of biological evolution toward forms of increasing complexity, there is perhaps one structure that has evolved more than any other: the *brain.* The brain is an extremely complex system which functions as an organizing center for the rest of the body as well as an autoanalytical instrument, which, as part of the nervous system, receives, processes, stores and distributes information. The brain may even generate information. A particular feature of the human brain is that it is superbly adapted for handling digital information. Although we may assume that the brain is the seat of consciousness and volition and the organ through which we perceive eternal reality, it must not be confused with the *mind,* defined as the intellectual power of humans, or the non-material universe of mental phenomena (perception, feelings, abstract reasoning, judgement, etc.). This boils down to the correlation between the physical mechanisms for handling information by the brain, and the assignment of meaning to that information, which is a mental or intellectual process. In fact, *intelligence* may be defined as the ability of a dissipative system to handle information. This issue is very relevant to the subject of organization and change in complex systems, since it is the mind that perceives the different kinds of organization and levels of complexity in the world (reality). For an analysis of this not yet fully understood problem, the reader is referred to the paper by Löwenhard.

A third level of complexity that we recognize in the world is that of social structures as we know them on Earth. Social systems exhibit both order and organization, although the level of each varies with animal species, being specially developed in certain species of insects and primates, and having reached an especially high level of sophistication in humans. If we compare social systems to physical systems, we may recognize that social systems are open dissipative systems far from equilibrium and exhibiting a self-organizing behavior. Most probably, social systems are characterized by non-linear relations among its factors with an appreciable amount of feedback.

To simplify the language, in the context of social systems we shall use the terms order and organization interchangeably, distinguishing between them only when necessary. The subsystems or components in social systems are individuals, usually of the same species, which interact (i.e. exchange information) among themselves and with the environment through electromagnetic (visual), mechanical (acoustical, tactile) and chemical (olfactory) agents, which produce different types of information, to which the common genetic code of the individuals generate similar responses, which we designate as *instinctive* behavior. Human societies are particularly interesting because in addition to the natural genetic response to physical agents, humans have developed means of establishing new levels of order beyond those spontaneously adopted because of genetic conditioning.

One of the key factors that have allowed humans to develop higher levels of order is the ability to exchange information in the codified form of both oral and written language, coupled of course with the ability for abstract thinking, i.e. the ability of the brain to handle abstract forms of codified information (hypotheses, theories, criteria, points of view, etc.). Without language, civilization would probably not exist, at least in the way we know it. With the emergence of language, which opened a broader range of possibility for learning and passing knowledge from one generation to another, the tempo of cultural and intellectual evolution became much faster than that of biological evolution.

In dealing with order and organization in human societies one has to distinguish two different kinds: social and economic. In the evolution of both types of order, a prime factor has been the human ability to generate new knowledge and apply it to produce a variety of materials and processes that do not occur naturally (agriculture, manufacture, transportation, communication, health, etc.). These are activities we designate generically as science and technology. It is through science and technology, a strictly human activity, that it has been possible to continuously develop new, highly sophisticated forms of social and economic order in human societies, forms that do not exist in any other type of social system. One interesting question, posed by Friedrich von Hayek, is whether or not humans have consciously controlled the evolution of their social and economic order. It is Hayek's position that man never consciously devised civilization (or social organization), but it was the understanding of "spontaneous order" that ultimately opened the road of cultural evolution. However the final answer to this question requires a deep historical analysis of how social and economic order has evolved since the emergence of the human species and the factors that have affected this evolution. But until the present, at least, human societies have certainly not been able to foresee or predict their development and future organization. In addition, since social systems are not linear, certain local fluctuations (inventions, discoveries, revolutions, wars, emergence of political leaders, etc.) may result in major changes; we cannot, in principle predict future knowledge–induced changes, since that would mean that we already possessed that knowledge now.

These factors related to the evolution of social and economic order and the role of science and technology (knowledge) in human societies are discussed in the papers by Ayres and Radnitzky and in the comments by Petroni and Georgescu-Roegen.

Although the problem of organization and change in complex systems is far from having been settled, the collection of papers and notes in this volume provides new insights and one hopes, may contribute to an integrated approach to the subject.

I

ORGANIZATION AND COMPLEXITY IN PHYSICAL SYSTEMS

1

Gravitation and the Origin of Large Structures in the Universe

JACOB D. BEKENSTEIN

1. THE EXPANDING UNIVERSE

The why of structure and organization in the physical world has always fascinated mankind. Only in this century was enough understood about the quantum world to allow an explanation of organization in everyday objects: the order in a salt crystal, the precisely architectured shape of a benzene molecule, etc. The organization shown by heavenly bodies also prompted early speculation on how matter has been segregated and organized into stars. Here the long-range force of gravity, not electromagnetism and quantum mechanics, is responsible. And who else but Isaac Newton should have been the first to put forth the idea that gravity has, over the eons, gathered matter, originally spread out homogeneously, into clumps which we see as stars (Koyre 1958). Newton was essentially right, but the actual situation is far more complicated than he envisaged. Complete understanding of the organization apparent in the astronomical world still eludes us.

The first point to make is that the structure has arisen in an expanding universe, a fact unknown to Newton. This has many consequences for our understanding of the process. Around the turn of the century the British physicist Sir James Jeans developed in detail the mathematical theory of the process Newton had described two centuries earlier (Jeans 1902, 1929). He showed that Newton's hunch was right, and that even when account is taken of the pressure exerted by the medium pervading the universe, condensations will still form. The only proviso is that the condensations involve a minimum mass (today we speak of the Jeans mass). In Jeans' scenario the initial medium must contain "seed" inhomogeneities or irregularities in order for condensations to appear at all. However, the amplification of the density contrast of an inhomogeneity relative to its surroundings (we shall speak of growth in its strength henceforth) is exponential in time, so that even weak seeds are effective. We know that in any seemingly homogeneous medium there must be some seeds, if only because of the particulate nature of matter and statistical fluctuations. Thus, if Jeans' study were the whole story, the problem of formation of structure in the cosmos would have been solved long ago.

The realization that our universe expands, first expressed by the great American astronomer Edwin Hubble (Hubble 1929), immeasurably complicated matters. A theory of the expansion became possible in terms of the theory of General Relativity that was completed by Albert Einstein in 1915 (Einstein 1916). Einstein applied his theory to cosmology very early (Einstein 1917), and it is well known that, committed as he was philosophically to viewing the universe as unchanging, he missed the chance to *predict* the expansion of the universe. This honor was claimed by the Russian mathematician Alexander Friedmann, who invented the cosmological models used today as a basis for the description of the universe's evolution (see the contribution by Fritzsch in this volume).

Friedmann's models, which are based on General Relativity, indicate that the universe began in a state of virtually infinite density, and afterwards expanded by a very large factor. One can speak of the universe when it was a thousandth, or even a billionth of its present size. The availability of General Relativity led the Russian physicist Evgenii Lifshitz to reconsider Jeans' calculation in the framework of Friedmann's models. He found that inhomogeneities still grow in strength, but no longer exponentially in time (Lifshitz 1946). In effect, the expansion fights tooth and nail against gravity, and almost succeeds in neutralizing the Newton-Jeans growth. Lifshitz established (and this has been confirmed time and again by many others) that the strength of inhomogeneities grows in direct proportion to the size of the universe. For example, to achieve a thousandfold amplification, a seed must have developed during a thousandfold expansion of the universe.

So what? Let us assume the seeds were present at an early enough stage in the universe, so that by now enough expansion has taken place to amplify them into strong inhomogeneities. Actually, such a scenario would be acceptable if the universe contained only matter. But the universe is also full of radiation—not only electromagnetic radiation (photons), but also neutrino and gravitational radiations. An important role in our considerations is played by the famous microwave radiation background. It was first observed in 1965 by Arno Penzias and Robert Wilson (Penzias and Wilson 1965) a feat which won them the 1978 Nobel Prize in

Physics (for a fuller account refer to Sexl's paper in this volume). This radiation changes the terms of our problem entirely.

Virtually all scientists agree that the background is radiation that severed contact with the emitting matter long ago, when the universe was much smaller than today (1000 times smaller is a good guess). Now we trace backwards the expansion of the universe. The matter in it becomes denser in inverse proportion to the cube of the universe's size. Not so the radiation; its energy density grows faster because photons gain energy as their wavelength shrinks with the universe. We need not go back very far in this imaginary odyssey before the density of energy in radiation overwhelms that of matter. The picture is now of a universe dominated in its early dynamics by radiation.

Now when Lifshitz's calculation is redone in the radiation-dominated universe, it predicts *no* growth of inhomogeneities. Growth sets in only late in history when matter begins to dominate the dynamics. The earliest this can have happened is when the universe was about 10,000 times smaller than it is at present. Thus seeds can have been magnified by at most a factor of 10,000. In view of this limitation, could the structure seen now have grown from purely statistical fluctuations? No. For galaxies and clusters of galaxies exhibit density contrasts (fraction by which density is different) with respect to their surroundings which exceed unity. Hence the "seeds" from which they arose must have had density contrasts no smaller than 10^{-4}. But by the square root law of fluctuations, only an aggregation of 10^8 particles or fewer is expected to show a fluctuation in density at the 10^{-4} level. But masses of material out of which a star or galaxy could come involve numbers of particles many orders of magnitude larger, with correspondingly smaller fluctuations. Statistical seeds cannot have given rise to stars, or any larger objects, in the expanding universe!

The conclusion must be that early in the universe's expansion, when radiation still held sway, there must already have been seed inhomogeneities much stronger than statistical inhomogeneities. This is how cosmologists today look at the origin of structure in the universe. This viewpoint leaves much to be desired because it relies on "initial conditions" to explain organization. Yet, as a pragmatical philosophy it has proved fruitful, and of late a rationalization for it has emerged from the so-called "inflationary" cosmological model which will be described briefly in Section 5.

2. THE REALM OF THE GALAXIES

Having mentioned the difficulty facing Newton's conjecture about the origin of organization because of the expansion of the universe, let us turn

Figure 1-1. NGC 2903, some 15 million light years distant from us, is a disk galaxy with well-developed spiral structure. Reproduced with permission from a plate exposed by Dr. A. Meisels with the 1-meter telescope of the Wise Observatory, Israel.

and ask what does the universe look like at present. As late as the 1920's it was accepted that stars are the basic building blocks in the heavens. In fact, when Einstein invented relativistic cosmology, he always imagined a universe of homogeneously distributed stars. With Hubble's demonstration (Hubble 1926) that the spiral "nebulae" are distant analogues of our own stellar system, the Milky Way galaxy, it became evident that galaxies are the basic units in the universe. Stars may be linked to cells of an organism (galaxy). The analogy just drawn is not an idle one. Multiple lines of evidence suggest that stars in a galaxy were formed after their mother galaxy had become a separate entity in the medium pervading the universe. And just as cells in an organism die and are replaced, so stars in a galaxy may die (witness the supernova), and stars are born continuously in a large fraction of the galaxies. So if galaxies are the units in the universe, we are faced with two questions: What do the inner structures of galaxies look like, and how did they arise? How are galaxies organized in the universe?

Let us take up the first question in this section. Just as the organisms, galaxies are of many species and genera. To avoid getting lost in the

Figure 1-2. M 94, a spiral galaxy dominated by its spheroidal component, is a member of the nearby Canes Venatici I cloud of galaxies. From a plate by the author exposed at Wise Observatory.

"taxonomy" of galaxies (also originally due to Hubble), let it be said at the outset that the majority of galaxies are composed of a roundish component, the spheroid, and a disk rotating about the center of the spheroidal component. In *spiral* galaxies such as our own (see Figures 1-1, 1-2, 1-3, 1-4), this division is very appropriate, though here and there there are spirals whose visible spheroid is minute. *Elliptical* galaxies are almost purely spheroidal (though there are a number of ellipticals sporting small disks in their central regions). And a small percentage of galaxies are *irregular* with no easily defined shape (see Figure 1-4), and do not fit easily into the spheroid-disk paradigm. By contrast the large group of *lenticular* galaxies have clear spheroid-disk morphology though lacking spiral structure entirely.

What forces shaped most galaxies according to the spheroid-disk motif? The prevailing view among astrophysicists might be summarized thus: As in Newton's original proposal, the gas filling the universe began to grow condensations under the action of gravity, and the condensations then collapsed upon themselves. These were *protogalaxies*, and they must have been roughly spherical. As the gas collapsed, it lost energy to radia-

Figure 1-3. M 65 (upper) and NGC 3627 are two spiral members of the small M 66 group of galaxies. Note the extensive spheroidal component of M 65 and the disturbed shape of NGC 3627. Reproduced from a Wise Observatory plate by Dr. A. Meisels with his permission.

tion and thereby cooled. Since the Jeans mass decreases with decreasing temperature, it would have dropped rapidly. Then parts of the original protogalaxy found themselves, in terms of mass, below the Jeans mass. The protogalaxy would then tend to fragment into several lumps. This process may have repeated until lumps with starlike masses appeared, and stars formed. All this must have been accomplished as the collapse went on. The fresh stars, once formed, would move only under the influence of gravity and, in effect, would form a "gas" of stars. And just as a gas fully fills the receptacle confining it, so would the stars fill the entire volume

Figure 1-4. NGC 4657 (lower left corner), an example of an irregular galaxy, and NGC 4631 (center), a spiral galaxy seen edge-on, are members of the Canes Venatici II cloud of galaxies. Also visible is NGC 4627, a small satellite elliptical galaxy, as a small roundish smudge just above NGC 4631. The streak through the photograph is the trail of a meteor that traversed the telescope field in the course of the 3-hour exposure of the plate by Dr. O. Lahav at Wise Observatory. Reproduced with his permission.

occupied by the protogalaxy when star formation began. Thus was the spheroid formed.

No process is perfectly efficient: some of the protogalaxy's gas must have escaped condensation into stars, and continued to collapse. It stands to reason that the protogalaxy had some angular momentum. At least one mechanism, tidal interaction, is known which could have given angular momentum to the protogalaxies before they separated much (Peebles 1980). The leftover gas would have some of this angular momentum, and would thus be prevented from falling to the center of the spheroid. Instead, it would have settled into a flattened rotating disk in the plane perpendicular to the angular momentum vector. In the disk, the gas cooled by radiation, and must also have started to form stars, though in a protracted manner. In this way, disks were formed.

Why are some galaxies (ellipticals) nearly all spheroid and no disk? The prevalent opinion is that their low angular momentum promoted very efficient star formation during protogalaxy collapse, so that no gas was left for the disk. By contrast a high angular momentum would have prevented the radial collapse, resulting in collapse to a disk instead. In this manner one can understand the nearly pure disk spiral galaxies.

We now turn to the question of spiral structure, surely the most aesthetically pleasing feature in galaxies. How does this highly organized structure arise? The first point to make is that spiral arms in galaxies are delineated by young stars and regions of gas; old stars are not found there. This immediately suggests that the spirals are not material structures, but rather some sort of wave. Were they material spirals, they would disappear soon since stars cannot remain young forever, and new stars cannot be formed at the high rate required to keep the bulk of the stellar population in the spiral arms young over billions of years. Furthermore, any material structure inscribed on a rotating galaxy disk could not last long. All galactic disks rotate differentially, that is, the angular velocity steadily decreases with distance from the center, at least outside the very central regions. This uneven rotation would wind up material arms and erase them over a period of some 10^8 years. Galaxies are suspected to be some 10^{10} years old, so spiral structure would be a rare occurrence if the spirals were material. This is belied by the facts: a major portion of disk galaxies have spiral structure.

The suggestion that the spirals are traveling waves first came from the Swedish astronomer Bertil Lindblad (Lindblad 1927). An elaborate theory of "spiral density waves" was worked out only much later by Chia Chiao Lin and Frank Shu (Lin and Shu 1964). The basic idea of this well-developed theory is that a galactic disk made of stars and gas can serve as a propagation medium for spiral shaped waves which circulate around it rigidly (in contrast to the stars and gas which orbit around it differentially) at a steady angular velocity. The waves are density waves in the sense that gas swept up by them is compressed, and by Jeans' mechanism gives birth to stars. The newborn stars delineate the spiral. As they age, they are left behind and the wave induces new star formation to replace them. All this is very much like a conflagration sweeping through a dry forest. A distant observer, upon seeing the line of fire advancing through it, might regard it as some travelling material structure. In fact what advances is the front between the charred trees and the yet untouched ones. In a galaxy the spiral arms separate a region in which star "ignition" has just ended from one in which much gas awaits the chance to be turned into stars.

A striking confirmation of the theory is provided by the lenticular galaxies which are disk-spheroid galaxies with no spiral structure whatsoever. Optical and radiowave studies have verified that the disks of lenticulars are devoid of gas. Either early star formation was vigorous and consumed all the gas that fell onto the disk, or some catastrophe, like a near collision with a neighbor galaxy, has swept the gas out. At any rate, since there is no gas to make stars, no "conflagration" can propagate, and the spiral structure cannot express itself.

The mathematical theory of spiral waves (Toomre 1977) makes it clear that the waves propagate as a result of the interplay of gravitation, pressure and rotation in the disk. Without gravity there would be no spiral waves, just as without gravity no waves could propagate on the surface of a pond. Although the spiral wave theory has had successes, it is still unable to give an account of the *origin* of the waves. Propagation of the spirals, once formed, is understood; the mechanism that triggers them is not. Of the various triggers suggested (a quickly rotating central bar in the galaxy and perturbation from another galaxy are two examples), none seems to be universal.

Although we have stressed the galactic level of structure, it is well to point out that the stellar component of galaxies is not amorphous when examined at small scales. Stars are grouped into doubles, triplets and associations. And there are clusters of stars with populations ranging from hundreds to hundreds of thousands. There is, however, evidence that clusters and associations can disperse, so that the organization just mentioned may be ephemeral (Fall and Rees 1977). So we now turn our attention from galaxy interiors outward.

3. THE FABRIC OF THE UNIVERSE

We now turn to the second question raised in the last section: how are galaxies organized in the universe? The early impression of astronomers was of a rather homogeneous distribution of galaxies over the sky if allowance was made for obscuration associated with the Milky Way itself. Out of this impression arose the *Cosmological Principle* which states that, on a very large scale, matter in the universe is distributed homogeneously. Of course on smaller scales matter is distributed irregularly. One of the key questions of cosmology is where to draw the line between these two regimes.

By the 1930's it was known that some galaxies appear in pairs, and that there are small groups as well as large clusters of galaxies. One of the large clusters, the Coma Cluster, played an important role in the early discovery by Fritz Zwicky, an American astronomer of Swiss origin, of a discrepancy between the mass seen in extragalactic systems, and the mass that should be there on dynamical grounds (Zwicky 1933). With the completion of the Palomar Observatory photographic survey of the sky in the 1950's, it became crystal clear that clusters, far from being an occasional feature, are quite prevalent in the universe.

Much speculation attended the question of whether the hierarchy of clumping continues to higher levels: clusters of clusters, etc. In particular, one should mention Gerard de Vaucouleurs' farsighted belief (de Vaucouleurs 1953) that our own group of galaxies, the Local Group, is part of a large *supercluster* which also includes the populous Virgo Cluster at a distance of some 30 million light years. The concept of superclusters was not very popular in the 1960's and early 1970's. A well known cosmology text of that period, citing the giants of astronomy, claims ". . . the hierarchy stops at clusters of galaxies or at most at clusters of clusters of galaxies, and shows no evidence of inhomogeneities of larger scale . . ." (Weinberg 1972).

The tide started turning in the mid-1970's. At that time James Peebles at Princeton analyzed systematically the correlation of positions of galaxies as seen in the sky and came to the conclusion that even loose galaxies are not sprinkled over the heavens at random (Peebles 1980). Rather, there is a clear tendency for galaxies to "hang together" even if the eye does not reveal a well-defined group. The correlation function, which expresses this finding quantitatively, has by now become one of the basic tools for understanding organization in the universe, and is also regarded as a rich source of information about the early universe. The correlation function approach shows that there is more organization among galaxies than meets the eye. But it does not reveal the full fabric of the universe because it is based on a two-dimensional map of galaxies.

Up to the mid-1970's positions of galaxies projected on the heavenly sphere could easily be determined, but distances could be established moderately accurately only for a small minority. At that time the development of "mass production" techniques for measuring distances to galaxies via the redshift shown by their spectra allowed astronomers to compose an extensive three-dimensional map of the universe (Huchra *et al.* 1983). Two great surprises followed. First, it was found that galaxies and clusters tend to fall on chain-like or sheet-like structures. These were named superclusters (Oort 1983). Thus was de Vaucouleurs' insight verified and extended. To the best of present knowledge, superclusters are the largest structures in the universe. Many stretch out over distances of tens of millions of light years and encompass tens of thousands of galaxies. The superclusters form a veritable maze in space, making up the filaments of the cosmic fabric. The second discovery was that in between superclusters, space is virtually empty: very few galaxies have been detected in these voids. The largest known void (Kirshner *et. al.* 1981) spans nearly 300 million light years of galaxy-free space (although it must be pointed out that the presence of significant amounts of gas in the voids has not been ruled out).

This, then, is the fabric of the universe. How was it formed? The first question that must be confronted is a modern version of the proverbial query: which came first, the chicken or the egg? Did galaxies form first and then clump to form clusters which then grouped into superclusters, or did superclusters form first and then fragment into clusters which themselves went on to fragment into galaxies? Both schemes can be based on the Newton-Jeans process. The distinction between them must arise from the scale of the important inhomogeneities in the matter filling the universe in primordial times. If the salient inhomogeneities involved masses of the order of a galaxy's, it is a good guess that galaxies formed first and then clumped in response to their mutual attraction. If, by contrast, the significant inhomogeneities involved masses equivalent to tens'of thousands of galaxies, it would be a safe guess that superclusters emerged first and galaxies were born from them by repeated fragmentation.

No consensus has been reached yet by cosmologists discussing these possibilities. Two cosmological scenarios contend today for primacy in explaining the large scale organization of the universe. First we have the so called *hierarchical scenario* espoused by Peebles and many of his colleagues (Peebles 1980, Gott and Rees 1975). It assumes that the primeval inhomogeneities were matter density inhomogeneities in which small scales were most salient, and large scales less so, but with a smooth transition in strength from scale to scale (technically the density contrast is proportional to some inverse power of the scale). Under such conditions galaxies would form first from the small-scale inhomogeneities, and would then begin to cluster under the influence of the weaker but larger-scale inhomogeneities. It is even possible in this scenario that galaxies were not the first structures to form, but rather objects with masses similar to today's globular star clusters, which then went on to cluster into galaxies (Fall and Rees 1977).

The rival scenario is the *pancake scenario* espoused by the late prominent Soviet physicist Yakov Zel'dovich and his colleagues (Zel'dovich 1972, Doroshkevich, Sunyaev and Zel'dovich 1974). The pancake scenario (the rationale for the name will be made clear below) assumes that the primeval inhomogeneities were *joint* matter and radiation irregularities (remember that early on, radiation was more intense than today). Small-scale inhomogeneities of this type were susceptible to erasure during the epoch, some 3×10^5 years after the expansion began, in which radiation stopped interacting directly with matter as a result of the recombination of ions and electrons into atoms. Calculations first carried out by Joseph Silk (Silk 1968) showed that inhomogeneities involving masses less than some 10^{15} solar masses will not survive past the recombination epoch. Therefore, in this scenario the first structures to form have masses comparable to those of superclusters (thousands of galactic masses). Clusters and galaxies appear later by repeated fragmentation.

How do these scenarios fare when confronted with the evidence? One check of the hierarchical scenario is possible by numerical simulations in large computers which follow the motion of a large assemblage of particles (galaxies or smaller entities) subject to Newtonian gravitation and in a steadily expanding background. Numerous "N-body simulations" of this type have been carried out, and the general impression is that the combination of expansion and gravitational attraction is indeed responsible for the tendency of galaxies to form stable clumps as observed. The specific form of the correlation function found by Peebles from the data is also explained (Gott 1979). Some of the simulations even show voids, but the observed maze-like organization of the superclusters is hard to explain.

Unlike the previous approach which studies the motion of discrete particles, any simulation relevant to the pancake scenario has to take into account that the matter about to form a supercluster is still gaseous (no stars or galaxies exist yet, by definition). The dynamics is thus complicated by fluid-dynamic effects. These, together with the universal expansion, make it natural for the incipient supercluster to collapse, not spherically, but to a highly flattened structure—a colossal pancake. A shock, followed by cooling of the gas due to radiation ensues; both facilitate the fragmentation of the pancake into future clusters and galaxies. Neighboring pancakes may intersect, and the dense loci of crossing are especially susceptible to fragmentation. Thus chains of galaxies and voids between them have a natural place in the pancake scenario.

However, the pancake scenario has also had setbacks. Observational constraints on the strength of primeval matter-radiation inhomogeneities (see Section 4) have forced theorists to modify the scenario by supposing that the "matter" the scenario deals with is mostly not ordinary elements, but rather a species of neutrinos endowed with a small rest mass. (Neutrinos have been usually regarded as massless; however, modern theories of elementary particles allow the neutrino to have mass, and some experimental evidence for it has been claimed.) This hypothesis allows the constraints to be sidestepped neatly. But the modified scenario has lately been shown to be incapable of explaining the precise form of the galaxy correlation function (White *et al.* 1984).

Elementary particles also play a role in a new version of the hierarchical scenario which, unlike the original version, seems quite successful in explaining the filamentary nature of the large structures. This "cold matter" picture calls for matter made up mostly of some massive elementary particle which has yet to be detected in the laboratory. One candidate is the elusive axion. It is too early to pass a final verdict on this approach, except to point out that it is typical of the current trend that weaves the physics of elementary particles and cosmology into a common cloth.

We may also mention Ostriker's maverick *explosion scenario* (Ostriker and Cowie 1981, Schwarz, Ostriker and Yahil 1975). It holds that the origin of the large linear structures is in the intersection of expanding shells propelled by violent explosions of a class of primordial supermassive objects. It is a sobering thought that detonations akin to the supernovae that end the lives of massive stars may be responsible for the birth of the superclusters of galaxies.

4. LOOKING INTO THE PAST

Observations of very distant objects in the universe are tantamount to use of a time machine that takes us back to the time when the light was just leaving those objects. Can such a look back to the era of galaxy formation tell us whether galaxies or superclusters came first? Can it help us verify that there were really inhomogeneities long before galaxies or superclusters became evident?

To answer the first question one would like to detect both galaxies and superclusters at very large distances to tell which kind of object is seen earlier on. The measure of distance is, as we mentioned, the redshift displayed by the object's spectrum. Redshift is defined as the fractional excess of the wavelengths of the spectral lines over their laboratory values. (Accordingly the redshift is given by $z = \Delta\lambda/\lambda$. Using the expression for the Doppler effect and Hubble's law it is possible to relate the redshift to the distance and thus to the time of emission [NE].) The mathematics of Friedmann's models are such that the observed redshift plus one equals the factor by which the universe has expanded since the light being studied was emitted.

Present earthbound instruments are only able to see isolated galaxies out to a redshift of about unity (meaning that one sees them some six billion years in the past when the universe was half of today's size). There is wide agreement that this is not reaching deep enough into the past to allow us to tell directly whether galaxies came first. Doubtlessly, with the projected launch in 1989 of the Hubble Space Telescope by NASA, the prospects for this approach will improve.

Even from Earth's surface progress may be made by other avenues. Quasars, those bright beacons shining early in the universe's history, can now be detected at redshifts exceeding 4 (that is we see them as they were some 9 billion years ago when the universe was a fifth of its present size). The weight of opinion now is that a quasar is a violently energetic outburst in a galaxy's nucleus. If true, this means we can indirectly see some galaxies at redshifts which are becoming relevant for answering our query. One way to check whether superclusters came first has been developed by Patrick Osmer (Osmer 1983): find enough high-redshift quasars to decide whether they tend to cluster as if they belonged to superclusters. That program is still in its infancy, but may be able to enlighten us within a few years.

And now for our second question: is there evidence for the presence of inhomogeneities long before galaxies and superclusters took shape? To answer this we must evidently look out to very high redshifts, and the only messenger from those regions (or rather epochs) known to us is the microwave background radiation we alluded to earlier.

A striking feature of this radiation is its purely thermal spectrum: it looks just like radiation emitted by a black body at a temperature of 2.7 Kelvin. As mentioned in Section 1, we can infer that the energy density of the radiation (and its temperature) grows very rapidly as we go back in time. The equations of General Relativity allow us to extrapolate this trend back almost to the point when the density and temperature were infinite and the universe had zero radius (see Fritzsch's contribution in this volume). Thus the beginning of the universe was associated with a blinding intensity of radiation—hence the name "primeval fireball" sometimes given to the radiation background. At early times the radiation was in intimate control with matter (in physicist's jargon there was thermodynamic equilibrium), and this led to its striking thermal character today. But the contact must have been severed as the primordial hot plasma recombined into ionized gas at the epoch at a redshift of 1,000 or so when the temperature was reduced by the expansion to some 3,000 Kelvin. Since then the radiation must have been traveling unhindered through the expanding universe.

Any inhomogeneity present both in the matter and radiation before they decoupled must have left an imprint on the freed radiation. Today this should be reflected in variations of the radiation's intensity over the sky. In this way one can expect to see directly the inhomogeneities at very early times, in fact, at a redshift of 1,000, corresponding to the recombination epoch. (This is much farther than can be probed by telescopes looking for galaxies.) Yet a second striking feature of the background radiation is its isotropy (extreme uniformity with respect to direction) on all angular scales. For example, recent measurements (Uson and Wilkinson 1984) have shown that, over angles of a few arc-minutes, the radiation intensity is uniform to an accuracy of a few thousandths of a percent. Very smooth indeed! One can calculate that at a redshift of 1,000 an angle of a few arc-minutes corresponds to a region encompassing a supercluster-sized mass.

So, if the original pancake scenario were right in that there were *joint* radiation-matter inhomogeneities, then the density contrast achieved by the matter's inhomogeneities, after the magnification associated with a 1,000-fold expansion of the universe, would be only a few percent today. Yet the superclusters today have a much higher density contrast with respect to their surroundings. The scenario thus runs into trouble. It is precisely for this reason that the modified pancake scenario involving massive neutrinos (see Section 3) was given serious consideration.

The original hierarchical scenario is less badly hit by the microwave background observations because it posits matter inhomogeneities only, and the observed smoothness of the radiation intensity does not directly clash with this assumption. However, to explain superclustering, if it can do that at all, this scenario must posit matter inhomogeneities with a density contrast of 0.1 percent at a redshift of 1,000 which extend over supercluster scales. Such matter irregularities, when they go into motion, must induce comparable irregularities in the radiation via the Doppler effect (Davis 1980). Thus, it is generally agreed, a small improvement in the measurement of the radiation isotropy will cause trouble for the hierarchical scenario in its original form. This has motivated the introduction of the "cold matter" restatement of the scenario (Section 3).

It is not out of the question, in view of the eventful history of the two major scenarios, that they may both collapse under the assaults of future observations. In such an eventuality, the less popular explosion scenario may come to the fore. It relies only on primeval inhomogeneities on small scales (corresponding to the mass of a supermassive star—much smaller than a galaxy's). Technically, it is very difficult to establish accurate isotropy limits on the corresponding angular scale of a small fraction of an arc-second, so it is unlikely that the scenario will fall on this score. In the explosion scenario the large-scale structure comes from the ejected shells, so it does not require primordial inhomogeneities on scales susceptible to observational scrutiny of the microwave background. However, it remains to be seen, when details of the explosion scenario are worked out in depth, whether it does not run aground on unexpected effects.

5. AFTER THE BEGINNING

Assuming a particular type of initial inhomogeneity has proved a handy procedure for cosmologists in their attempts to understand organization in the heavens. Yet much thought has gone into trying to explain where the initial inhomogeneities came from. We mentioned that the simplest explanation, that they are statistical fluctuations in the distribution of particles, fails dismally. Alternative explanations have usually posited an irregularity in some other physical quantity (magnetic field, matter velocity . . .) which then "infects" the matter density. This is, evidently, only postponing the problem. At some point one must come to terms with the real issue: in fundamental terms what were the initial conditions in the universe like, and how did the required inhomogeneities arise from them?

What did the universe look like immediately after emergence from the beginning? If we do not wish to introduce *ad hoc* assumptions, there is very little leeway here: the universe must have been completely homogeneous and isotropic (looking the same not only at all locations, but also in all directions). To have it otherwise would require specification of initial parameters describing the inhomogeneities and anisotropies. Since the universe is not just an example of a class of systems, but the only universe, such parameters would take on the role of physical laws. But having so many laws would clearly prove inimical to a rational picture of cosmology.

Although I have presented this view matter-of-factly, it is hardly the majority view today. Perhaps more popular is Misner's hypothesis (Misner 1968) that initially the universe was highly chaotic—showing marked inhomogeneity at all scales—and only became smooth—both homogeneous and isotropic—through complex dissipative processes. It is only when we appeal to thermodynamics that the strength of the contrary hypothesis—highly smooth initial universe—becomes apparent.

The striking lesson of thermodynamics is its second law: in a closed system the entropy—the measure of disorder—cannot decrease, and will usually increase if the system undergoes a change. We defer for the moment the question of whether the universe is a closed system in any sense, and presume the second law to be valid for it. It is perhaps ironic that despite the wide applicability of the second law in science, a clear-cut explanation of it in terms of dynamical laws has never been found. The main reason is that all physical dynamics (with a small exception—the superweak interaction thought to be responsible for the K-meson oscillations) are symmetric under time reversal. Thus processes proceeding forward in time and backward in time are not dynamically different. Hence the dynamics cannot be exclusively responsible for the increase of entropy. It is actually the boundary conditions that set the direction of "arrow of time," that is, the temporal sense in which entropy increases. In Ludwig Boltzmann's celebrated H theorem, which showed how entropy increase comes about in molecular dynamics, it was his assumption of an initial lack of correlations (molecular chaos) that set the arrow of time.

As emphasized long ago by David Layzer (Layzer 1971), and more recently by Roger Penrose (Penrose 1979), in the context of cosmology the appropriate boundary condition to impose so that entropy will increase as the universe expands is that the entropy be low initially. This means that the universe must be created in a highly regular and smooth state, one lacking irregularities which would translate into a contribution to the entropy. It is simplest to interpret this initial condition to apply both to the universe's gravitational field (or, what is equivalent, its spacetime geometry), and to its material contents.

The geometry will be smoothest if the universe, initially, fits a perfect Friedmann model: homogeneous and isotropic (Penrose 1979). The matter will be smoothest if it is in a perfectly homogeneous quantum state. Statistical fluctuations in the number of particles in a given volume are antagonistic to perfect homogeneity. It follows that the matter quantum state should be a *vacuum*, a state devoid of any particles. In view of recent developments in field theory (Birrell and Davies 1982), we know that a vacuum state in an expanding universe is not necessarily vacuous:

it carries energy and exerts pressure as would a material gas. The vacuum is actually a zero-temperature state because it is devoid of quanta which we might think of as thermal excitations.

The proposal that the universe must have started cold apparently goes back to Layzer. It sounds paradoxical in view of the widespread belief, documented in Sections 1 and 4, that the early universe passed through a very hot state. Nevertheless, the need for such an initially cold homogeneous quantum state for the matter in the universe is clear. Reconciliation with the evidence for an early hot era may be achieved if at some very early epoch the cold smooth low-entropy state could transform itself into a hot state of higher entropy (this must take place earlier than redshift 10^{10} to preserve the highly successful picture of helium formation in the hot early universe—see Sexl's and Fritzsch's contributions).

This, then, is the prescription for making peace between thermodynamically suitable boundary conditions and the strong evidence for a hot early universe. It sounds far-fetched, but it has actually been advocated on entirely different grounds in the inflationary cosmological model propounded by Alan Guth (Guth 1981) and Andre Linde (Linde 1982) among others (again see Fritzsch's paper). In inflationary cosmology the universe starts with a completely homogeneous and isotropic gravitational field (a de Sitter geometry, a special case of the Friedmann model), and initially contains only a curious field, called the Higgs field by particle physicists (see Fritzsch's contribution for a full characterization), in a cold vacuum state. This state of the field is directly responsible for a very early and exponentially rapid (inflationary) expansion of the universe, an expansion which plays an important role in solving several thorny problems of cosmology. What needs concern us here is the view of inflationary cosmology that the rapid expansion terminates in conjunction with thermalization of the vacuum state of the Higgs field at a high redshift (about 10^{26}). Matter and radiation are created at the expense of the energy of the Higgs field; the new state is a high-entropy hot state. The cold low-entropy universe thus turns into a hot high-entropy universe as required by our previous discussion.

A bonus of the inflationary scenario is that it provides an elegant genesis for the inhomogeneities required for the formation of large structures in the universe. According to detailed calculations (Bardeen, Steinhardt and Turner 1983) the quantum fluctuations of the Higgs field in its original vacuum state, fluctuations dictated by physical law, are transformed into inhomogeneities of the matter and radiation that is created as inflation ends. Not only that, but the calculated inhomogeneities have the correct distribution by strength or density contrast: their strength decreases with increasing scale according to a law, first suggested by Edward Harrison (Harrison 1970) and Zel'dovich (1972), which is most appropriate for the required initial spectrum of inhomogeneities. This is an unexpected and most welcome success of the inflationary cosmology. Still troubling these endeavors is the fact that the predicted overall strength of the inhomogeneities is too high by far, but there are signs that this problem may find a resolution (Hawking 1985).

6. A MEASURE OF ORDER

Thus the inflationary cosmology can explain the passage of the universe from thermodynamically reasonable initial conditions to a state pervaded by hot matter with some inhomogeneity. This state is to serve as raw material for the formation of large structures.

A paradox appears at this stage. It is well known that a system in thermodynamic equilibrium, such as the matter at the epoch in question is most likely to have been, has attained the maximum allowed value of its entropy. According to the usual information-theoretic interpretation, if the entropy takes on its maximum value, the information obtainable about the detailed state of the system is nil. One then wonders how the matter in question eventually evolved into large structures (galaxies, galaxy clusters, superclusters) which are highly organized systems requiring a lot of information for their specification. Put another way, how can the matter in question go from a state of maximal entropy to one considerably below maximal entropy. Does not this violate the second law of thermodynamics?

A routine retort to a query of this kind is that the universe is an open system, so that the second law does not apply to it, and hence there is no paradox. It appears that this viewpoint obscures the real issue. It is true that if the universe is spatially infinite (and the empirical evidence leans in this direction), then it is not closed in a strict sense. However, another evident feature of the universe is that very distant objects recede from us with velocities very similar to those required by Hubble's picture of a uniformly expanding universe. This means that on a large scale (larger than superclusters) matter transfer between separate locations is negligible. In addition, if our position in the universe is not privileged, we know from the low velocity of our galaxy with respect to the thermal background radiation (about 300 km/sec, small compared to relative galaxy velocities in the local supercluster) that all over the universe, radiation hardly flows with respect to the matter. Thus there is no important radiation transfer between separate locations. The conclusion is that any large region in the universe, defined by the galaxies it contains rather than by volume, will not exchange much matter or energy with its surroundings. That region is thus nearly closed in a thermodynamic sense.

The law of entropy increase should thus operate for each such large region in the universe. Since such regions today do contain highly organized structures, we come back to the paradox. How do organized systems arise from matter already at the maximal entropy level without running afoul of the second law? One possible resolution was pointed out long ago: the maximal level of entropy is not set once and for all, but is continually raised by the expansion of the universe (Tolman 1934). In his contribution to this volume, Sexl describes a homely, everyday analog of this phenomenon.

That the maximal allowed entropy is continually rising in the universe is made particularly clear by the well-known theorem (Tolman 1934, Layzer 1971) that the expansion removes any system of particles, which are neither non-relativistic nor ultrarelativistic, from thermodynamic equilibrium. Since this equilibrium is a maximal entropy situation for given constraints, the removal from equilibrium can only be accomplished by a raising of the maximal entropy level. The level cannot be lowered because the actual entropy cannot decrease. In fact, because of the departure from equilibrium, the actual entropy should increase steadily. Thus in cosmology one requires a restatement of Rudolph Clausius' formulation of the second law: entropy increases steadily instead of tending to a maximum.

As the maximal entropy level is raised, the region in question acquires a potential for information content measured by the difference between the maximal entropy and the actual entropy. Thus the expansion opens up the opportunity for organization in what would otherwise remain formless matter. According to this viewpoint, galaxies, clusters of galaxies and superclusters are creatures, not just of the ability of gravitation to gather distant matter together, but also of the information-generating ability of the Hubble expansion. In his paper Sexl takes a similar view.

I believe that though the resolution just described, which has been offered at various times in the literature (Tolman 1934, Layzer 1971), has elements of the truth, it cannot be the whole truth. Much of the organization at the cosmic level appears after the universal expansion has lost its grip on the matter. For example, it is believed that galaxy disks and spiral structure developed only after the protogalaxies became detached from the expanding universal medium and collapsed upon themselves. But did the maximal entropy level continues to grow during the collapse phase as required?

In classical thermodynamics an increase in maximal entropy level is associated, either with an increase in the volume occupied by the system, or with an increase in the range allowed to the momenta of the particles composing it (phase space). In the collapsing protogalaxy, volume is contracting, so only the second factor can be conducive to raising the maximal entropy level.

The range allowed to the momenta increases with the magnitude of the kinetic energy of the system. In fact, the combined kinetic and thermal energy of the collapsing protogalaxy does increase, mostly as a result of the steady decrease of the (negative) gravitational potential energy. This trend is in the right sense to increase the entropy. In fact, it is precisely the unbounded decrease of the potential energy which is held responsible for the "gravothermal catastrophe" which Newtonian assemblages of masses can undergo (Lynden-Bell and Wood 1968), a catastrophe which results in unbounded growth of the entropy. Thus, factors promoting the rise of the maximal entropy level are present in protogalaxy collapse. But it is important to note that they depend critically on gravitation.

This brings me to suggest that no picture of the growth of organization in systems ruled by gravitation is complete unless it includes a "gravitational entropy" in its considerations. For it seems unreasonable to rely on gravitation to extend the entropy limits of the matter, while denying it any part in the entropy of the system. Of course, gravitational entropy was once an unthinkable concept, but with the general acceptance of black hole entropy (Bekenstein 1973, Hawking 1975) as a *bona fide* entropy in gravitational physics, the psychological hurdles have been removed. Another similar entropy may be associated with gravitational systems which do not include black holes, similar in that it is quantified by the geometric properties of gravitation, rather than by properties of matter. If so, any argument about the growth of organization in gravitating systems will be incomplete if it fails to include gravitational entropy in the information–theoretic considerations we mentioned.

It was Penrose (1979) who first suggested, on different grounds, a local gravitational entropy quantified by the Weyl tensor, the measure of "wrinkling" of spacetime due to gravitation. To his arguments we may add one directly relevant to our subject. We stressed the importance of homogeneous initial state for the matter to provide the right boundary conditions for operation of the second law. Now a homogeneous matter state is possible only in a homogeneous and isotropic spacetime, for any irregularities in its geometry would feed back to the matter. The homogeneous isotropic (Friedmann) spacetime has a vanishing Weyl tensor. In later epochs the Weyl tensor departs from zero in regions where mass congregates. The larger the departure from homogeneity, the larger will Weyl's tensor be for a given mass. It is tempting to see in the growth evidenced by the Weyl tensor the increase expected of an entropy. It may even be that the growth of this gravitational entropy is the factor that allows structure to appear in the matter—with consequent decrease of the material entropy—without causing a conflict with the second law. Gravitational entropy may thus be one key to the origin of large structures in the universe.

It must be stressed, however, that no generally accepted formula relating gravitational entropy to the Weyl tensor is known as yet, and, therefore, the concept of generic gravitational entropy has yet to be put to the crucial test.

ACKNOWLEDGMENTS

I am indebted to Professors M. Alonso, H. Fritzsch, N. Kurti, P. Lowenhard, the late R. Sexl, and P. Sussman for comments and useful suggestions. My thanks are also due to the Director of the Wise Observatory of Tel Aviv University for allocations of observing time.

REFERENCES

Bardeen, J. *et al.* 1983. "Spontaneous Creation of Almost Scale Free Density Perturbations in an Inflationary Universe." *Physical Review* D28:679.

Bekenstein, J. 1973. "Black Holes and Entropy." *Physical Review* D7:2333.

Birrell, N. and Davies, P. 1928. *Quantum Fields in Curved Space.* Cambridge: Cambridge University Press.

Davis, M. 1980. "Lower Limits to Fluctuations in the Microwave Background Radiation Induced by Recombination." *Physica Scripta* 21:717.

Doroshkevich, A. *et al.* 1974. "The Formation of Galaxies in Friedmannian Universes." Edited by M. Longair in *Confrontation of Cosmological Theories with Observational Data.* Dordrecht: Reidel.

Einstein, A. 1916. "Die Grundlage der allgemeinen Relativitetstheorie (The Foundation of the General Theory of Relativity)." *Annalen der Physik* 49:769.

Einstein, A. 1917. "Kosmologische Betrachtungen zur allgemeinen Relativitetstheorie (Cosmological Considerations about the General Theory of Relativity)." *Sitzungs Berichte der Preussische Akademie der Wissenschaten* 1:142.

Fall, M. and Rees, M. 1977. "Survival and Disruption of Galactic Substructure." *Monthly Notices of Royal Astronomical Society* 181:37P.

Friedmann, A. 1922. "Uber die Möglichkeit einer Welt mit Konstanter negativer Krummung des Raumes (On the Possibility of a World with Constant Negative Space Curvature)." *Zeitschrift fur Physik* 21:326.

Gott, R. and Rees, M. 1975. "A Theory of Galaxy Formation and Clustering." *Astronomy and Astrophysics* 45:365.

Gott, R. 1979. "Computer Simulation of the Universe." *Comments on Astrophysics* 8:55.

Guth, A. 1981. "The Inflationary Universe: A Possible Solution to the Horizon and Flatness Problems." *Physical Review* D23:347.

Harrison, E. 1970. "Fluctuations at the Threshold of Classical Cosmology." *Physical Review* D1:2726.

Hawking, S. 1975. "Particle Creation by Black Holes." *Communications on Mathematical Physics* 43:199.

Hawking, S. 1985. "Limits on Inflationary Models of the Universe." *Physics Letters* 150B:339.

Hubble, E. 1926. "Extragalactic Nebulae." *Astrophysical Journal* 64:321.

Hubble, E. 1929. "A Relation Between Distance and Radial Velocity Among Extra-Galactic Nebulae." *Proceedings of the National Academy of Sciences* 15:168.

Huchra, J. *et al.* 1983. "A Survey of Galaxy Redshifts: IV. The Data." *Astrophysical Journal Supplement* 52:89.

Jeans, J. 1902. "On the Stability of Spherical Nebulae." *Philosophical Transactions of the Royal Society of London* 199:1.

Jeans, J. 1929. *Astronomy and Cosmology.* Cambridge: Cambridge University Press.

Kirshner, R. *et al.* 1981. "A Million Cubic Magaparsec Void in Boötes?" *Astrophysical Journal* 248:L57.

Koyre, A. 1958. *From the Closed World to the Infinite Universe.* New York: Harper and Row.

Layzer, D. 1971. "Cosmogonic Processes." Edited by M. Cretien *et al.* in *Astrophysics and General Relativity.* Volume 2. New York: Gordon and Breach.

Lifshiftz, E. 1946. "On the Gravitational Stability of the Expanding Universe." *Zhurnal Eksperimentalnoi Teoretishkoi Fiziki* 16:187 (*Soviet Journal of Physics* 10:116).

Lin, C. and Shu, F. 1964. "On the Spiral Structure of Disk Galaxies." *Astrophysical Journal* 140:646.

Lindblad, B. 1927. "The Small Oscillations of a Rotating Stellar System and the Development of Spiral Arms." *Bulletin of Uppsala Astronomical Observatory* 19:1.

Linde, A. 1982. "A New inflationary Universe Scenario: A Possible Solution of the Horizon, Flatness, Isotropy and Primordial Monopole Problems." *Physics Letters* 1088:389.

Lynden-Bell, D. and Wood, R. 1968. "The Gravo-thermal Catastrophe in Isothermal Spheres and the Onset of Red-Giant Structure for Stellar Systems." *Monthly Notices of Royal Astronomical Society* 138:495.

Misner, C. 1968. "The Isotropy of the Universe." *Astrophysical Journal* 151:431.

Oort, J. 1983. "Superclusters." *Annual Reviews of Astronomy and Astrophysics* 21:373.

Osmer, P. 1983. "Quasars and Superclusters." Edited by G. Abell and G. Chincarini in *Early Evolution of the Universe and its Present Structure.* Dordrecht: Reidel.

Ostriker, J. and Cowie, L. 1981. "Galaxy Formation in an Intergalactic Medium Dominated by Explosions." *Astrophysical Journal* 243:L127.

Peebles, P. 1980. *The Large Scale Structure of the Universe.* Princeton: Princeton University Press.

Penrose, R. 1979. "Singularities and Time-Asymmetry." Edited by S. Hawking and W. Israel in *General Relativity—An Einstein Centenary Survey.* Cambridge: Cambridge University Press.

Penzias, A. and Wilson, R. 1965. "A Measurement of Excess Antenna Temperature at 4080 MHz." *Astrophysical Journal* 142:419.

Schwarz, J. *et al.* 1975. "Explosive Events in the Early Universe." *Astrophysical Journal* 201:1.

Silk, J. 1968. "Cosmic Black-Body Radiation and Galaxy Formation." *Astrophysical Journal* 151:459.

Tolman, R. 1934. *Relativity, Thermodynamics and Cosmology.* London: Oxford University Press.

Toomre, A. 1977. "Theories of Spiral Structure." *Annual Reviews of Astronomy and Astrophysics* 15:437.

Uson, J. and Wilkinson, D. 1984. "Small Scale Isotropy of the Cosmic Microwave Background at 19.5 GHz." *Astrophysical Journal* 283:471.

Vaucouleurs, G. 1953. "Evidence for a Local Supergalaxy." *Astronomical Journal* 58:30.

Weinberg, S. 1972. *Gravitation and Cosmology.* New York: Wiley.

White, S. *et al.* 1984. "The Size of Clusters in a Neutrino Dominated Universe." *Monthly Notices of Royal Astronomical Society* 209:27P.

Zel'dovich, Y. 1972. "A Hypothesis, Unifying the Structure and Entropy of the Universe." *Monthly Notices of Royal Astronomical Society* 160:1P.

Zwicky, F. 1933. "Die Rotverschiebung von Ekstragalaktische Nebeln (The Redshift of Extragalactic Nebulae)." *Helvetica Physica Acta* 6:110.

2

On the Origin of Order in the Universe

ROMAN U. SEXL*

1. INTRODUCTION

During the 19th century several important discoveries related to the evolution of our world and the Universe took place. These discoveries took many forms: In biology Charles Darwin (1809–1882) published in 1859 his epoch-making book *On the Origin of Species;* in geology Charles Lyell (1797–1875) contributed to our knowledge of the changes in the appearance of the earth with his treatise *The Principles of Geology* published during 1830–1833; and in physics, the formulation of the second law of thermodynamics and the introduction of the concept of entropy by Rudolph Chausius [1850] and Lord Kelvin [1851] based on the work of Sadi Carnot [1824] seemed to imply the irreversible running-down of the cosmic clockwork. The "heat death" of the universe was apparently unavoidable and the steady increase of entropy a precise measure for the progress of the greatest doomsday machine ever envisaged.

This view of the world led to severe problems in a time when the understanding of the atom, a concept present since antiquity, put us on the verge of a scientific breakthrough. The very existence of atoms threatened the progress of mankind and the universe, as measured by the ever increasing entropy.

*Due to a severe illness and ultimately death, Prof. Sexl has not been able to revise the first draft of his paper. However since it contains many important ideas, it has been decided to publish it with some minor corrections and a few editorial notes, which appear in parentheses or as footnotes.

This threat took several forms. In France, Henry Poincaré pointed out, around 1900, that eternal recurrence was unavoidable and that a universe made up of atoms had necessarily to retrace its own path again and again resulting in a cyclic universe. The old idea of a cyclic time, present ever since the Mayas built their magnificent observatories, had apparently been borne out by the laws of physics.

Universal evolution and eternal recurrence collided in philosophical circles. The German philosopher Friedrich Nietzsche (1844–1900) studied natural science. He was a firm believer in a world eternally repeated in a senseless play and derived a moral principle from these ideas. In a world where every event is repeated eternally every human deed has to be performed so that it can be repeated eternally.

Reversibility was the other threat to the atomic order of nature. In Vienna, the physicist Joseph Loschmidt (1821–1895) pointed out that the time-reversible motion of the atoms would necessarily lead to a world in which time would have no preferred sense and would run both ways— although this is hard to envisage.

Reversibility and eternal recurrence endangered the evolutionary universe and the notion of entropy, the precise measure of its progress towards the ultimate heat death. Ludwig Boltzmann, the main proponent of the atomic theory, had to fight many hard and bitter battles of which the one at the *Naturforscherversammlung* in Lübeck in 1894 became most famous.

2. BOLTZMANN'S ATOMIC UNIVERSE

Boltzmann was an ardent admirer of Darwin and extended his ideas to new and unconventional realms, like the evolution of the world of ideas and consciousness. At the same time he was the main proponent of the atomic theory that seemed to endanger the very concept of progress and evolution towards order.

Both schools of physical thought prevailing at the end of the 19th century were in conflict with the idea of evolution: at the very heart of thermodynamics was the second law, formulated mathematically as the constant and unavoidable increase in entropy. Since entropy is considered a measure of disorder, this implied the steady destruction of order, and not its creation in an evolutionary process as envisaged by biology. Were the laws of physics inapplicable to biology? Was physics, and especially thermodynamics, presenting the final and convincing proof for a *vis vitalis*, for *entelechy*, a special force characteristic of living beings and unknown to the inorganic world?

On the other hand there were the recurrence and reversibility paradoxes characteristic of the atomic point of view. Could evolution be a recurrent process? This seemed unimaginable.

Ludwig Boltzmann tried to find a way out of this dilemma and to reconcile evolution, the second law, and atomism. His universe was an eternal and infinite one that had suffered the heat death* already. It was a universe in thermal equilibrium, in eternal slumber. But it was an infinite universe, and in such a universe local fluctuations—"small" regions with important deviations from the global equilibrium—could exist. It was Boltzmann's idea that he did live in such a fluctuation, one that extended over all the regions of the sky that were visible to the best telescopes of his day. Our region of the universe was one which was just returning to equilibrium, and this is what he thought we observe and formulate in the second law of thermodynamics. There must be other regions of the universe which are not approaching equilibrium but in which a fluctuation is just gaining strength and increasing. In such a region the second law would still be valid and time would flow in a direction opposite to the one known to us.

This was Boltzmann's way out of the dilemma—a desperate way, but unavoidable at a time when the evolution of the universe itself was still unknown and the Big Bang unheard of.

3. COSMIC EVOLUTION

When Albert Einstein (1876–1955) arrived at his theory of Special Relativity in 1905 and ten years later at General Relativity, the skies were still the symbols of eternity and immutability for science, and particularly for physics. When Einstein started to work out the cosmological implications of his ideas in 1917 he still envisaged an eternal and essentially unchangeable universe—much as Boltzmann had done several decades earlier. The only difference between Einstein's and Boltzmann's views was the connection between matter and the curvature of space-time. While Boltzmann had speculated about the possibility of a curved space, Einstein had found out the definitive relation between curvature and the distribution of matter in his theory of gravitation, i.e. in General Relativity.

Einstein's ideas led him into trouble immediately. In order to construct a stationary and unchangeable cosmos he had to supplement his field equations of gravitation with a new *ad hoc* term. He called it the *cosmological constant* at first, and his "greatest blunder" later. This term was to prevent the universe from either collapsing or exploding and con-

---

*This term *heat death* as used by R. S. is equivalent to thermal equilibrium. More precisely, a consequence of the heat death of the universe would be that it has reached a state of global thermal equilibrium, in which nothing else should happen.

sisted, technically speaking, of a negative density of matter that was supposed to fill the universe uniformly, causing the universal repulsion necessary to overcome the universal attraction that would cause the world to collapse if only ordinary matter were present.

The death of the "Einstein universe" was caused by Alexander Friedmann (1888–1925), a Russian mathematician, who worked out the cosmological implications of Einstein's General Relativity without invoking the strange cosmological matter density Einstein had used.

Friedmann's universe was born in a Big Bang and either expanded eternally or recollapsed into a state of infinite density—the relativistic doomsday—depending on certain parameters, such as the average mass density of the universe. An eternally expanding universe is "open," while a recollapsing or cyclic universe is "closed."

Friedmann's universe was born experimentally when Edwin Hubble discovered, in 1929, the expansion of the universe and calculated the time that had passed since the Big Bang. His result was that the universe had existed for at most 2 billion years, i.e. it was supposed to be about half as old as we currently believe the Earth is. Subsequently, the progress of cosmology continuously revised this number upwards and current estimates for the age of universe are around 15 to 20 billion years.

This increase in the estimated age of the universe by a factor of ten is due to the continuous refinement of assumptions and ideas about stars and galaxies. Lacking better knowledge, the simplest possible assumptions had always been used as, for example, that the brightest galaxies in each cluster always had the same intrinsic brightness. With increasing knowledge about stars and galaxies it was possible to revise these and other assumptions and the result was a steady climb in the estimated age of the universe.

4. THE EARLY UNIVERSE

The idea of the origin of the universe in a Big Bang was speculation at first and it took a long time before it was taken seriously. The extrapolation of the expansion curve of the universe that had been observed for a few decades to billions of years seemed to be too outrageous to be considered part of exact science.

It was George Gamov who in 1948 had the courage to publish his speculations about the origin of the chemical elements in an early, hot phase of the universe. Extrapolating the present expansion backwards into the past he obtained temperatures of several billion degrees in the first minutes after the Big Bang, sufficient to "cook" the chemical elements using protons and neutrons as ingredients. His idea that *all* of the chemical elements observed today were produced in the initial hot phase of the cosmos had to be revised later, but the key ideas remained valid: we believe even now that the lightest elements, helium and lithium, were produced in the initial fireball. The abundances calculated from this theory agree with observation to a high degree of accuracy.

The real test for Gamov's ideas occurred in 1965 when Robert Dicke at Princeton University decided to look for the remains of the initial fireball that should be present even now in the form of a "cosmic background radiation" filling the universe. The initially extremely hot radiation would have been cooled down by the expansion of the universe. The temperature of this relic radiation had been predicted by Gamov to be 5 K.

The rest of the story has often been told. Penzias and Wilson, working at Bell laboratories, not far from Princeton University, accidentally discovered in 1965 the radiation that Dicke wanted to measure during their search for satellite signals. It corresponds to a temperature of 2.7K, a bit lower than that predicted by Gamov. They were rewarded with the Nobel prize of 1978 for this discovery, which became the keystone in our present understanding of the history of the universe.

We shall not concentrate here on this story and its implications for the history of the early universe. We shall leave out all the fascinating ideas and speculations that have recently came up concerning the very early universe and the inflationary scenario invented to overcome some of the difficulties of the standard Big Bang theory. (See the chapters by J. D. Bekenstein and H. Fritzsch in this volume for more detailed analysis of the inflationary universe.)

We shall concentrate here on another aspect of the cosmic evolution—the origin of structure. How could long- and short-range structures originate in a universe initially filled completely and uniformly with a gas in thermal equilibrium? Is the initial period after the Big Bang the heat death envisaged by the doomsday scientists of the 19th century? Is the heat death a matter of the past rather than the future?

5. ENTROPY IN THE UNIVERSE

The apparent resurrection from heat death is not the only thermodynamic paradox in our understanding of the universe.* There is a second one which has been discussed in the literature for decades: How does entropy change in an expanding and recollapsing world?

*R. S. is implicitly assuming that the universe is cyclic and successively expands and contracts although not necessarily repeating itself in each cycle. This is a hypothesis for which there is insufficient evidence.

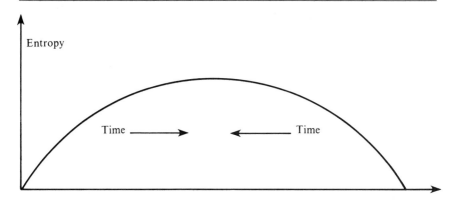

Figure 2-1. Entropy and time direction in an expanding and recollapsing universe: the cyclic concept

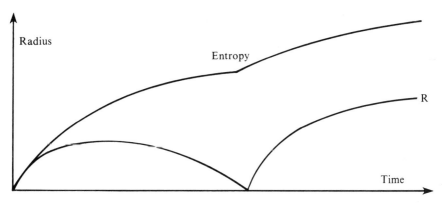

Figure 2-2. Entropy and expansion in an (almost) cyclic universe according to standard thermodynamics.

This question is intimately related with the problem of the direction of time as discussed by Boltzmann in his first attempt to cope with the problem of the order and structure observed in the world. Some authors have speculated that time is *per definitionem* directed toward increasing entropy (the thermodynamic arrow of time). Recall that Clausius synthesized in 1865 the two laws of Thermodynamics by stating that "the energy of the universe is constant but its entropy increases continuously."

Granting this idea, an interesting point of view suggests itself concerning the behavior of entropy in an expanding and later recollapsing (closed) universe: Could it be that entropy increases during the expansion phase of our world and reaches a maximum when the expansion of the world reaches its maximum? Could it be that the entropy of the world decreases thereafter and that the universe reaches its initial state again upon collapsing? In this case a cyclic universe would be possible (Figure 2-1). As indicated before, the concept seemed so attractive to Nietzsche that he developed a whole moral philosophy from it.

A second possible answer was first worked out by Richard Tolman in 1934 and later elaborated in detail by various other authors. This approach is related more closely to standard thermodynamics. In this model, one calculates the entropy increase of an initially hot gas that is first expanded and then recompressed by the cosmic expansion (and subsequent contraction).

This approach shows that entropy increases continuously even in the recontracting phase of the universe (Figure 2-2). An exactly cyclic universe is impossible and the periods of expansion and recontraction of the universe become longer and longer as time proceeds.

Both approaches at first leave one central question unanswered: how can structure originate in a universe that has initially been in a state of thermal equilibrium and in which entropy and thus disorder tend to become maximal?

6. ORDER IN THE UNIVERSE

We have formulated the central question concerning the origin of order in the universe before in the form: is the heat death already behind us?

We can reformulate this question as follows: If entropy is increasing continuously during the cosmic expansion, why was the initial state of our world a state of low entropy? After all, thermal equilibrium already existed in the beginning and all the degrees of freedom of the matter filling the cosmos had—on average—the same energy per degree of freedom. In order to clarify this problem let us look at a simple model that will show the essential source of order. Consider a gas in a container closed by a movable piston (Figure 2-3). The motion of this piston will represent the expansion in our model.

Initially the gas is in thermal equilibrium—heat death has occurred. Then the expansion sets in. The gas starts to follow the piston and cur-

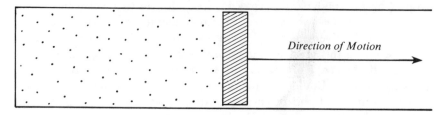

Figure 2-3. A simple model of cosmic expansion: gas enclosed in a container with a movable piston.

rents, local density variations etc. are the consequence. Hydrodynamic structures, such as eddies, will indicate that the heat death is now a matter of the past. In the real universe these eddies will be galaxies or clusters of galaxies and the full spectrum of objects in the universe will emerge. Thus we reach the following conclusion: *The expansion of the universe is the source of all structure and order.*

The low entropy of the initial universe is to be found mainly in its small size—i.e. the highly specified information about the position (and motion) of the constituent particles.

Resurrection from heat death is explained by the fact that all degrees of freedom have initially the same average energy—except for one: the cosmic expansion itself. This consideration still requires an explanation how, out of a state of thermal equilibrium, expansion sets in with the corresponding appearance of fluctuations.

Whether and when the gas will leave its thermal equilibrium depends on the speed of the expansion. If the expansion is slow (as in classical reversible processes) so that the internal processes within the gas can continuously adapt to the changing external conditions the equilibrium will be maintained. This was the case in the first million years of the universe. At that time it was not so much that the expansion was slow, but that the gas was heated to relativistic temperatures. All particles had speeds approaching the velocity of light and were therefore able to adjust rapidly and continuously to the changing conditions in the universe. This changed only about one million years after the Big Bang, the time of origin of the structures.

What about the recollapse of the universe? What happens if we push the piston back in an recompress the gas? The fact that equilibrium had not always been maintained during the expansion process implies that irreversible processes have occurred which will have raised the temperature of the gas. The recollapse will therefore be different—slower—than the expansion and the gas will not return to its original state. When it is recompressed to its starting volume it will be hotter than at the Big Bang.

7. STRUCTURE IN THE UNIVERSE

Our considerations have shown us the source of order in the universe. The possibility of order has been demonstrated thereby, but not the types of order and structure that would originate. What are the structures that are observed in the universe and how can they be classified and explained?

The simplest classification scheme for structures is one grouping all bodies according to size (radius) and mass. Atomic nuclei are the smallest structures at a radius of about 10^{-25}m. Atoms are roughly five orders of

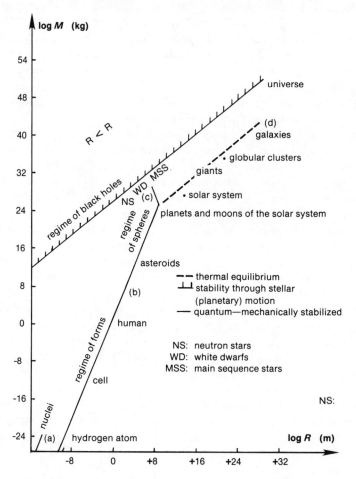

Figure 2-4. Masses and Radii of the objects in the universe. It should be noted that lines (a), (b) and (c) correspond to compact systems, resulting from strong, electromagnetic and gravitational interactions, while (d) corresponds to dispersed systems.

magnitude larger. Masses of atomic nuclei range from 10^{-24}kg for hydrogen to about 240 times this mass for uranium (Figure 2-4). More massive nuclei do not exist naturally since atomic nuclei tend to be unstable beyond this limit. (This restricts the masses of atoms to about the same range of values.) Larger objects that might then be classified and plotted in a mass-radius diagram might be a virus, a speck of dust, a grain of salt, a fly, birds, dogs, men, elephants, rocks, moons, planets, and so on. Plotting their radii and masses one obtains a straight line in a log (mass) vs. log (radius) diagram, highlighting their basic unifying structure: all these objects consist of atoms (Figure 3-4, line [b]).

The atomic order in our part of the world extends from a single atom up to Jupiter, the largest planet of our solar system, and the sun. More than 54 orders of magnitude are spanned by the straight line (b) representing the (practically) constant and universal density of roughly 1,000 kg/m³ of these objects made up of atoms.

If the mass goes beyond these limits (line [c]) then the radius of the object becomes smaller and smaller as the mass increases: The gravitational field is so intense that it slowly overcomes the other internal forces in the object and compresses the internal structure of its atoms. Finally the limit is reached. When the object—a white dwarf—has a mass of more than 57 orders of magnitude, the *Chandrasekhar limit* of the mass is reached. No object beyond this limit can resist the gravitational collapse.

The most fascinating connections between quantum mechanics and gravitational field theory are seen in analyzing the numerical relations here and seeing the connection between the microworld of atoms and the macroworld of stars.

This connection can be derived by studying the energy of an atom in a star: When the atom is compressed strongly by the gravitational field of the star then the energy of the particles contained in the atom becomes relativistic and its kinetic energy is *pc*, where *p* is the momentum of the particle and *c* is the speed of light. The electric potential energy of the atom is of the order of $-e^2/r$ and its gravitational potential energy within the star is on the order of $-GMm/R$, where *M* is the mass and *R* the radius of the star in which the atom of mass is contained. Taking into account the uncertainty relation $pr = h$, where *h* is the Planck's constant, for the momentum in the atom we obtain

$$E = hc/r - e^2/r - GMm/R \qquad (2\text{-}1)$$

If there are *N* atoms in the star then the radius *R* and the mass *M* of the star are related to the radius *r* and mass *m* of the atom by

$$R = N^{1/3}r \qquad M = Nm \qquad (2\text{-}2)$$

Inserting this into the above equation we obtain for the order of magnitude of the total energy *E* of the atom in the star,

$$E = hc/r - GN^{2/3}m^2/r \qquad (2\text{-}3)$$

Here we have neglected the term proportional to e^2, since the term proportional to *hc*, i.e. the energy due to the uncertainty relation, is two orders of magnitude larger than the energy due to the electrostatic interaction. (Recall that $\alpha = 2\pi e^2/hc = 1/137$.)

There is a maximum number of atoms N that can be contained in the star; this is the Chandrasekhar number limit. It is obtained simply by setting $E = 0$ and leads to

$$N = (hc/Gm^2)^{3/2} = 10^{57} \qquad (2\text{-}4)$$

The corresponding mass of the star is

$$M = mN = 10^{30} \text{ kg} \qquad (2\text{-}5)$$

which gives the Chandrasekhar mass limit.

Our result shows the fascinating connection between the microphysics—the atomic and quantum mechanical structure of the universe—and the maximum size of stars that can be observed in the universe.

Order in the universe can be due to two things: the origin of compact structures can be explained by the connection between microphysics and cosmology. Other structures—the size of black holes or of galaxies—remains undetermined by the microphysics. It is the history of the universe, its thermodynamics and its early structure that determine the presence of such structures.

3

Order in the Physical Universe

GEORG SUSSMAN
(This note is an extension of the preceding chapter by Roman Sexl.)

I would like to begin by stating that I accept, of course, the overall picture which Dr. Sexl has presented, and I also agree with most of his more detailed statements. What I especially like in his presentation is his explanation of the universal mass-volume diagram in logarithmic scales with their vastly varying orders of magnitude. But let me, for the sake of discussion, concentrate on our minor differences of opinion and on some points which I should like to amend or simply add.

First of all, we may inquire more closely into the primordial origin of all of these physical magnitudes, which means asking for the numerical values of the fundamental constants of nature. Some of these numbers are codetermined by conventions like the definition of meter or kilogram, but others are really natural in the sense of being independent of our accidental choices of metrological units. A typical example is Sommerfeld's fine structure constant $\alpha = 2\pi e^2/ch \approx 1/137$. More recent measurements[1] yielded an admirably precise value, $1/\alpha = 137.0359(6)$, its error being less than one part per million. This is an *absolute value* which seems to hint at some hidden unity of the physical forces. Most physicists hope that science will be able, sooner or later, to calculate such a natural number from new principles which we are eagerly looking for. But there are some colleagues who guess that α might be somehow an accidental number, a result of God's playing dice (so to say, with Einstein). In any case it is a thought-provoking and illuminating endeavor to imagine how the universal order would look like if $1/\alpha$ had another value, say 200 instead of the 137 which it happens to have in our universe.[2] In Sexl's paper, α occurs implicitly in Equation 2-1 as the ratio of the first to the second term on the right-hand side of that equation. Sexl goes on to neglect the second term in comparison with the first one, as being about 137 times smaller, and so this middle term no longer shows up in the final expression of the energy E, later in the page. This is quite right, but in other circumstances α cannot be neglected; its order of magnitude determines, for example, the size a of the hydrogen atom which lies at the very bottom of Sexl's diagram. The pertinent formula is $a_1 = \alpha\, h/2\pi cm$ where m is the mass of the electron and, as before, c the velocity of light and h Planck's quantum of action. A change of α would affect the temporal and energetic scales as well as the spatial ones. The whole microscopic structure of the universe including the laws of organic chemistry and biology may change quite sensitively.

Another fundamental constant of this kind is the ratio M/m between the mass of the proton and that of the electron. It happens to be about 1850, and we do not know whether or not a different value would violate some fundamental principles. It is not clear to me either how deeply the fabric of our universe would be affected by a change of this number—be it real in time, or in our imagination only.

Yet there is no doubt about the importance of the gravitational attraction between an electron and a proton in relation to their electrical attraction. This coefficient $G = \gamma mM/e^2$, a natural measure of Newton's gravitational constant G, has the extremely small value of about $10^{-40} \approx 2^{-730} \approx e^{-82}$. About fifty years ago Dirac proposed that this number might decrease during the cosmic evolution. This interesting idea seems to conflict with the more recent observations and estimations. A similar (and probably related) fate had Heisenberg's vision that at the Compton length of the proton, which is about 10^{-15}m, our continuous space notions should be replaced by some kind of geometrical atomism. Now we are pretty sure that Minkowski's smooth space-time structure stays valid until at least 10^{-17}m, which is a hundred times smaller than Heisenberg's value. Nowadays we usually guess that a discrete structure of space and time should obtain at a much smaller scale, as an effect of Einstein's gravitational force combined with quantum theory. This amounts to the Planck length $l = \sqrt{Gh/2\pi c^3}$ of about 3×10^{-36}m, and the corresponding Planck time $\tau = l/c \approx 10^{-44}$s.

These considerations stress the deep importance of that mysterious number, 10^{-40}. How likely is this tiny ε the unique solution of some fundamental (eigenvalue) equation? Be that as it may, had ε a different numerical value (which is, to be sure, independent of any metrological conventions), that universe would not equal our universe. Recent studies seem to indicate surprisingly narrow margin to be observed in order to avoid drastic changes. Imagine, for example, a decrease of ε by one decadic order of magnitude, from 10^{-40} to 10^{-41}. If we view this on a logarithmic scale, which seems to be the appropriate thing to do in this case, what we see is a relatively small change only, namely from -40 to -41. Nevertheless, the physical conditions in the possible planetary systems would have to undergo dramatic changes. These would probably suffice to destroy the probability of any organic life, or the like, in the universe.

Contemplations of this kind have been summarized by some authors under the heading of a new approach to natural philosophy, called the *anthropic principle*. Roughly speaking, it proposes to look at those conditions which the so-called laws of nature must meet in order that the existence of humans or other intelligent populations is not prohibited (or, which is the same thing here, physically prevented). The main obstacle in this field is, of course, our lack of phantasy or, which is almost the same, our poor mathematical craft or power together with our less than perfect experimental and observational experience. All this notwithstanding, the field is not as dark as one could all too easily surmise. As a typical example, let me mention the chemical basis of organic life. (By the way: the preorganic level of order is not dead, but alive on a lower level, which I like to call the *dynamical* level of life, followed by the *vegetative,* the *animal,* and the *intellectual* level.) As you know, organic chemistry is centered around carbon, which is just one of the chemical elements chosen out of one hundred others. For a long time many people talked about an analogue of organic chemistry based on silicon, a chemical element whose atoms exert, like those of carbon, for valency bonds. But now we are rather sure that there can be no organic life (no self reproduction by means of digital information processes) centered around silicon. (The artificial life, or even intelligence, based on the chips from the Silicon Valley are quite another thing: It is artificial, man made, and not spontaneously grown). That kind of order which is called organic life depends on the well balanced slightly excited electronic shell structure of the carbon atom. This electron configuration $(1s)^2 (2s)(2p)^3$ of the carbon shell must be fine tuned in a very fortunate way. Distort it slightly, and all the wonders of the long molecular chains and reactions are gone. Such are the structural origins of order in the universe.

Its temporal origins are, of course, also of the utmost importance. In our days the sciences find them, as Sexl explains, in the original cosmological singularity and during the ensuing spatial expansion which gave rise to atoms, galaxies, stars, planets, rivers, plants, animals, and humans. This cosmic process with emerging order structures is quite consistent with an overall increase of entropy, which can be regarded as a measure of disorder. Organic beings are able to eat negative entropy and store part of it within their own architectures. Negative entropy may be interpreted as the information that is contained in the thermodynamic state (as opposed to the dynamic state which has always a vanishing entropy). There is thus no contradiction between the emergence or transvolution (the so-called evolution) of higher and higher structures, and the second law of thermodynamics.

The other atomistic dilemma of the entropy concept is much more serious: According to the second law of thermodynamics the entropy of a thermally isolated system (not in equilibrium) has to increase irreversibly in time.[3] How can this phenomenon be made consistent with the well proven reversibility and quasi-periodicity of the atomic motions? Boltzmann's proposal, so nicely explained by Sexl, is not convincing, as von Weizsäcker has pointed out many years ago: By believing in Darwinism, Boltzmann contradicted himself with an overwhelming probability, because we can imagine a vast majority of cosmic fluctuations which are much smaller than the Darwinian ones, and are consistent with all our experiences, and are much more probable. Weizsäcker then arrived at a phenomenological philosophy of time, close to that of Husserl, Bergson, or Heidegger. But I agree with Sexl that we should look for a cosmological solution of the thermostatistical problem, which is based on a more realistic cosmology than that which prevailed between Laplace and Boltzmann. An important point here is that our dynamical universe may no longer be treated as an isolated system not even with respect to energy and much less so with respect to entropy. Since about 1970, I have argued that an increasing cosmic volume could very well be a strong cause of entropy production. Sexl's piston picture is a nice illustration of this kind of argument.

What I do not understand in Sexl's work and what seems to me rather unlikely, is the model of an oscillating universe with an ever increasing entropy. In a cyclic or almost cyclic universe one should expect an infinity of cycles before that one which we are living in. Then there is no reason to assume that the entropy content of the universe should steadily increase from left to right, that is, from what we humans call past to what we call future. Any argument in favor of one direction of time would favor the opposite direction as well or as badly.

In this context Sexl's piston picture becomes convincing only if it is supplemented by an atomistic or microscopic model analogous to that given by Boltzmann in his famous "Gastheorie," where he used his statistical collision equation based on what he called "molecular chaos." A better name would be "semi-chaos" instead of "chaos," because his assumption is, as the Ehrenfests have made clear, asymmetric with respect to (what we call) past and future. As I have pointed out in my contribution "Irreversibility and Quantum Theory," ICUS X (1981), the temporal asymmetry of Boltzmann's statistical equation can be understood only by an appeal to the cosmological arrow of time, as evidenced by the galactic space expansion and the cosmothermal background radiation. An intermediate step in this chain of reasoning is the electromagnetic time arrow of the Sommerfeld causality. According to this empirical law, which is an asymmetric strengthening of the better-known Einstein causality, an (electromagnetic) effect cannot temporarily precede its (electromagnetic) cause. Now it is essential to realize that this chain of reasoning applies to the final Big Bang as well as to the original one. This means that the time flow should gradually die out when the universe approaches its maximum volume and that "after" that it should continuously build up in the opposite direction. Next assume that there are (or will be, if we stick to our provincial language) some intelligent creatures in the other hemicosmos, which is by no means sure according to the anthropic principle with its small probabilities. But if we make that assumption, then these very strange colleagues of ours would experience a time arrow that is in the opposite direction, according to our temporal concepts, which become rather abstract anyway if extended to the whole universe. But this difficulty of our subjective intuition is not much harder than for example Einstein's twin paradox which has been understood and experimentally confirmed long ago. When the Phoenicians sailed around Africa they were surprised to find the sun in the north, and their contemporaries (including Herodotus) laughed at their report—quite wrongly as was realized soon after in Alexandria. In a similar way the direction of time may very well be different in various parts of the universe.

NOTES

1. The most accurate ones use the quantized Hall effect, which was discovered by von Klitzing a few years ago and awarded the 1985 Nobel prize in physics.
2. There is an old jocular equation, $2 \times 137 = 1 + 273$, allegedly connecting Somerfeld's constant with Kelvin's value in centigrades of the absolute zero in an amusing way.
3. This is not only a definition of the time direction, but a substantial proposition, because the orientation of time may be defined otherwise, e.g., by the outgoing waves of any radiation.

4

Particle Physics and Cosmic Evolution

HARALD FRITZSCH

1. COSMOLOGY: THE STANDARD MODEL

Modern cosmology is based on the idea of the "hot Big Bang" first discussed by George Gamov in 1948. It is founded on a few, but important experimental facts that we shall review briefly.

The Expanding Universe

Distant galaxies are receding from us with a speed proportional to their distance from us. Since the discovery of this phenomenon in 1929 by Hubble and his collaborators, the experimental data have become rather precise. We relate the velocities of the distant galaxies, determined by redshift measurements, to the corresponding distances with the linear "Hubble Law":

$$v = H_o r$$

The Hubble parameter H_o has been determined to within a factor of two to be

$$H_o \approx 50 \text{ to } 100 \text{ km s}^{-1} \text{ Mpc}^{-1}$$

where Mpc stands for megaparsec (1 pc $= 3.08572 \times 10^3$ km $= 3.2615$ light years).

The recession of the galaxies is interpreted as a consequence of the expansion of the universe, which according to the measured values of H_o started about 10 to 20 billion years ago.

Photons in Intergalactic Space

The observation of an isotropic electromagnetic radiation with a Planck spectrum of 2.7 K strongly supports the idea that the universe has been very hot in the past. On the average there are about 400 photons per cm^3, carrying an energy of 0.25 eV/cm^3 which corresponds to about $^1/_{1600}$ of the total average energy density in the universe. In the standard "hot Big Bang" scenario these photons are relics of the Big Bang. The number density of photons $n(\gamma)$ in the universe is much larger than the number density of nucleons $n(N)$. One estimates that

$$\frac{\text{number of photons}}{\text{number of nucleons}} = \frac{n(\gamma)}{n(N)} \sim 10^9 \text{ to } 10^{10}$$

Helium Abundance

It is well known that the elements heavier than helium are produced by stars burning. This explains why the relative abundances of these elements vary greatly throughout the universe. On the other hand, helium is very abundant (slightly more than $^1/_4$ of all matter in the universe is helium), and distributed rather uniformly. The only satisfactory explanation for this phenomenon is to suppose that the helium was formed shortly (about 100 s) after the Big Bang, when the matter in the universe was present in form of a hot isotropic and homogeneous plasma of mostly nucleons and electrons. By the time the temperature of the plasma drops to less than 10^9 K or 10^{-4} GeV (10^5 eV) (about 10 to 100 s), deuterons can be formed without being broken up shortly afterwards by the radiation. Consequently, all neutrons combine with protons to form deuterons. The latter react quickly among each other, so that within about 200 seconds virtually all deuterons disappear and helium nuclei are produced. The relative amount of helium produced depends only on the relative number of neutrons present at the time when the temperature drops below 10^9K. On the other hand, the number of neutrons in the plasma depends solely on the neutron proton mass difference, and to some extent on the time elapsed since the formation of the neutrons (about 10^{-5} s after the Big Bang = free neutrons are not stable and decay with a half-life $\tau_{1/2}$ = 10.6 ± 0.2 min). At the time of deuteron formation one expects that of every 16 nucleons, about 14 are protons and 2 are neutrons.

During the helium production 4 of every 16 nucleons form a helium nucleus. Thus about 25 percent of all nuclear matter is transformed into helium. During the past 10 or 20 billion years the burning of hydrogen into helium in the stars led to an increase of the helium content of the universe to about 27–28 percent. Thus about 90 percent of the helium observed in the universe today is of primodial origin; it is a relic of the hot and dense plasma which filled the universe hundreds of seconds after the beginning.

Space-Time Geometry and Energy-Matter Density

We shall assume that the interplay between the space-time geometry and the matter content of the universe is correctly described by Einstein's theory of General Relativity. The latter allows, of course, an immense number of possible cosmological models, due to the complexity of matter distributions one may envisage. The situation is enormously simplified if one assumes that the universe is isotropic and homogeneous. Of course, we know from daily experience that this is not true on a small scale. However once the scale of the extension of superclusters of galaxies, say 500 million light years, is passed, the universe does seem to be isotropic and homogeneous.

The possible geometries of a homogeneous and isotropic universe can be described in a rather simple way. Three different possibilities can be distinguished:

    A. A finite universe with a positive curvature
    B. An infinite universe with zero curvature
    C. An infinite universe with negative curvature.

The interplay between geometry and matter density described by Einstein's field equations leads to the following conclusions:

1) If the matter density ρ of the universe is larger than a certain critical matter density ρ_c, given essentially by Hubble's constant, the universe is of type A. In this case, the expansion eventually stops and, due to the gravitational attraction, the galaxies start to approach each other.

2) Case B is realized if the matter density is exactly equal to the critical density. In this case the expansion of the universe slows down more and more but never stops.

3) In case C the matter density of the universe is less than the critical density, and there is not enough matter in the universe to bring the expansion to an end.

Using the presently accepted value of the Hubble constant, the critical matter density comes to about $\rho_c = 10^{-29} \text{g/cm}^3$. Direct estimates of the mass density in the universe give $\rho \approx 10^{-31} g/cm^3$, or about 10^3–$10^4 eV/cm^3$. Taking into account matter not seen directly, but indirectly due to its gravitational effect, the matter density can be brought up to about $10^{-30} g/cm^3$. Thus it seems that the matter density in the observed universe is only about $1/10$ of the critical mass density, and the universe is of type C. Due to the uncertainties involved in the various estimates of ρ and H, this is the most likely situation, but by no means certain. The matter density is related to the rate of expansion of the universe.

The presence of the "photon sea" in the universe suggests that the cosmos was very hot shortly after the Big Bang: the further we go back in the history of the universe, the larger the temperature. (Temperature is used as a measure of the average particle energy, the exact relation depending on certain factors that need not to be considered here.) We therefore expect that, immediately after the start, the matter in the universe can be described in terms of a very hot plasma of the matter constituents. According to our modern view, matter consists of leptons, quarks and a number of force-carrying bosons. This implies that we can describe the cosmological development in terms of a hot plasma of leptons, quarks and bosons. If the temperature is large enough, these objects can be treated like massless quanta (because their energies are much larger than their rest energies). In this case the matter density ρ is proportional to the fourth power of the temperature:

$$\rho = \frac{\pi^2}{30} g T^4$$

The parameter g is a measure of the effective number of spin degrees of freedom and is given by

$$g = n_b + \frac{7}{8} n_f$$

where n_b and n_f are the number of bosonic and fermionic degrees of freedom, respectively; antiparticles are counted separately.

Simple estimates indicate that at $t \approx 10^{-11}$ s after the Big Bang the temperature dropped down to 10^{15} K, corresponding to an average energy of the particles of 100 GeV. This energy is about the energy explored in the modern high energy physics laboratories. Thus we can say that the insights into the substructure of matter gained in particle physics allow us to extrapolate the cosmological development back to about 10^{-11} s after the beginning. Further extrapolations to earlier times can only be made by relying on specific theories which have not yet been tested experimentally.

2. PARTICLE PHYSICS: THE STANDARD MODEL

Matter consists of quarks and leptons. Using high energy accelerators, we have been able to explore the structure of matter down to distances of the order of 10^{-16} cm, corresponding to energies on the order of 100 GeV. All particle physics phenomena can be described in terms of the *standard model*: a combination of the electroweak gauge theory of electromagnetic and weak interactions, and quantum chromodynamics (QCD), the gauge theory of quarks and gluons, which seems to be the correct field theory for the strong interaction.

Thus far, five different quarks have been found. Only two quarks, the "up" and "down" quarks u and d, act as the constituents of nuclear matter and are essentially massless. The nucleons each consist of three quarks: the proton, uud, and the neutron, ddu. The π-mesons consist of quarks-antiquark pairs, e.g., the π^+ meson is ($\bar{d}u$). The other three quarks, s ("strange"), c ("charm"), and b ("bottom"), are relatively heavy and act as constituents of highly unstable matter. Theorists suppose that a sixth quark t ("top") exists. These six quarks can be nicely arranged with the six observed leptons in the following way:

$$\text{leptons} \qquad \text{quarks}$$
$$\begin{pmatrix} \nu_e & \nu_\mu & \nu_\tau \\ e^- & \mu^- & \tau^- \end{pmatrix} \qquad \begin{pmatrix} u & c & t \\ d & s & b \end{pmatrix}$$

Hadrons and Quantum Chromodynamics (QCD)

Quarks carry an attribute not carried by leptons: "color." The latter is nothing but a nickname for the fact that each quark can appear in three different editions. The interactions between the quarks are described by the exchange of gluons—massless spin-one objects within the magic property of being able to change the colors of the quarks. Such a theory is an example of a *gauge theory*. Theories of this type were first discussed by H. Weyl around 1920, and by O. Klein in the thirties. The first actual gauge theory was introduced by Yang and Mills in 1954.

The gauge theory of colored quarks is quantum chromodynamics (QCD). The QCD gauge force acts universally on all quarks. The gluons mediate the strong force and are responsible for the permanent binding of the quarks and gluons to colorless hadrons. The strong nuclear forces among hadrons are indirect manifestations of the color force.

During the last few years, the most impressive success in high energy physics has been the verification of the predictions of quantum chromodynamics for hadronic physics. QCD has developed from a hypothetical scheme to a realistic theory of the hadrons and of their inter-actions.

The strong interaction coupling constant g_s has been determined recently in lepton-hadron scattering experiments and in the e^+e^- annihila-tion with a relatively good accuracy. One finds at an energy of about 30 GeV that $g_s^2/4\pi = \alpha_s \approx 0.15$-$0.20$. Both in the lepton-hadron scattering and in e^+e^- annihilation experiments, one observes effects (e.g. scaling violations) due to gluon radiation from quarks, which are the QCD ana-logs of the well-known QED *bremsstrahlung*. Furthermore, we have found evidence for the production of quark-antiquark pairs by gluons (the QCD analog of e^+e^- production by photons via the Bethe-Heitler process), e.g. by observing the production of particles with charm and bottom quarks in hadronic collisions. In addition, there are indications that gluons couple directly to gluons, as predicted by the QCD gauge theory. One can draw this conclusion by investigating the change of the gluon distribution func-tion of the proton at increasing energies.

Quantum chromodynamics has the interesting property that the in-teraction between the quarks decreases as the energy increases. At suffi-ciently high energies, more specifically at energies above a few GeV, hadronic matter can be described to a good approximation in terms of a gas of free quarks and gluons. All the complexities of nuclear physics disappear at high energies or high temperatures. This constitutes an enor-mous simplification for cosmological studies.

Electroweak Forces

The gauge theory of the electroweak forces describes three different kinds of interactions, the weak *charged-current* interaction mediated by $W^\pm$-boson exchange, the weak *neutral current* interaction, mediated by Z-boson ex-change, and the electromagnetic interaction mediated by photon ex-change. The gauge symmetry is SU(2) × U(1). It is valid only at energies much greater than 100 GeV. At lower energies it is spontaneously broken. As a consequence, the W and Z particles are massive (masses of order 100 GeV). These masses are determined by the vacuum expectation value $<0|\varphi|0>$ of a scalar *Higgs field* φ, which in turn is determined phenome-nologically by the observed value of the Fermi constant G_F, introduced by Fermi in his theory of β-decay, which measures the strength of the weak interaction:

$$\frac{1}{2<0|\varphi|0>^2} = \frac{G_F}{\sqrt{2}}, \qquad (<0|\varphi|0> = 246 \text{ GeV}).$$

The SU(2) gauge force acts universally on all left-handed quarks and leptons which transform as SU(2) doublets. The right-handed quarks and leptons are singlets. As a consequence, parity is violated maximally. It is unknown why this is the case, nor do we know whether parity conservation is restored at some high energy scale.

The U(1) force acts differently on the various kinds of quarks and leptons. The coupling strength is determined by the electric charge. Charge quantization is not required. Thus on the level of the electroweak gauge theory it remains unclear why, for example, the charge of the u quark is exactly equal to $2/3$ of the positron charge.

A remarkable feature of the observed leptons and quarks is their classification into three different families:

$$\text{I} \quad \begin{pmatrix} \nu_e & u_r & u_g & u_b \\ e^- & d_r & d_g & d_b \end{pmatrix}$$

$$\text{II} \quad \begin{pmatrix} \nu_\mu & c_r & c_g & c_b \\ \mu^- & s_r & s_g & s_b \end{pmatrix}$$

$$\text{III} \quad \begin{pmatrix} \nu_\tau & t_r & t_g & t_b \\ \tau^- & b_r & b_g & b_b \end{pmatrix}$$

Where r, g and b correspond to red, green and blue quark colors, respectively.

Within each family the sum of the electric charges vanishes. The existence of the three families, in particular the fact that the leptons and quarks in each family seem to have identical properties, apart from the various lepton-and quark masses, remains one of the great puzzles in high energy physics.

The W and Z particles were discovered in 1983 at the CERN $\bar{p}p$ collider. Their masses coincide with the masses predicted by the standard electroweak theory. Whether the spontaneous symmetry breaking mechanism for generating masses is correct is yet unknown. The associated neutral Higgs particle has not been found yet.

The mass generation via spontaneous symmetry breaking has an interesting property: it disappears if one is dealing with a system of interacting weak bosons placed in a hot environment. If the temperature is larger than the typical scale of 300 GeV ($\sim 10^{15}$K), the vacuum expectation value of the scalar field disappears, and correspondingly the W and Z masses vanish, as well as all lepton and quark masses. Of course, the associated temperature is extremely high. It can hardly be reached in any physical situation other than the first instants after the Big Bang.

3. UNITY OF QUARKS AND LEPTONS

A popular way to extrapolate to the physics at energies much larger than 100 GeV is to suppose that a unified description of the leptons and quarks can be achieved, following a line similar to the electroweak theory, which gives a unified description of the electromagnetic and weak forces due to the spontaneous breaking of the electroweak gauge symmetry. It might well be that quarks and leptons are related by a large symmetry which is valid only at very small distances. The differences between leptons and quarks observed at distances on the order of 10^{-16} cm or larger would then be attributed to a spontaneous breakdown of this symmetry. Our aim is to embed both the QCD gauge group $SU(3)^c$ and the electroweak gauge group $SU(2) \times U(1)$ in a larger group G.

The program following those lines, called the *grand unification* of all interactions, is very ambitious in that it proposes to unify all interactions within one theoretical framework. In this theory all observed interactions except gravity—e.g., the long-range electromagnetic force, the short-range weak forces and the strong interactions—are interpreted as different manifestations of the same underlying fundamental force.

If one starts out from the observed set of leptons, quarks and bosons, the program of grand unification can be realized in two ways, which are closely related to each other and are described by the symmetry groups $SU(5)$ or $SO(10)$.

One possible symmetry among leptons and quarks is described by the group $SU(5)$. The fermions in one family (2 leptons, 2 quarks) form a system of 15 objects, taking into account the color degree of freedom explicitly. The large symmetry $SU(5)$ implies that these fermions are divided into two classes—one class of five fermions and one class of ten (Figure 4-1). Each of these classes consists of both leptons and quarks, i.e. a unification of them is achieved once the large symmetry becomes relevant.

The $SO(10)$ scheme is more stringent than the previous one in the sense that all fermions of one family, altogether 16 objects, are related to each other by the symmetry (Figure 4-2). Compared to $SU(5)$ the symmetry is larger, and there exist several different ways to adjust the parameters of the theory to observable quantities. This is relevant for, among other things, the problem of proton decay.

A general feature of the type of theories discussed above is the constraint that the large symmetry uniting quarks and leptons becomes relevant only at extremely high energies. The onset of the lepton-quark symmetry is given by the mass of those gauge bosons, the so-called X-bosons, which cause transitions between leptons and quarks. Various experimental constraints require these bosons to be extremely heavy, at least

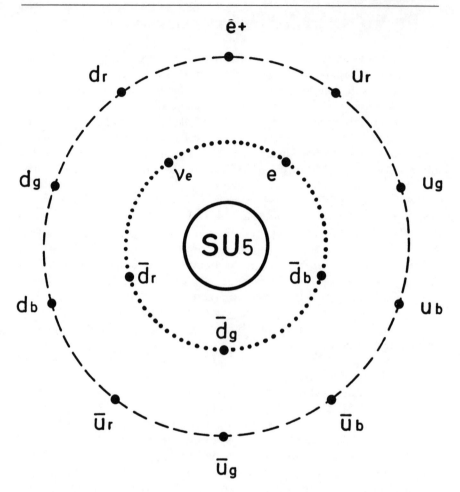

Figure 4-1: Two classes of fermions, one consisting of five and one consisting of ten objects, appear as the fundamental units in the SU(5) scheme.

10^{14} GeV. Due to the large mass of these bosons all processes in which lepton-quark transitions are involved are strongly suppressed. The most interesting process of this kind is the decay of the proton.

In the SU(5) scheme the lifetime of the proton can be estimated rather precisely to be

$$\tau(\text{proton}) = (4 \times 10^{31 \pm 1.3}) \left(\frac{\Lambda}{0.16 \text{ GeV}}\right)^4 \text{ years}$$

where Λ is an energy parameter appearing in QCD, to be determined by

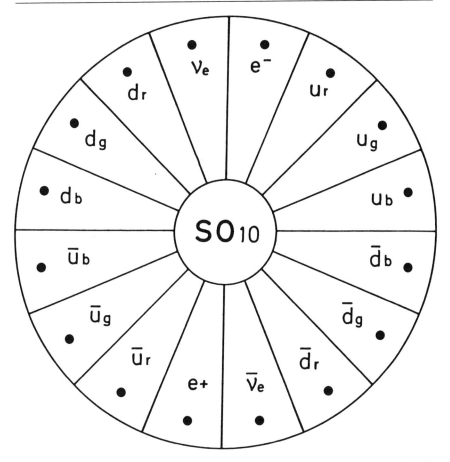

Figure 4-2: The 16 fundamental particles are related to each other by the SO(10) symmetry.

experiment. The best value of Λ is about 0.16 GeV, hence the proton lifetime is expected to be about 10^{31} years, in disagreement with experiment which suggests $\tau > 10^{31}$ years.

In the SO(10) scheme the decay of the proton proceeds essentially along similar lines as in the SU(5) scheme. However one may expect the proton lifetime to be larger than 10^{31} years. It may even be above 10^{33} years. At present it seems that the SU(5) theory is unlikely to be correct. However the SO(10) scheme could be the correct way of achieving a unification of QCD and the electroweak interactions.

We should like to emphasize that the theories of grand unification discussed here can be supplemented by incorporating supersymmetry, a specific symmetry relating fermions and bosons. This effectively means adding more particles, the supersymmetric partners of the observed leptons, quarks and bosons, which have not been observed experimentally and for this reason are required to be very massive. Supersymmetric theories are of special interest since they can be viewed as part of a larger theory, *supergravity*—a theory uniting gravity and the other interactions.

Recently it has been found that all interactions including gravity can be described rather uniquely if the basic objects in the theory are not one-dimensional, but two-dimensional. These string-like objects are called *super-strings*. However, specific discussion of this theory cannot be presented here.

Probably the most interesting application of the idea of a unified interaction becoming relevant at a large energy scale ($>10^{14}$ GeV) is the *spontaneous generation* of baryonic matter in the universe. In particular, the decays of superheavy gauge bosons or superheavy scalars can produce a net baryon number. The idea is that soon after the "Big Bang" the baryon number violating interactions came into equilibrium, and any initial baryon asymmetry (if present) was washed out. If the expansion rate of the universe is fast compared to the decay rate of the superheavy particles, the latter drop out of equilibrium, and a net baryon number is generated, as discussed later.

Another way of achieving a unity of quarks and leptons is to consider composite models. Quarks and leptons may consist of smaller constituents. Experimental constraints require the bound state radii of quarks and leptons to be less than about 10^{-16} cm. This length scale corresponds to an energy scale of about 10^3 GeV. In some models of this type even the weak bosons are considered as bound states, in which case the 1 TeV energy scale arises as the natural scale for the inverse radii of the bound states. Such ideas have direct implications for cosmology. Shortly (about 10^{-13} s) after the big bang, when the temperature of the universe was still above 1 TeV (or 10^{16} K), the matter in the universe would have been present in form of a gas of lepton-quark constituents. In particular, the mechanism for the generation of a non-zero baryon number in the universe would depend on details of the dynamics of the constituents.

Which way our understanding of particle physics might go in the future depends in particular on the new insights which will be gained at the beginning of the nineties when new accelerators like LEP (CERN, Geneva) and HERA (DESY, Hamburg) start to operate.

4. THE UNIVERSE BACKWARD IN TIME

High energy physics allows us to extrapolate the development of the universe backward in time until about 10^{-11} s after the Big Bang, a time at which the temperature of the universe was about 100 GeV or 10^{15} K. Further extrapolations depend on specific theoretical frameworks, which

During the time interval 10^{-5} to 5×10^5 years a number of impor-
have not yet been tested. In this chapter I shall describe the development
of the universe starting from our present time.

At present matter consists of nucleons, electrons, photons, neutrinos
and perhaps other neutral particles not yet detected. There is no evidence
that antimatter is present in large quantities. The gravitational dynamics
of the universe is governed by the total energy density ρ, which can be
decomposed into its different components:

$$\rho \;=\; \underset{\text{nucleons}}{\rho_n} \;+\; \underset{\text{electrons}}{\rho_e^-} \;+\; \underset{\text{photons}}{\rho_\gamma} \;+\; \underset{\text{neutrinos}}{\rho_\nu} \;+\; \underset{\substack{\text{other} \\ \text{unknown} \\ \text{particles}}}{\bar{\rho}}$$

The energy density provided by the nuclear matter is on the average
about 400 eV/cm^3. As explained before, this corresponds to the ratio

$$\frac{\text{number of photons}}{\text{number of nucleons}} \approx 10^9 \text{ to } 10^{10}.$$

The nuclear matter density dominates the energy density, unless
massive neutrinos or other neutral particles are important. It is much less
(< 10 percent) than the *critical energy density*, i.e., the density required in
order to have a closed universe. The latter is estimated to be $\sim 10^3$ to 10^4
eV/cm^3.

If neutrinos are massive, one expects the neutrino sea (analogous to
the photon sea) to contribute to the energy density an amount $\rho_\nu \sim 230$
m_ν cm^{-3}, for each kind of neutrino of mass m_ν. The restriction $\rho_\nu < \rho_e$ leads
to the constraint:

$$\underset{\text{neutrinos}}{\Sigma m_\nu} \;\lesssim\; 50 \text{ eV}.$$

Today the energy density is dominated by nonrelativistic particles
(mainly nucleons) and perhaps neutrinos or other particles. At earlier
times the relativistic particles take over, since $\rho \sim T^4$ and $T \sim R^{-1}$ where
R is the radius of the universe; it follows that $\rho \sim R^{-4}$, which should be
compared with $\rho \sim R^{-3}$ for nonrelativistic matter. The energy density of
the photon sea exceeds the nuclear density about 500,000 years ($\sim 2 \times 10^{13}$s) after the Big Bang, when the temperature dropped below 0.3 eV
(10^3 K).

tant changes took place in the universe, which will be mentioned here
briefly:

    a. Nucleosynthesis; formation of deuterium and helium at $t \sim 2 \times 10^2$ s.
    b. The disappearance of the positrons by e^+e^--annihilation at $t \sim 10$ s.
    c. The decoupling of the neutrinos at $t \sim 1$ s.
    d. Decay of all strongly interacting particles except nucleons at t $\sim 10^{-5}$ s).

As has already been mentioned, nucleosynthesis, generating in particular a sizeable amount of helium, is one of the important features of the
hot Big Bang cosmology.

At about t = 10^{-3} s the universe was filled with a plasma with a
temperature of $T \sim 30$ MeV or 3×10^{11} K composed of electrons,
positrons, photons, neutrinos and nucleons. If we go back in time to $t \sim 10^{-6}$ s, $T \sim 1$ GeV $\sim 10^{13}$ K, other particles begin to play a rôle (pions,
muons). If one treats the pions naively as pointlike objects, one arrives at
the conclusion that at $T \sim 1$ GeV (or 10^{13} K) the tiny volume of one cubic
fermi (1 fm = 10^{-13} cm) would be inhabited by fifty pions. According to
our present understanding of the strong interactions this is impossible,
since pions like any other strongly interacting particles consist of quarks
which are confined inside a finite volume with the extension of about 1
fm. We conclude that during the time interval 10^{-6} s to 10^{-4} s the hadronic
matter went through a phase transition. If the temperature is above 1
GeV (10^{13} K), no free hadrons exist. Instead, the hadronic matter is represented by a gas of nearly free quarks and gluons, a special state of
matter which I like to call *chromoplasma*. It was in thermal equilibrium
with the other light, non-strongly-interacting particles (photons, e^-, e^+
etc.). The chromoplasma consisted of quarks and antiquarks of the u, d
and *s- flavors*. The densities of s-quarks and s-quarks were exactly the
same, while for u and d-flavors there was a tiny excess of quarks over
antiquarks:

$$\frac{n(u) + n(d)}{n(\bar{u}) + n(\bar{d})} - 1 \sim 10^{-9}$$

The baryon-antibaryon asymmetry observed in our present universe
can be traced back to this tiny excess of quarks in the chromoplasma.

At $T \sim 1$ GeV (or 10^{-6} s) only the three light quark flavors u, d, s
were present in the chromoplasma. At higher temperatures ($t \sim 10^{-8}$ s or
$T \sim 30$ GeV = 3×10^{14} K) the new quark flavors c and b contribute,
and at $T > 100$ GeV presumably the sixth quark flavor t starts to play its

rôle. (Thus far the existence of the t-quark has not been confirmed by experiment.)

If the temperature of the universe drops significantly below 1 GeV, the chromoplasma starts to disappear, and individual hadrons form. Due to our lack of understanding of nonperturbative aspects of QCD, dynamical details of this phase transition are not known. Preliminary studies indicate that this may be a first order phase transition, the transition temperature being on the order of 150 to 250 MeV (or about 10^{12} K).

Details of the phase transition can be obtained by new experimental studies, notably by investigating high energy collisions of heavy nuclei. One expects that in a frontal collision of two heavy nuclei, part of the colliding hadronic matter undergoes a transition to the chromoplasma phase, provided the critical temperature is reached. The plasma would cool down rapidly until the condensation of the quarks, antiquarks and gluons into individual hadrons (mostly pions) sets in. Possible signals for the formation of the chromoplasma would be the production of an unusual number of γ-rays and of e^+e^- or $\mu^+\mu^-$ pairs by the annihilation of the quarks and antiquarks in the chromoplasma. Experiments are now under way at CERN.

The chromoplasma in the universe must have undergone the transition to the hadronic phase around $t \sim 10^{-5}$ s. Presumably a large number of pions must have been formed during the phase transition, as well as the nucleons which are the constituents of nuclear matter in the universe today. The pions decay weakly or electromagnetically, and these decays mark the end of the life of the antiquarks in the universe. Afterwards, the hadronic matter is present only in form of nucleons consisting of quarks.

It is well-known that cosmic rays contain a small flux of antiprotons ($\bar{p}$). Although the exact magnitude of the $\bar{p}$-flux in the primary cosmic rays is still controversial, it is consistent to suppose that all antiprotons observed in the universe today are products of high energy collisions of nucleons (either cosmic ray collisions or collisions in man-made accelerators). The antiquarks which belonged to the most prominent inhabitants of the universe at $t \lesssim 10^{-5}$ s all disappeared suddenly at the time of the transition from chromoplasma to hadrons.

In view of our limited knowledge both from experiment and theory about the phase transition it cannot be ruled out that besides the nucleons, other exotic pieces of electrically neutral quark matter, in particular matter involving a non-vanishing density of strange quarks, have survived the chromodynamic phase transition. As speculated by a number of theorists, this new type of nuclear matter could manifest itself in the existence of neutral *quark nuggets* of macroscopic size. They could even provide the dominant part of the "missing matter" in the universe.

During the period from 10^{-12} s to 10^{-6} s the temperature of the universe dropped from 1 TeV (10^3 GeV) to about 1 GeV. This drop of tem-

perature affected mostly the electromagnetic and weak properties of
matter. At energies above 100 GeV, i.e. above the masses for the W and Z
bosons, one expects the weak interaction to be of essentially the same
strength as the electromagnetic interaction. The W and Z masses are
proportional to the vacuum expectation value of the Higgs field, which
disappears at sufficiently high temperatures, as discussed before. As a
result, at $t < 10^{-12}$ s, all four gauge bosons—Z, W$^\pm$ and γ—are massless;
likewise the quarks and leptons. If this picture is correct, *the appearance of
masses is due to a new phase transition, the electroweak phase transition.*

The dynamical details of the electroweak phase transition depend
greatly on whether the SU(2) × U(1) theory is indeed a microscopic
theory of the fermions and bosons. In various schemes of composite leptons, quarks and bosons the 1 TeV energy scale corresponds to the inverse
radius of the leptons and quarks. If this is the case, the matter in the
universe at $T > 1$ TeV (or 10^{16} K) would be represented by a dense gas of
lepton-quark constituents.

5. THE GENESIS OF BARYONS

Today there exists clear evidence that the observed matter in the universe
consists of u and d quarks and electrons. Large quantities of antimatter
do not seem to exist.

In the standard SU(3) × SU(2) × U(1) model, the number of
quarks minus the number of antiquarks is exactly conserved. (This implies the *conservation of* baryon number). During the hot phase of the chromoplasma the quarks dominated slightly over the antiquarks by a tiny
amount on the order of 10^{-9} to 10^{-10}. As long as the physics of matter is
described by the standard model, there is no way to explain the net baryonic charge of the universe. Rather, it must be considered a boundary
condition for the Big Bang.

It would be much more satisfactory to obtain the baryon number as
a result of the dynamics of matter shortly after the Big Bang. Any framework achieving this must incorporate three features:

a. Baryon number conservation cannot be strictly maintained.
b. Charge conjugation (C) and the CP-symmetry must be violated.
c. The relevant processes cannot be in thermal equilibrium.

The first two conditions are easy to understand since the aim is to
generate more quarks than antiquarks, violating both the C and CP symmetry. The third condition is necessary in order to avoid the CPT-theorem
which implies equal masses for particles and antiparticles, hence strictly
equal abundances in thermal equilibrium.

A simple mechanism for baryon number generation exists if we suppose that the idea of grand unification makes sense. Around 10^{-36} s after

the Big Bang, the temperature dropped below the grand unification mass scale of the order of 10^{14} to 10^{15} GeV or 10^{28} K. As long as the temperature is still above that energy, the matter in the universe will be present in form of a hot plasma of leptons, quarks and their antiparticles as well as photons, gluons, weak bosons and a new type of boson, called the X boson, which carries both color, electric and weak charges. The latter are responsible for the unification of the strong and electroweak interactions.

As the temperature of the universe drops below 10^{15} GeV or 10^{28} K, the X bosons decay, thereby violating the conditions of thermal equilibrium. These decays will violate both C and CP, since those symmetries are violated by the electroweak interactions. A drastic way to envisage what happens is as follows. Suppose we start out from an $X\overline{X}$ pair. The X-particle may, for example, decay into two u-quarks, and the $\overline{X}$-particle into a d-quark and an electron: $X \rightarrow uu$, $\overline{X} \rightarrow de^-$. The net result is: $X\overline{X} \rightarrow (uud) + e^- = p + e^-$. From equal amounts of matter and antimatter we obtain effectively a proton and an electron, i.e. hydrogen.

Although the chain discussed above is a very simplified one, it clearly displays the generation of baryon number. The violation of CP will guarantee that the other reaction $X\overline{X} \rightarrow (\overline{u}\overline{u}\overline{d}) + e^+$ is slightly suppressed in rate. Unfortunately, quantitative estimates of the amount of baryonic charge generated by this mechanism depend on unknown parameters, e.g. the amount of CP-violation in the X-decay, or the X-mass, which in turn determines the decay rate of the proton. Guesses in the literature range from $n_B/n_\gamma \sim 10^{-6}$ to 10^{-12}, the observed value being $\sim 10^{-9}$ to 10^{-10}.

It is interesting to note that the picture of baryon genesis discussed above is intimately connected with the idea of the unity of quarks and leptons at some high energy scale. We do not know whether the theories of unification based on the symmetries SU(5) or SO(10) give an adequate description of what happens at high energy. Perhaps the unity of quarks and leptons is achieved in some other way, e.g. within the composite model approach. But the chances are good that the baryon number of the universe and the unification idea are closely related. Consequently the proton should not be stable. Eventually the decay must be observed in laboratory experiments.

6. COSMOLOGICAL PUZZLES AND INFLATION

The Problem of Flatness

If we suppose the universe to be isotropic and homogeneous on a large scale, one can distinguish among three different cases, as we discussed in Section 1.

A. The actual matter density ρ in the universe is larger than the critical mass density ρ_c introduced above ($\rho > \rho_c$), which is defined by

$$\rho_c = \frac{3 \, H_o^2}{8\pi \, G} \approx 10^{-29} \text{ g/cm}^3.$$

In this case our three dimensional space is of the elliptic type, i.e. it is closed (finite), and the expansion of the universe will eventually come to a halt, followed by a phase of universal contraction.

B. The actual matter density is equal to the critical one ($\rho = \rho_c$). In this case the three-dimensional space is flat and infinite. The expansion slows down continuously without coming to a halt.

C. The actual matter density is less than the critical mass density ($\rho < \rho_c$). In this case our three dimensional space is infinite (open) and of hyperbolic type; the universe continues to expand forever. An experimental determination of the matter density in our galactic neighborhood gives $\rho \approx 10^{-30}$ g/cm^3, about one-tenth of the critical mass density. This suggests that we are probably in an open universe; even the case $\rho = \rho_c$ is not very likely.

It is interesting to consider the dimensionless quantity $\Omega = \rho/\rho_c$ as a function of time. The standard cosmological model implies:

$$\frac{\Omega - 1}{(\Omega - 1)_{\text{today}}} = \left(\frac{T}{T_{\text{today}}}\right)^{-n}$$

where T is the temperature in the universe at a certain time t, and T_{today} is today's temperature (2.7 K). The exponent n is unity as long as the energy density in the universe is dominated by nonrelativistic particles (*matter-dominated epoch*), and changes to two if the energy density is dominated by radiation.

Today $\Omega - 1$ is a number of order one, say between zero and one. However at earlier time Ω must be much closer to one. For example, at the time of primordial nucleosynthesis ($T \approx 10^9$ K) one finds $\Omega - 1 = 0(10^{-17})$. At $T \approx 10^{32}$ K (the Planck temperature) one has $\Omega - 1 = 0(10^{-63})$.

To require Ω to be extremely close to one at earlier times such that it is still of order one today, and not some absurd number, requires an artificial fine tuning, which looks very ugly from a theoretical point of view (the *flatness problem*). However no problem of this kind exists if Ω is exactly equal to one at all times, e.g. as a consequence of an underlying physical principle.

The Horizon Problem

The photon sea in the universe is very isotropic (to an accuracy of one part in ten thousand). On the other hand a quick calculation shows that only regions in the sky which are less than $2°$ apart could have been in contact with each other 300,000 years (10^{13} s) after the Big Bang, i.e. at the time when the photons decoupled. In view of the large scale inhomogeneities of the observed matter in the universe the isotropy of the 3 K radiation is a puzzle.

The Inflationary Universe

A popular way to solve both the flatness and the horizon problem is the idea of the *inflationary universe*. Suppose the symmetry of a grand unified theory of quarks and leptons is broken by a scalar Higgs field φ which acquires a vacuum expectation value $<0|\varphi|0>$. The latter depends on specific properties of the effective potential for the φ-field, which plays the rôle of an ordering parameter of the system. At temperatures above a certain critical temperature T_c the vacuum expectation value $<0|\varphi|0>$ is zero—the symmetry is unbroken.

If the temperature drops below T_c, a phase transition takes place, and due to a quantum mechanical tunneling phenomenon the vacuum expectation value becomes different from zero: $<0|\varphi|0> \neq 0$. The system makes a transition from a symmetric phase to an asymmetrical one. Suppose we identify the latter phase with the state of the universe today. From observations we know that the energy density of the vacuum, i.e. the cosmological term Λ, must be very small (if different from zero at all). In any case it must be significantly less than the critical density.

However, the vacuum energy density of a system involving a Higgs field φ depends on the effective potential V_{eff} and hence on σ. The potential difference ΔV_{eff} between the unbroken and broken phases describes the difference between the vacuum energy density of the two phases. Since the broken phase $\Lambda \approx 0$, it follows that in the unbroken phase the cosmological term $\Lambda = 8\pi G \Delta V_{eff}$ must correspond to $T_c \sim 10^{14}$ GeV (10^{27} K). However, one must bear in mind that this argument does not explain why Λ is zero or nearly zero in the universe today. The smallness of Λ today, i.e. in the broken phase of the universe, is a great puzzle.

A constant cosmological term Λ implies a constant Hubble parameter H_o, which in turn leads to an exponential expansion of the universe: $R(t) \sim e^{H_o t}$. The typical time scale for this expansion is of the order of $H_o^{-1} \sim 10^8$ to 10^9 Planck time units.

During the inflationary era, which is estimated to last about 10^{-32} s, the size of the universe increased by a factor of about 10^{50}. Afterwards the transition to the broken symmetry phase took place. The tremendous energy density of the unbroken phase was released in the production of particles.

The inflation of the size of the universe by a factor of as large as 10^{50} solves the problem of the isotropic 3 K radiation. Before inflation, the region which later on becomes the universe we observe today is small enough for a thermal equilibrium to be achieved.

If an inflation took place early in the history of the universe, one expects the ratio $\Omega = \rho/\rho_c$ to be essentially one. The inflation causes the space to become nearly flat. Although many observers believe Ω to be significantly less than 1, e.g. $\Omega \approx 0.1$, the case $\Omega = 1$ is certainly not yet excluded.

In the simplest inflation scenario, described above, serious problems exist. In particular, one expects, in analogy to similar situations in solid state physics, that the phase transitions at $T_c \sim 10^{14}$ GeV (10^{27} K) would proceed via a nucleation of bubbles of the new phase, resulting in the creation of severe inhomogeneities, which are not seen in the universe today. These problems can be solved in the so-called *new inflationary universe model.* Here a very special type of Higgs potential is required so that a particular smooth phase transition occurs, allowing a sizable supercooling effect. The reheating temperature depends on specific details of the effective potential. Nevertheless, I think it is fair to say that an attractive particle physics model of the inflationary universe has not yet been constructed.

The idea of the inflationary universe is very promising, since the evolution of the universe is essentially independent of the details of the initial conditions, which are washed out by the inflation. It is quite possible that the universe started out in a highly chaotic state. Certain parts would undergo inflation, thus creating regions which are fairly smooth and regular. Due to huge factors of order 10^{50} playing a rôle, such a region would be large enough to encompass the entire observable universe.

Another interesting aspect of the inflationary scenario is the concept of matter and energy of the universe as relics of a phase transition, representing the latent heat liberated by the transition. In such models, it is quite plausible that the gravitational energy of the universe cancels all other energy, so that the universe has zero energy. A creation of the universe out of nothing may well be possible.

7. CONCLUSION

It is quite clear that in recent decades cosmology has turned from a speculative field into a real science of the dynamical evolution of the universe. Due to the progress made in our understanding of the structure of matter and the dynamical issues of the forces in nature, we are able to trace back the history of the universe to very early times. Thus far, the structure of matter is explored to a distances on the order of 10^{-16} cm, corresponding to an energy scale of about 100 GeV. The standard cosmological model implies that the temperature of the universe dropped below 100 GeV or

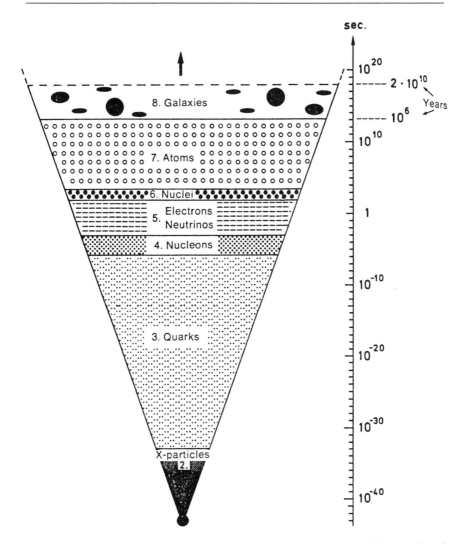

Figure 4-3: A schematic drawing of the evolution of the cosmos. Eight epochs of cosmic evolution are represented, beginning with the first, 10^{-43} seconds following the Big Bang, and continuing to the present epoch, which is marked by the presence of galaxies.
From: H. Fritzsch, *The Creation of Matter* (New York: Basic Books; 1984). Reprinted with permission of the publisher.

10^{15} K at about 10^{-11} s after creation. Thus we may say that the cosmological development is reasonably well understood since $t \approx 10^{-11}$ s. As far as earlier times are concerned, only theoretical extrapolations can be made. However the chances are good that at least some of the speculations we discussed, such as grand unification and the associated phase transition, the mechanism of baryogenesis via X-particle interactions, or the inflation of the universe, may have contact with reality. On the other hand, I am not satisfied with the way we have to rely on the standard mechanism for the dynamical symmetry breaking. Thus far, no scalar Higgs particles have been observed, and chances are that the symmetry breaking is caused by dynamical effects in which no explicit new particles are needed. If this is the case, ideas such as baryogenesis and inflation have to be modified. Furthermore, a serious problem remains entirely unsolved. If indeed inflation is caused by a mechanism which can be described effectively by a cosmological term, it is completely unclear why this term is absent in our observed universe.

Combining theoretical speculations with knowledge from experimental high energy physics, one may divide the cosmological development into eight periods. This "eightfold way" of the evolution of the universe is shown in Figure 4–3. The first epoch (10^{-43} s – 10^{-36} s) is the epoch in which quantum gravity is important. not much is known about it. It is followed by the period (10^{-36} s – 10^{-11} s) in which grand unification is relevant (perhaps inflation and baryogenesis). The third epoch (10^{-11} s – 10^{-6} s) corresponds to the epoch of the electroweak and chromodynamic plasma. in the fourth epoch (10^{-6} s – 10^{-3} s) protons and neutrons are formed. The final traces of antimatter (positrons) disappear during the fifth period (10^{-3} s – 10^2 s). The sixth epoch (10^2 s – 10^4 s) is the one of nucleosynthesis. During the seventh epoch (10^4 s – 10^{13} s) atoms are formed. The photon sea decouples from matter. Today we live in the eighth epoch ($> 10^{13}$ s) in which macroscopic structures like galaxies, stars and planets come into existence.

The principal feature of the present, eighth epoch of cosmic evolution is *structure*—a characteristic of the universe not found during the first million years (10^{13} s). During the first seven eras the structure of the cosmos underwent little change. Energy and matter were distributed homogeneously; the universe was filled with uniform radiation. The only evidence of temporal evolution was found in the expansion of the cosmos and the continuous drop in temperature.

At the beginning of the eighth epoch the universe was composed of a relatively hot gas made up of hydrogen and helium atoms. Today, about 20 billion years or 10^{18} seconds after the Big Bang, the cosmos is filled with galaxies, stars, planets, and such complex structures as ourselves. *The eighth epoch can rightly be called the epoch of structures, of organized systems.*

As far as the very early universe is concerned, many questions remain to be answered, in particular questions about the details of the generation of baryon number and about the possible rôle of the spontaneous symmetry breaking during the yet hypothetical inflationary period. We have not mentioned the important rôle which massive neutrinos or other massive neutral particles might have played in the early universe and in the development of the large scale structure of the universe (galactic clusters, etc.).

Recently, many theorists have become interested in so-called superstring theories, in which the basic elements of the theory are not pointlike particles, but two dimensional objects, the *superstrings*. Interesting models of this type have a curious property: the basic interactions factor into two parts, one describing the particles and interactions we observe (*ordinary matter*), the other describing a shadow world, interacting with ordinary matter only through gravity. *Shadow matter* can only be felt by its gravitational effect, and massive shadow objects ("shadow stars") could make an important contribution to the mass density in the universe. Thus the large-scale structure of the universe could be influenced, perhaps even determined, by the shadow world.

Although many uncertainties about the cosmic evolution still exist, the prospects seem good for explaining the observed features of the universe and its development on the basis of the physical laws of nature, without referring to a special set of initial conditions. The question remains: Who invented the physical laws, the rules which govern the behavior of matter and the space-time structure of the universe?

APPENDIX: MATTER DENSITY AND LARGE-SCALE STRUCTURE

It is assumed that the dynamics of the gravitational force, of space and time, is governed by Einstein's field equations of general relativity:

$$R_{\mu\nu} - \tfrac{1}{2}Rg_{\mu\nu} + \Lambda g_{\mu\nu} = 8\pi \, G \, T_{\mu\nu} \qquad (A-1)$$

where $R_{\mu\nu}$ is the contracted curvature tensor, $R = R_\mu^\mu$, $g_{\mu\nu}$ is the metric tensor; Λ is the cosmological constant and G is Newton's constant for gravity.

The cosmological constant Λ was introduced originally by Einstein in order to obtain a static solution of (A-1). After the discovery of the expansion of the universe the motivation for introducing the Λ-term was lost, and in cosmological considerations Λ is usually set to zero. As we shall see, a Λ term might have been present shortly after the Big Bang and might have played a crucial rôle in the dynamics of the inflationary universe.

Assuming that the universe on a large scale is isotropic and homogeneous, the line element can be written as:

$$ds^2 = dt^2 - R^2(t) \, d\sigma^2 \qquad (A-2)$$

where R is a scale factor ("radius"), related to the Hubble parameter $H = \dot{R}/R$, and $d\sigma^2$ is the line element of a three-dimensional space of constant curvature (independent of time). Introducing radial and angular variables, (15-2) can be rewritten as:

$$d\sigma^2 = \frac{dr^2}{1 - k\left(\dfrac{r^2}{R^2}\right)} + r^2(d\theta^2 + \sin^2\theta d\varphi^2) \qquad (A-3)$$

where the parameter k can assume three different values:

    a. $k = +1$ (positive curvature, finite universe)
    b. $k = 0$ (flat space, infinite universe)
    c. $k = -1$ (negative curvature, infinite universe).

Einstein's field equations lead to the Friedmann equations for R:

$$\left(\frac{\dot{R}}{R}\right)^2 = H^2 = \frac{8\pi \, G}{3}\,\rho + \frac{1}{3}\,\Lambda - \frac{k}{R^2} \qquad (A-4)$$

$$\frac{d}{dt}\,(\rho R^3) + p\,\frac{d}{dt}\,(R^3) = 0 \qquad (A-5)$$

where ρ is the matter density in the universe, and p is the pressure.

In order to determine $R(t)$ from equation (A-4), one needs a relation between ρ and R, which can only be derived from the specific properties of the matter in the universe at the corresponding time.

At the present epoch one can neglect the pressure terms in the matter energy-momentum-tensor, in which case one obtains from (A-5) $\rho R^3 =$ constant or more conventionally

$$\frac{4\pi}{3} \rho = \frac{M}{R^3} \tag{A-6}$$

Assuming Λ negligible, one finds that the sign of k is related to the density in the universe:

$$\begin{aligned}
k &= -1 \quad \text{for } \rho < \rho_c \\
k &= 0 \quad \text{for } \rho = \rho_c \\
k &= +1 \quad \text{for } \rho > \rho_c
\end{aligned} \tag{A-7}$$

where $\rho_c = \dfrac{3 \, H^2}{8\pi \, G}$, corresponding to $\Lambda = 0$ in Eq. (A-4).

In the early universe where ρ is large, the spatial curvature term kR^{-2} in (A-4) can be neglected, and (A-4) reduces to:

$$\left(\frac{\dot{R}}{R}\right)^2 = \frac{8\pi \, G}{3} \rho + \frac{1}{3} \Lambda \tag{A-8}$$

It is important to stress that both the Einstein equations (A-1) and their consequence, the Friedmann equations (A-4, 7) are valid only in the range where quantum effects can be neglected. This is the case if

$$\rho \ll M_p^4, \text{ or } (\dot{R}/R) \ll t_p^{-1}, \tag{A-9}$$

where M_p is given by

$$M_p = (\sqrt{G})^{-1} = 1.22 \times 10^{19} \text{ GeV (we set } h = c = 1). \tag{A-10}$$

This is the so-called Planck energy, corresponding in time units to the Planck time t_p:

$$t_p = 5.4 \times 10^{-44} \text{ s.} \tag{A-11}$$

Thus the Friedmann equation (A-8) cannot be integrated backward to the time at which ρ exceeds M_p^4. At present, it is not possible to make statements about the very early universe ($t < t_p$), i.e. about the period at which quantum fluctuations of space and time are strong enough to destroy our conventional notions about space-time structure. I shall identify the beginning of the cosmic time with the time at which the energy density drops below M_p^4.

If we set $\Lambda = 0$ and define the curvature $K = k/R^2$, the Hubble parameter $H = \dot{R}/R$ and the deceleration parameter $q = (-\ddot{R}/RH^2)\ddot{R}/RH^2$, one finds:

$$K = H^2(2q-1), \; 4\pi \, G\rho = 3H^2q. \tag{A-12}$$

If space is flat ($k = 0$), the deceleration parameter is fixed: $q = 1/2$, and one has from (15-8) with $\Lambda = 0$, or (15-12),

$$8\pi \, G\rho = 3H^2. \tag{A-13}$$

In this case the age of the universe is given by $t = 2/3H^{-1}$ and the "radius" R varies in time as $R/R_o = (t/t_o)^{2/3}$.

REFERENCES

Standard Cosmology

Goldsmith, D. and Wagoner, R. 1982. *Cosmic Horizons*. San Francisco: W. Freeman Company.

Hawking, S. and Ellis, G. 1973. *The Large Scale Structure of Space-Time*. Cambridge: Cambridge University Press.

Narlikar, J. 1977. *The Structure of the Universe*. London: Oxford University Press.

Narlikar, J. 1983. *Introduction to Cosmology*. Boston: Jones and Bartlett.

Peebles, P. 1971. *Physical Cosmology*. Princeton: Princeton University Press.

Sciama, D. 1971. *Modern Cosmology*. Cambridge: Cambridge University Press.

Silk, J. 1980. *The Big Bang*. San Francisco: W. H. Freeman.

Weinberg, S. 1972. *Gravitation and Cosmology*. New York: John Wiley/Sons.

Particle Physics, Standard model

General

Fritzsch, H. 1983. *Quarks*. New York: Basic Books.

Specialized:

Cheng, T. and Li Ling-Fong 1984. *Gauge Theory of Elementary Particle Physics*. Oxford: Clarendon Press.

Halzen, F. and Martin, A. 1984. *Quarks and Leptons*. New York: John Wiley/Sons.

Quigg, C. 1983. *Gauge Theories of the Strong, Weak and Electromagnetic Interactions*. Benjamin Cummings.

Particle Physics, Grand Unification and Cosmology

General:

Fritzsch, H. 1984. *The Creation of Matter*. New York: Basic Books.

Specialized:

Adouze, J. *et al.* editors, 1982. *Birth of the Universe*. Gif-sur-Yvette: Editions Frontiers.

Gibbons, G. *et al.* editors, 1983. *The Very Early Universe*. Cambridge: University Press.

Kolb, E. *et al.* editors, 1984. *Inner Space—Outer Space*. Chicago: University of Chicago Press.

Turner, M. 1985. "Cosmology and Particle Physics," in: *Quarks, Leptons and Beyond.* Edited by Fritzsch, H. et al. New York and London: Plenum Press.

Wolfendale, A. editor, 1982. *Progress in Cosmology.* Boston and London: D. Reidel Publ. Co.

Inflationary Universe

General:

Guth, A. and Steinhardt, P. 1984. *Scientific American* 250:3.

Specialized:

Guth, A. 1981. *Physical Review* D 23:347.
Linde, A. 1984. *Rep. Prog. Phys.*

II

ORGANIZATION AND COMPLEXITY IN LIVING SYSTEMS

5

The Origin of Life: The Emergence of Organized Self-Replicating Molecular Systems

BULENT ATALAY

Life is an interaction between nucleic acids and proteins, that is biochemically speaking . . .

Cyril Ponnamperuma (1981)

Humankind has long been preoccupied with the origin of life. Every religion known bespeaks of a time before life existed: Each has its own set of myths. Soil, in the form of dust, mud or clay appears to be a virtually ubiquitous building ingredient. In the Bible it was the "dust of the ground" that formed man. One novel alternative was offered by the Mayan epic in which the gods had initially created mankind from clay, but with rain their creations disintegrated. The gods tried again, forming their creations out of straw, only to see them perish in a spontaneous fire. Success was finally achieved when maize was used as the major ingredient for modeling living creatures.

Aristotle in *Metaphysics* explained that fireflies had issued from morning dew, a theory which found acceptance later among medieval scholastics, and later still among a number of seventeenth century scientists, including William Harvey, Rene Descartes, Isaac Newton and Johannes Baptista von Helmont. In fact, von Helmont added from his own careful observation that a mixture of grain and dirty laundry, incubated for twenty-one days, would result in spontaneous generation of life. He reported soberly, "Mice . . . neither weanlings, nor sucklings, nor premature . . . jump out fully formed." The twenty-one day period, however, was critical.

Yet twenty-five centuries earlier, the Greek philosopher Anaximander had shown remarkable prescience in suggesting that human beings had emerged from the sea; so, too, had the Indian sages who recorded similar beliefs in the *Ṛg-Veda* and the *Atharva-Veda*. These claims, however, were born more of mysticism than of rational deduction like the claims of Aristotle or von Helmont.

Serious scientific investigation concerning the origin of life dates from the time of Darwin and Wallace in the last century and culminated in the notion that each living species is traceable to its immediate predecessor, that life comes from life. In this sense, the necessary regression should take all living species back to a common ancestor. But then one is confronted inevitably by the ultimate question of the first living organism coming from the nonliving. This question certainly gave substantial pause to a scientific community already reeling from the Darwinian picture, perhaps because of a perception of the gap which exists between the living and nonliving.

Then in the nineteenth century, Pasteur demonstrated the impossibility of the growth of microorganisms in a sterile medium, and thereby disproved the theory of spontaneous generation. He announced his discovery to the French Academy of Sciences in 1861, saying, "Never will the doctrine of spontaneous generation recover from this mortal blow." But by "spontaneous generation" Pasteur referred to creation of complete biological systems—whether fireflies from morning dew or mice from dirty undergarments.

1. CHEMICAL EVOLUTION

It was not until the early 1920's with the work of the Soviet biochemist A. I. Oparin and the British biologist J. B. S. Haldane that seminal ideas again began to emerge. The two researchers independently theorized that components of living entities could more readily be formed in the earth's hydrogen-rich primordial conditions than in the oxygen-dominated conditions that came later. In their models, before there were systems able to evolve indefinitely under natural selection, a period of *chemical evolution* took place, leading gradually to an accumulation of a stock of the types of organic molecules characteristic of all living organisms.[1] Oparin's work pointed to the formation of organic molecules (such as the oils and waxes which constitute petroleum deposits) in an atmosphere abounding in hydrogen and methane. Haldane's work was complementary to Oparin's in saying that organic molecules could more readily be produced and amassed in an atmosphere devoid of free oxygen, which would react with and degrade the organic molecules. Both models attributed to external

perturbations, such as ultraviolet light, the energy for the requisite endo-
thermic reactions.

Here, two ironies present themselves immediately: First, according
to this picture the atmosphere which is suitable and necessary for present-
day life is precisely wrong for spawning life in the first place; and conversely much life, as we know it, would perish if it were subjected to the
oxygen-free atmosphere which made it possible. Seemingly just as ironic
is that solar ultraviolet radiation, which in fact readily destroys molecules
including those essential to life, would have been the primary energy
source driving the chemical reactions which produced organic molecules
in the first place.

The early atmosphere may have included the elements hydrogen,
carbon, oxygen, and nitrogen in the chemical combinations methane
(CH_4), ammonia (NH_3), water vapor (H_2O) and free hydrogen (H_2), a
great deal of which would have escaped the earth's gravitational field.
There was no free oxygen (O_2). This mixture of gases is quite similar in its
composition to the present atmospheres of Jupiter, Saturn, and Saturn's
moon Titan. This primeval atmosphere was drastically modified by the
action of various energy sources. These include ultraviolet and X-ray
radiation from the sun, cosmic radiation, lightning, geothermal sources
such as hot springs and volcanoes, terrestrial radioactivity in rocks and
shock waves generated by the collision of meteorites. Free oxygen did not
appear until plant life capable of photosynthesis developed.

Experiments demonstrating the viability of such a model have been
carried out repeatedly since 1953 when S. Miller and H. Urey first passed
electrical discharges through a mixture of gases simulating the atmosphere of the primitive earth.

Their experiments, replete with vaporizing and condensing stages
representing the water cycle in nature, accomplished the synthesis of
water-soluble organic molecules from at least fifteen percent of the carbon
atoms originally present in the methane. In all, four of twenty amino
acids which constitute proteins had been produced. For example, glycine
(NH_2CH_2COOH) was produced in the reaction

$$NH_3 + 2CH_4 + 2H_2O + (energy) \longrightarrow NH_2CH_2COOH + 5H_2.$$

One objection to the Miller-Urey hypothesis has been that it presupposes a rich admixture of hydrogen in the primordial atmosphere, an
assumption which may not be valid in light of this element's propensity to
escape the gravity of the earth. This objection, however, may not represent a serious problem. P. Abelson has shown that complex organic molecules can be formed in a weak reducing atmosphere, one low in hydrogen
content. Carbon dioxide, carbon monoxide and nitrogen in the presence
of only small quantities of hydrogen, when irradiated with ultraviolet

light, can react to produce hydrogen cyanide (HCN) and water. The former (HCN), combining with itself in an alkaline bath (such as that presumably available in the early oceans), can also produce amino acids. Here the reaction is given by

$$3HCN + 2H_2O + energy \longrightarrow NH_2CH_2COOH + H_2HCN,$$

where the products are glycine and cyanamide molecules, respectively.

Although nucleic acids were not detected in the Miller-Urey experiments, it was shown by J. Oro in the early 1960's that cyanide (HCN) molecules could join together to form adenine, one of the bases of DNA and RNA. Meanwhile, another of the organic molecules synthesized by Miller and Urey, formaldehyde (CH_2O) had been known for the past century to possess an affinity to join together to form ribose, another constituent of RNA. Recently, actual nucleotides which make up the DNA and RNA molecules, and in turn genes, were found by C. Ponnamperuma, along with amino acids, in experiments of the Miller-Urey sort. Using improved detection techniques, designed for analysis of organic molecules in meteorites, Ponnamperuma found all four bases which comprise DNA—adenine, cystosine, guanine and thymine—and a fifth, uracil, which substitutes for thymine in RNA. Evidently, nucleic acids were being formed along with the amino acids all along; the experiments themselves were not new, but the detection techniques were more sensitive.

As for the new techniques' application to the study of meteorites themselves, there was revealed the existence in those extraterrestrial materials of traces of both amino acids and nucleic acids, molecules clearly formed in the lifeless conditions of interstellar space.

2. POLYMERIZATION

The preceding discussions illuminate the possible mechanisms for the formation of organic molecules, which are the building blocks needed for the next stage in the creation of life, namely the assembly of macromolecules—proteins and the double helix of the DNA molecule.

This process, "polymerization," represents a far greater puzzle, and invites more speculation and more model building, than had the variety of mechanisms which created the organic molecules in the first place. It has been incontrovertibly shown, on one hand, that simple primordial molecules can be transformed into more complex organic molecules,[2] and on the other, that DNA placed in a suitable bath will replicate.[3] But the actual assembling of DNA from constituent molecules has not been achieved in a laboratory.

The prevailing model for this essential intermediate step is still somewhat vague. It envisions the accumulation of the various important organic molecules at the edges of shallow ponds by a process of evaporation and/or freezing. There the organization into polymers is thought to have occurred, perhaps around particles of clay that offer the maximum surface area for a given grain size and by adsorption accomplish an enrichment in the concentrations of the organic molecules at their surface. Furthermore, these clays are capable chemically of catalyzing a variety of reactions among the adsorbed organic molecules. The actual organization of component pieces into macromolecules may be brought about by the lattice structure of the clay. The mineral montmorillonite, for example, which abounds on this planet, has been shown to align some organic substances such as guanine and adenosine in ways which promote polymerization. But to date the possible relevance of all this to the origin of life is merely speculative.

So, too, is the work of the past several decades, especially by S. Fox, showing that if high concentrations of amino acids are heated, the molecules will link together in protein-like polymers. Immersion of these polymers in water results in the formation of minute spheres, "microspherules," evocative of bacterial cells. One might conjecture that these serve as a prototype for membrane-bound cells, capable of enclosing nucleic acids. But the next step toward life would be to incorporate the self-replicating system within these proto-cells, a system capable of directing the formation, maintenance and renewal of the entire cell.

Then also, one can offer an alternative scenario to a primordial soup as the spawning ground for the first organisms. Instead of warm shallow ponds sitting below an atmosphere rich in ammonia and methane, conditions which have long since disappeared, the correct site (or an additional site) for the origin of life may have been superheated seawater at great ocean depths, conditions which still exist on earth. H. Yanagawa recently reported that protein-like spheres had been produced in the laboratory from amino acids in an environment of 240° C and 130 atmospheres. Such conditions exist naturally around hydrothermal vents deep in oceans, where plumes of hot water and dissolved chemicals spew forth. The implication is that life is still being created in the sea.

3. CRYSTALS OF CLAY: GENETIC TAKEOVER

The traditional view of the origin of life and the one which has been generally favored by biochemists ever since Oparin and Haldane propounded their ideas, and Miller and Urey gave these ideas weight, has been the two-phase theory consisting of molecular or chemical evolution of organic molecules, followed by their polymerization.

In any event there are two incontrovertible facts:

1. The most central molecules of life are essentially the same in all organisms on earth today. This is the principle of the "Unity of Biochemistry."
2. It takes only twenty-eight basic building-block molecules to comprise life, and these can be synthesized under conditions simulating the primitive earth.

These happy facts notwithstanding, there is the problem of explaining their polymerization into extremely sophisticated structures, the proteins and the nucleic acids, possessing an entirely symbiotic relationship. And then there is the corollary question of whether it was the proteins or the nucleic acids that came first.

A. G. Cairns-Smith (1984, 1985) has offered a model which reverses the order of prebiotic evolution, in putting phase two, the polymerization, ahead of phase one, the formation of organic molecules. Thus the scaffolding precedes the accumulation of the building blocks. The scaffolding is provided by inorganic clay minerals. Cairns-Smith calls examples of the Principle of the Unity of Biochemistry "red herrings," or misleading clues. The originality of his approach and the fundamental nature of the questions he poses most certainly warrant consideration of his model.

According to Cairns-Smith the complexity of the structures of the proteins and nucleic acids, and the existence of a unique code for converting RNA messages into protein sequences (even though innumerable others can be envisioned), suggest that all life now on earth descended from a common ancestor, which was quite high on the evolutionary tree, and the central biochemical system was fixed by that time. Meanwhile the curious interdependent kind of complexity, with the ability to have remained fixed for so long, suggests that this "high tech" engineering was itself the product of evolution, and that the Unity of Biochemistry reflects a much later stage of evolution and not its beginning.

As for our ability to simulate the synthesis of the various organic molecules essential to life, Cairns-Smith points out that these molecules are but minor constituents of the tars produced in Miller-Urey type experiments, and that it is difficult to imagine that normal geological processes, which would ordinarily make the organic mixture even more of a jumble, would instead separate and concentrate them.

The model calls for three requirements for the first organisms:

1. They must be able to evolve,

2. They must be "low tech," and
3. They must consist of inorganic chemicals, i.e. minerals.

These lead him to conclude that the first organisms were naked genes of some unknown inorganic material. These then would have evolved to control their immediate environments by specifying the production of increasingly elaborate phenotypes, which would have helped in their survival and propagation.

Certain clay minerals have the suitable combination of structural characteristics, growth patterns and cleavage properties. Defects in crystal structure could supply multiple, stable alternative configurations for the storage of information. Clay minerals are crystallized from dilute solutions of silicic acid and hydrated metal ions formed by the weathering of rocks. The two mechanisms which power the formation of clay minerals are the geologic cycle, in which radioactivity inside the earth bakes sediments and thrusts them above the surface, and the water cycle, in which the action of the sun causes the evaporation of water from the sea, followed by its condensation in the atmosphere.

The introduction of organic molecules, e.g. amino acids and di- and tricarboxylic acids, can make metal ions such as aluminum more soluble in water, and thereby provides a catalytic service for clay synthesis. This could explain there was, in time, a genetic takeover of inorganic genes by organic ones.

The actual takeover machinery in Cairns-Smith's view was photosynthesis, which took carbon dioxide from the atmosphere to make molecules such as formic acid. The formation of more complicated molecules, the nucleotides, before the existence of enzymes, is a question open to speculation. Also open to speculation are 1) why crystal genes are no longer with us and 2) what experiments one can perform to test the model. About the first question, Cairns-Smith offers several possible answers, including that there are perhaps no crystal genes, or they have evolved into unrecognizable forms, or suitable conditions for their formation no longer exist. About the second question, the author reports that NASA biochemists have found that zinc and copper can mediate the binding of nucleotides to clays, and that ions in clay can have selective catalytic effects on amino acids. It is also reported that clays subjected to cycles of wetting and drying can cause linking in the amino acid glycine.

Some of the experimental results concerning clay, in fact, can be used by the proponents of the chemical evolution model to support their thesis that the crystal structure of clay can direct the polymerization of the already-formed organic molecules. One test that would be most revealing would be provided by the discovery of crystal genes. This could reveal the plausibility of the mineral versions of replicating systems.

4. UNRESOLVED QUESTIONS AND
A MATHEMATICAL MODEL

A number of questions emerge and become significant. With a view toward framing these questions with some degree of precision, a mathematical model formulated essentially for this purpose will be considered.

Sophisticated mathematics for population genetics was developed
early, around the time of Oparin and Haldane's work, by R. A. Fisher
(1930). It was refined further by M. Kimura (1970), and notably applied
to aging in cells by Kirkwood (1980). A mathematical model specifically
for the origin of life was formulated by F. J. Dyson (1982). It is this last
treatment that will be considered here. It should be reiterated at the outset that this is a model, rather than a theory, for the origin of life. The
latter would call for a detailed examination of reaction rates and dissociation rates and much more knowledge of the primitive earth than is presently available.

Before sketching out the mathematics underlying Dyson's model,
some of the questions which the model may aspire to answer will be
identified. The questions in most cases are significant for the "Genetic
Takeover Model" of the previous section.

1. As noted, organisms in the modern sense have two essential components: nucleic acids which are essential to genetic continuity,
   and proteins which have catalytic and structural functions. Their
   relationships, totally symbiotic and interdependent in organisms
   as we know them, lead to an obvious question: Were the first
   living creatures composed of just proteins, or just nucleic acids,
   or of a combination of the two?
2. At what state did random genetic drift give way to natural selection?
3. Is there (or was there ever) a violation of the central dogma of
   molecular biology, which observes that genetic information can
   pass from nucleic acids to nucleic acids or from nucleic acids to
   proteins, but cannot pass from proteins to nucleic acids or to
   proteins? (The information is contained in the nucleic acids, and
   not in the proteins.)
4. What is the origin of the nucleic acids?
5. How did these putative proto-organisms faithfully reproduce before the modern genetic apparatus evolved, and how did the
   present system evolve?

The assumptions underlying the Dyson model are the following:

1. Molecular or chemical evolution takes place in small "islands" or
   colonies. These could be colloidal droplets or solid particles, such

as those of clay, with molecules adsorbed on the surface. The islands exchange molecules with the environment, which acts as a source of chemical free energy to effect reactions.

2. Chemical evolution toward more organized polymerization in the island is by random genetic[4] drift and not by natural selection. (The latter process would be ascribed to a later development when the islands begin to grow and compete for nutrients.)

3. Each island contains a fixed number, N, of *monomers* or building-block molecular units. Some of the monomers may be free and others combined in random ways into polymers.

4. The population of polymers changes by discrete mutation, with monomers being added, subtracted or exchanged, one monomer at a time.

5. In normal living systems reactions are stimulated by enzymes. The efficiency of an enzyme in catalyzing a reaction is a function of its so-called *active site*. Thus a monomer will be regarded as *active* or *inactive* according to whether or not it is correctly placed as part of a structure catalyzing the synthesis of other catalytic structures. The multidimensional random walk of polymer mutation will be mapped onto a one-dimensional random walk by counting the numbers of active and inactive monomers.

With k designating the number of active monomers in a population of N monomers, the parameter $x = k/N$ will represent the fraction of active monomers in the population. Thus $0 \le x \le 1$. The larger k (or x) becomes, the more effective is the catalyzing structure. A simulated potential energy $U(x)$ is formulated with an unstable maximum point at β, and a pair of minima at α and γ (see Appendix). Thus $U(\alpha)$ and $U(\beta)$ represent two different levels of organization. Starting from a random population of monomers, each island will approach the relatively disordered state of limited molecular organization at $x = \alpha$ rapidly, and remain there for a long time, executing statistical fluctuations about the disordered state. With very low probability there will take place large enough statistical fluctuations to carry the population over the saddle point to the *ordered state*, that is one of higher organization. Then in the ordered state there will again be statistical fluctuations, which, after some time, will take it back over the saddle point to the disordered state. Without the activation of an enzyme, the population cannot jump over the saddle point.

Regarding, in some sense, the ordered state at $x = \gamma$ as representing the living state of the population (i.e. a catalytic structure characteristic of living systems), transition from $x = \alpha$ to $x = \gamma$ is the crucial step in the origin of life; the transitions in the reverse direction, that of death.

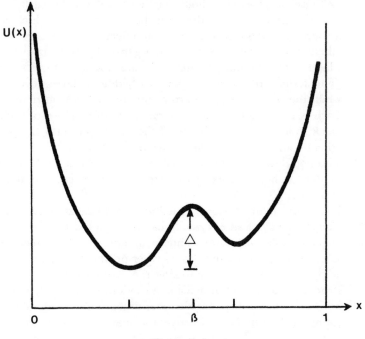

Figure 5-1

The population distribution will be centered around the two minima at $x = \alpha$ and γ, and will have an approximately Gaussian form. In terms of this distribution one can proceed to find the ratio of the populations in the ordered to the disordered states. However, it is not the size of the ordered population that is crucial to the question of the origin of life as much as the rates of transition in the two directions. For this, we need the transition rate for the disordered to the ordered state, i.e., the probability per mutation, (polymerization or increase of order), that a population crosses the barrier from α to γ (see equation A4 in the Appendix). In terms of the barrier height $\Delta = U(\beta) - U(\alpha)$, a parameter related to the activation energy, the meantime for a population to make the transition from disorder to order is computed (see equation A6).

In the absence of any real clues for the number of island populations that may have been present and their duration time, one can only supply 'reasonable' guesses. With Dyson's suggestion of perhaps 10^{10} islands existing for 10^5 mutation times, N monomers would have made the disorder to order transition with an upper limit given by N_c, where

$$N < N_c = 30/\Delta \qquad (1)$$

$U(x)$ is expressed in terms of an autocatalytic function $\varphi(x)$, which describes the autocatalytic capability (for polymerization) of the assemblage of active monomers. Thus the detailed chemical mechanisms by which population transitions occur are incorporated in the function $\varphi(x)$.

A mathematical description of $\varphi(x)$ is relegated to the Appendix. Let it suffice for now to say that $\varphi(x)$ is a monotonically increasing function defined for the closed interval $0 \leq x \leq 1$ crossing $\varphi(x) = x$ at the three points α, β, γ, with $0 < \alpha < \beta < \gamma < 1$. (See Figure 4A in the Appendix.)

In the absence of any detailed knowledge of prebiotic chemistry, a primitive $\varphi(x)$ is chosen based on two parameters a and b. The former specifies, as $(a + 1)$, the number of species of monomers; the latter, b, is the measure of their effectiveness in catalyzing reactions, a *discrimination factor.*

Since each catalyst lowers the activation energy for correct placement, an increase in the discrimination factor b manifests itself as a decrease in Δ. This, in turn, results in a corresponding increase in N_c.

The properties of $\varphi(x)$ impose certain constraints on the parameters a and b. For the discrimination factor a lower limit exists (see Appendix):

$$b > e^4 = 54.6 \qquad (2)$$

Thus a value of 10^2 for b would be reasonable for this prebiotic molecular evolution, compared with typical discrimination factors between 10^3 and 10^4 in present-day enzymes, which are suitable for the fine-tuned present-day organisms. In order to guarantee the existence of a pair of distinct stable ordered and disordered states, separated by a saddle point, hence to make the model viable, a lower limit on a emerges:

$$a > e^2 = 7.4 \qquad (3)$$

Thus, there must be nine or more species of monomers. Pure nucleic acid systems (constructed from four bases) without amino acids cannot be accommodated by the model. However, 10 to 20 amino acids, or a mixed system consisting of 10 or more amino acids and nucleotides can be accommodated. For $a \leq 7$, distinct ordered and disordered states cannot coexist. Either one finds a disordered equilibrium state (if the catalysts are weak), but no ordered state, suggesting that cells are incapable of living; or an ordered equilibrium state (if the catalysts are strong), but no disordered state, suggesting here that the cells are incapable of dying. The problems of interest span the range from "marginally alive" ($\alpha, \beta = \gamma$), to the symmetric ($\alpha, \beta = 0.5, \gamma$), to the "marginally immortal" ($\alpha = \beta, \gamma$). Defining a pair of parameters $A = \ln a$ and $B = \ln b$, these problems all lie in a wedge shaped area in A-B space (see Figure 5A in the Appendix).

In the "marginally alive" case there is no minimum in $U(x)$ at γ but rather a point of inflection at $\beta = \gamma$ (Figure 5-2). In the "marginally immortal" case, there is no minimum at $x = \alpha$, but a point of inflection at $\alpha = \beta$ (Figure 5-3). An infinitesimally stronger catalyst in the marginally alive case would produce the disorder-order transitions. Conversely, an infinitesimally weaker catalyst in the marginally immortal case would produce the order-disorder transitions.

1. For $a = 8$ (i.e. nine species of monomers):
    a) The marginally alive model with a discrimination factor $b = 62.9$ yields the critical values $\alpha = 0.32$, $\beta = \gamma = 0.59$ (this is to be interpreted as 32 percent of the catalysts in the disordered state are active, and 59 percent of the catalysts in the ordered states are active). The barrier height $\Delta = 0.002695$ and a maximum population of $N_c = 11,131$ can make the disorder→order transition.
    b) The symmetric model with a discrimination value $b = a^2 = 64$ yields $\alpha = 0.33$, $\beta = 0.50$, $\gamma = 0.67$. The barrier height is reduced to $\Delta = 0.001129$ and the maximum population making the transition increases to $N_c = 26,566$.
    c) Finally in the case of the marginally immortal, an enzyme discrimination factor of $b = 65.7$ yields $\alpha = \beta = 0.39$, $\gamma = 0.70$. The barrier height $\Delta = 0$ and the maximum number making the transition becomes infinite.

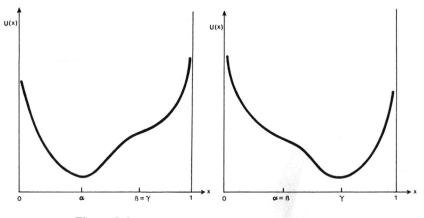

Figure 5-2   Figure 5-3

2. For $a = 19$, corresponding to 20 species of monomers, and akin to the present organisms with 20 amino acids:
   a) The marginally alive model with an enzyme discrimination factor of $b = 219.3$ yields $\alpha = 0.07$ and $\beta = \gamma = 0.75$. The barrier height Δ is 0.1906 and the maximum number making the transition N_c is 157.
   b) The symmetric model with a discrimination factor $b = a^2 = 361$ yields $\alpha = 0.08$, $\beta = 0.50$ and $\gamma = 0.92$. The barrier height is lowered to 0.1051 and the maximum population is raised to 285.
   c) The marginally immortal case with the discrimination factor $b = 3195$ yields $\alpha = \beta = 0.16$ and $\gamma = 0.99$. The barrier height Δ vanishes, and the maximum population becomes infinity.
3. For an intermediate case with $a = 10$, (11 species), and $b = 100$, the symmetric model $\alpha = 0.20$, $\beta = 0.50$ and $\gamma = 0.80$ presents a barrier height $\Delta = 0.0145$ and a maximum population making the transition $N_c = 2068$. The significance of the α and γ is that in the disordered state 20 percent of the monomers are active and in the ordered state it is 80 percent that are active.

The implication of the mathematical model is that nucleic acids with four species of nucleotides alone could not have conspired to evolve into organisms. Amino acids, however, numbering nine or more, and polymerized into protoenzymes with a polypeptide structure, could have reached the ordered state. Thus the Dyson model seems to suggest that enzymes preceded nucleic acids and genes.

The model does not allow for growth of a population of monomers within an island. Once an island population has reached the ordered state, however, one could visualize its passing into a new phase where chemicals from the environment could be absorbed and a growth in the island's population realized. Competition for nutrients between such islands could then follow, with those that suffer shortage of nutrients dying, and others flourishing. Thus, natural selection would come at this later state of evolution.

The central dogma of molecular biology is violated in that the enzymes are allowed to pass on the genetic information to other enzymes. The model suggests that at this prebiotic stage of evolution the central dogmas were not yet operational.

If this model is correct and amino acids did precede nucleic acids, organisms in the beginning may have used nucleotides such as adenine triphosphate (ATP) as energy carriers. A description of the recipe for assembling such nucleotides by way of an enzyme Q_β replicase appears in a paper by Biebricher *et al.* (1981).

It is possible to speculate about a number of different pathways along which the genetic code could have evolved. One possible channel would involve the non-specific binding of RNA to free amino acids, leading to transfer RNA, specific binding to catalytic sites leading to ribosomal RNA. In this particular pathway, described by Dyson, catalytic sites evolve from special-purpose to general-purpose by using transfer RNA instead of amino acids for recognition. Then the recognition unit splits off from the ribosomal RNA and becomes messenger RNA; the former becomes unique as the genetic code takes over the function of recognition.

As for the question of when the latest common ancestor of modern organisms emerged, it appears likely that the evolution of the genetic code was an extremely lengthy and tortuous process, the emergence of the ancestral prokaryotic cells taking much longer perhaps than the evolution of the prokaryotic to the eukaryotic, and subsequently multicellular, organisms. Evolution certainly would have been accelerated after the establishment of the genetic code.

At this juncture it should be pointed out that in the last few years the universality of the genetic code itself has come into question. In the early 1980's exceptions in mitochondria were found. Other exceptions were more recently reported in the genetic code of bacteria as well. The question which arises immediately is: did all organisms evolve from a single ancestor or did two (or more) separate evolutionary lines occur, commencing from separate origins? The existence of inordinate similarities in the genetic codes of all organisms suggests that the most plausible explanation is the former, and that in fact the branching occurred very late in the evolutionary process.

Concomitant with the question of how life began on earth is that of whether similar conditions have occurred elsewhere and hence whether extraterrestrial life exists. We live in a metagalaxy, the universe, of approximately 10^{23} stars. Although we have not directly seen a single planet outside of our solar system, our faith in the universality of physical laws, coupled with an admittedly incomplete understanding of the formation of our solar system suggests that planets are commonplace, and conditions suitable for life are also commonplace.

The earth represents the only successful experiment that we know of for the origin of life. Or can we really be certain of this? Indeed, in the early part of this century the Swedish chemist Svante Arrhenius proposed a theory of *panspermia,* in which he proposed that life originated elsewhere, spores having dispersed about as seeds, giving rise to life on earth. Arrhenius argued that these spores could have been propelled through interplanetary or interstellar space by electrostatic forces. The theory simply offers an alternative site for the primordial soup and does nothing to remove the formidable difficulties in resolving the plethora of questions. In fact, it introduces the additional problem of explaining how these spores survived the frigid cold (3K) of interstellar space, for any length of time, as well as unrelenting bombardment by cosmic and solar radiation. A whimsical scenario offered by Thomas Gold, however, alleviates the latter difficulties by suggesting that it was a spaceship of aliens who stopped off for a picnic on earth and left their crumbs behind. His theory has life evolving from these crumbs, and has been aptly named "Gold's Garbage Theory."

5. EPILOGUE

The foregoing scenarios point toward how, within the framework of physico-chemical processes, life could have originated, but also demonstrate that showing the *possibility* of a process is not the same as showing its *probability,* and certainly not its *inevitability.* Was the evolution of primitive life a necessary (therefore inevitable) consequence of the conditions from which it arose, or was there an ephemeral episode whose chances of occurrence in the first place were so unlikely that it might not occur again, given the same amount of time?

In Dyson's mathematical model, sizeable populations of monomers could make the transition from the disordered to the ordered state subject to reasonable conditions. (For example, with eleven species of monomers in the symmetric model "populations of around 2000 could make the transition without requiring a miracle.") In Ponnamperuma's experiments, nucleic acids were synthesized along with amino acids after electrical discharges were applied to gases simulating a primordial atmosphere. In Yanagawa's experiments protein microspherules were formed in superheated water, simulating conditions near hydrothermal vents in the ocean floor. The confluence of all of these results appears to reduce the origin of life to a level no less unlikely than an incident which took place in Cleveland in 1895: There were only two cars in the entire city and they collided.

APPENDIX

In terms of the parameter $x = k/N$, representing the fraction of active monomers in the population, a function $\varphi(x)$ is constructed. $\varphi(x)$ describes the *autocatalytic* capability (for polymerization) of the assemblage of active monomers. The function is chosen to depend on two parameters a and b, where $a + 1$ specifies the diversity of the population of monomers of which a are inactive; and b, called the *discrimination factor*, measures the precision of the polymerizing catalysts. The form of $\varphi(x)$ is based on a simple model in which each site in the island is assumed to be occupied by either an active or an inactive monomer. In the absence of autocatalysis, the probability that a site will be correctly occupied is

$$\varphi(0) = (1 + a)^{-1} \tag{A1}$$

If each catalyst can discriminate active from inactive monomers by a factor b, then the probability that a newly placed monomer will be active is given by

$$\varphi(1) = (1 + a/b)^{-1} \tag{A2}$$

For intermediate values of x, $0 \leq x \leq 1$,

$$\varphi(x) = (1 + ab^{-x})^{-1} \tag{A3}$$

Here each perfect catalyst is assumed to lower the activation energy (required for correct placement) of a monomer by

$$d = kT \ln(b) \tag{A4}$$

The function $\varphi(x)$ is a monotonically increasing function over the closed interval $0 < x < 1$. It is possible to show that the simulated potential energy $U(x)$ is given in terms of $\varphi(x)$ by

$$U(x) = \int \{\ln(y/(1 - y)) - \ln(\varphi(y)/(1 - \varphi(y)))\}dy \tag{A5}$$

$U(x)$ for the simple choice $\varphi(x)$ given by equation (A3) can be written as

$$U(x) = x\ln(x) - (1 - x)\ln(1 - x) + x\ln(a) - \tfrac{1}{2}\, x^2(\ln(b))^2 \tag{A6}$$

From equation (A5) it is very simple to verify that the maxima and minima of $U(x)$ are given by the equation

$$\varphi(x) = x \tag{A7}$$

This equation has three solutions, corresponding to $x = \alpha, \beta, \gamma$, with $0 < \alpha < \beta < \gamma < 1$. The condition that $\varphi(x)$ crosses $\varphi(x) = x$ at α, β, and γ:

$$\varphi'(\alpha) < 1, \; \varphi'(\beta) > 1, \; \varphi'(\gamma) < 1$$

Thus $\varphi(x)$ resembles the letter "S" stretched out an angle of $45°$ as in Figure 5-4.

The constraints on the number of monomers $(a + 1)$ and on the discrimination factor b arise from the restrictions imposed on $\varphi(x)$. A necessary (but not sufficient) condition for $\varphi(x)$ to cross $\varphi(x) = x$ three times is for $\varphi'(x)$ at the point of inflection to be greater than unity. We can compute this readily, recalling that $A = \ln a$ and $B = \ln b$,

$$\varphi(x) = (1 + e^{A-Bx})^{-1},$$
$$\varphi'(x) = Be^{A}(e^{-Bx}(1 + e^{A}e^{-Bx})^{-2})$$
$$\varphi''(x) = Be^{A}(-Be^{-Bx}(1 + e^{A}e^{-Bx})^{-2} + 2Be^{-Bx}(1 + e^{A}e^{-Bx})^{-3}) = 0$$
$$\frac{Be^{-Bx}}{(1 + e^{A}e^{-Bx})^{2}} = \frac{2Be^{-Bx}}{(1 + e^{A}e^{-Bx})^{3}}$$
$$e^{Bx} = e^{A} \text{ or } b^{x} = a,$$

which yields the point of inflection as $x = A/B = \ln a/\ln b$. Substituting this value into the first derivative, we obtain

$$\varphi'(x) = Be^{A}\{e^{-B(A/B)}/(1 + e^{A}e^{-B(A/B)})^{2}\} > 1.$$
$$Be^{A}e^{-A}/(1 + e^{A}e^{-A})^{2} > 1 \text{ or } B/2^{2} > 1$$

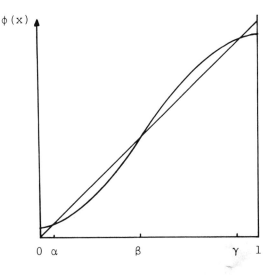

Figure 5-4. The autocatalytic function $\phi(x)$ as a function of the fraction of active monomers.

Finally, we have

$$B > 4, \text{ or } b > e^4 = 54.6 \tag{A8}$$

Meanwhile, another necessary condition for $\varphi(x)$ to have three solutions is that at the unstable saddle point $x = \beta$, $\varphi'(x) > 1$. A derivation similar to the foregoing yields a lower limit on A,

$$A > 2, a > e^2 = 7.4 \tag{A9}$$

    It can be shown that the transition rate from disorder to order is given by

$$\varepsilon = (2\pi N)^{-1}\{(1 - \varphi'(\alpha))\,(\varphi'(\beta) - 1)\,(\alpha - \alpha^2)/(\beta - \beta^2)\}\,\exp\,\{N(U(\alpha) - U(\beta))\} \tag{A10}$$

and the transition rate for the reverse process by

$$\eta = (2\pi N)^{-1}\{(1 - \varphi'(\gamma))(\varphi'(\beta) - 1)(\gamma - \gamma^2)/(\beta - \beta^2)\}\,\exp\,\{N(U(\gamma) - U(\beta))\} \tag{A11}$$

The ratio of the two rates (A10) and (A11), which is also the inverse of the population ratio, is given by

$$\frac{\eta}{\varepsilon} = \sqrt{\frac{(1 - \varphi'(\gamma))(\gamma - \gamma^2)}{(1 - \varphi'(\alpha))\,(\alpha - \alpha^2)}}\quad \exp\quad \}N(U(\gamma) - U(\alpha))\{ \tag{A12}$$

The mean time for a population to make the transition from disorder to order is given by

$$t = \tau e^{\Delta x} \tag{A13}$$

where τ is the average time between mutations at a given site. (For details of the derivation see Dyson (1982)).

NOTES

1. It was Darwin himself who had conceived of chemical evolution. He had written to a friend, Hooker: "We can conceive of a warm little pond with all sorts of ammonia and phosphoric salts—with light, heat, electricity, etc. present . . . a protein com-

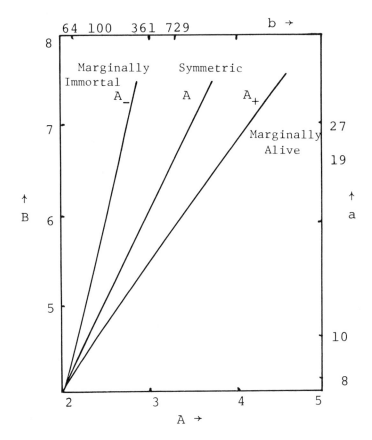

Figure 5-5. The wedge-shaped region in *A-B* space corresponds to the range of values for which the potential energy curve $U(x)$ has viable minima at x = α and γ, and a maximum at x = β. Thus order-disorder transitions become relevant only for this region.

pound already formed, ready to undergo more complex changes." (Ponnamperuma 1981)

2. "Organic" in the sense of those present in the organism.

3. "Suitable bath" for the *in vitro* (that is, free of intact living cells) synthesis of RNA would be a mixture of three ingredients: 1) A crude wheat germ (or RNA -) poly-merase enzyme preparation, 2) The buffer Tris-HC1 and salts, e.g. $MnC1_2$, $MgC1_2$, NH_4SO_4, and 3) Equal proportions of the nucleotides Guanine Triphosphate (GTP), Adenine Triphosphate (ATP), Uracil Triphosphate (UTP) and Cystosine Triphosphate (CTP).

4. "Genetic" in this sense is not meant to connote the existence of genes as much as the ability to transfer information.

REFERENCES

Bierbricher, C. *et al.* 1981. "Kinetic Analysis of Template Instructed and de novo RNA Synthesis by Q_B Replicase" *Journal of Molecular Biology* 148:391–410.

Cairns-Smith, A. 1984. *Genetic Takeover and the Mineral Origin of Life.* Cambridge: Cambridge University Press.

Cairnes-Smith, A. 1985. "The First Organism." *Scientific American,* June.

Dyson, F. 1982. "Origin of Life," *Journal of Molecular Evolution* 18:344–355.

Dyson, F. 1982. Lecture given at Oxford University, Department of Theoretical Physics, May.

Dyson, F. 1985. "Origin of Life," Cambridge University Press.

Fisher, R. 1930. *The General Theory of Natural Selection.* Dover Reprint Series (1958). New York: Dover Publications, Inc.

Kimura, M. 1970. *Mathematical Topics in Population Genetics.* Kojima, K., ed. New York: Springer-Verlag, pp. 178–209.

Kirkwood, T. 1980. "Error Propagation in Intracellular Transfer" *Journal of Theoretical Biology* 82:363–382.

Miller, S. and Orgell, L. 1974. *The Origin of Life on the Earth.* Englewood Cliffs: Prentice Hall.

Oparin, A. 1953. *Origin of Life.* Dover Reprint Series. New York: Dover Publications, Inc.

Ponnamperuma, C. 1981. "Search for Life in the Universe." Lecture given at Mary Washington College, Fredericksburg, VA, May.

Weiss, A. 1981. "Replication and Evolution in Inorganic Systems Angew" *Chem. Int. Engl.* 20:850–860.

6

Complexity of the Structure and Dynamics of the Genome

GUIDO PINCHEIRA

The outstanding progress in biological knowledge achieved in contemporary times has originated many provocative questions in relation to the concept of the unity of sciences. Some of these questions are related to "whether the structure and behavior of living systems are describable and predictable by the same laws that govern inanimate matter."

Many physicists have tried to interpret or to traduce the concept of the unity of sciences in physical terms. On the other hand, other scientists have postulated that the sameness of the physical and biological sciences is illusory and misleading. Eugene Wigner has stated that "present day physics and in particular quantum mechanics has a limited validity and it should be formulated in a somewhat probabilistic way, particularly so for a very macroscopic body."[1] Wigner has also indicated that "the laws of physics and the laws of quantum mechanics, in particular, apply only to isolated systems."[2]

Now, the idea of discussing the applicability of the laws and principles of inanimate matter to the living world also gives us the opportunity to analyze the degree of compatibility of the present laws of physics with fundamental aspects of living systems and to examine the possibility of a more fundamental science of nature with principles more suitable to the achievement of a unity of sciences. How can we demonstrate that the concepts of physics, even with some modifications, may serve as foundations for explanations of life phenomena?

A suitable starting point may be to consider biological macromolecules (nucleic acids, proteins, etc.) as physical objects of biological significance and to agree with Wigner that physics does not attempt to explain nature itself but only the *regularities* in the behavior of objects.[3]

LIVING SYSTEMS

General aspects

Living systems are unique examples of organization characterized by similarities and changes expressed in the appearance of the individuals or populations.

Living systems have a hierarchical structural organization. Different types of molecules give rise to membranes, chromosomes, cellular organelles (mitochondria, plastids, cilia, etc.), cells, tissues and so on.

These different levels of organization have different problems, they give rise to different questions and, of course, there is the possibility of achieving partial explanations for living phenomena.

In inanimate matter, we also have hierarchical organization of different units, such as electrons, neutrons, protons, nuclei, atoms, molecules and crystals; but the level of organization we find seems to be far more simple than in living matter, and, as such, more simple explanations, theories or laws may be sufficient to explain the phenomena.

In biology, the study of the different levels of living organizations has given rise to different branches of science: molecular biology, genetics, cytology, histology, physiology, etc. At the molecular level, the effort to understand living characteristics has been oriented through biochemistry, biophysics and, more recently, through biological physico-chemistry and quantum biology, indicating the growing contributions of chemistry and physics to biological knowledge.

Nevertheless, the complexity of the problem requires that the study of biological phenomena follows an integrative strategy of the contributions of these disciplines. The full understanding of a living character will be possible when the studies at a given level of biological organization are related to the problems originated at the other levels of organization of the biological systems. Sometimes it is possible that findings at a lower level of organization in biology do not add very much to the explanation of problems posed by higher levels of biological organization, which usually are more complex as a result of interactions of many other components. Biological systems would be rather simple to describe, if the components or units of the systems were not interacting.

The study of biological phenomena is also more complex, because efforts to elucidate proximate causes should be approached by projecting the possible findings to evolutionary causes. The importance of knowing how a genetic program is translated or processed is complementary to giving explanations about the origin of the genetic code and its changes through evolution. As Gerholm has said, "time is central in biological phenomena."[4]

The study of a complex biological system at the individual level must not neglect and should always consider the aspects of similar problems at the population level with an evolutionary perspective.

Biological proximate causes may be studied in physico-chemical terms, and as such it is possible that these processes follow the laws of physics. But considering the biological problems at the population level, it is essential to take into account other aspects, such as the variation between characters and between individuals, and because of this, the complexity of the problem reaches levels well beyond the range of physics. These aspects of change in biological systems almost invariably have a high content of probabilistic nature, and biological observations are subject to probability laws and a probabilistic conceptualization.

If we analyze the history of the progress in biology, we find that it is more frequent to speak of facts or concepts instead of laws.[5] In genetics this is the case, starting with the concept of the gene, a physiological concept that has experienced quite an evolution in the last thirty years.

Biologists very often organize new knowledge into a real network of concepts and, in relation to changes, these concepts almost invariably have a high content of probabilistic nature. Let us say, then, that biological knowledge has been able to progress on the basis of a probabilistic conceptualization that takes into consideration aspects of uncertainty in the occurrence of many events in living systems.

Similarities and variations in living systems may be examined at different levels during the ontogeny or development of an organism or at different times in a population. Nevertheless, these characteristics can be related or tracked back to mechanisms originated in the genetic endowment, designated as the *genome* or *genotype,* of an organism. This genome contains a program with the information and instructions to interact with environmental factors within the organism or external to it in order to determine the transient or permanent characteristics of the individual (phenotype). This process or system may be represented by the following scheme:

GENOME or GENOTYPE _____ PHENOTYPE (appearance of the organism)
                        ENVIRONMENT

In this sense, biological phenomena are preponderant expressions or relationships between the internal constituents of an organism with the external components of the physical world. As such, organisms may be considered *open systems,* able to maintain a certain degree of organization, even though their constituents and environment continually change. This is possible thanks to a continuous exchange of energy and information between organism and their environments.

Basic characteristics of living matter

Jacques Monod[6] has indicated three main characteristics of living matter: *reproductive invariance, teleonomic activities* and *autonomous morphogenesis.* These three characteristics are related to the physiological potential or performance of the genomic program of a living system.

Reproductive invariance expresses the capacity of the genome to create new genomes with *identical characteristics of structure, organization and coded information* to insure the preservation of characters specific for those living structures. This is achieved by the process of replication of the genetic material, a very complex phenomenon, not yet fully understood, but, according to more recent knowledge, subject to many possibilities for variations of the information coded.

Teleonomic activity is the capacity of the organism to transmit from generation to generation the content of the reproductive invariance characteristic of the species. In this respect, all the structures contributing to this purpose are teleonomic. That means, their purpose in being created is to perform, one way or another, transmission of such information. This characteristic is related to many physiological aspects oriented to the formation and function of hereditary units or structures, such as the gametes.

The property of autonomous morphogenesis is the capacity of the organism to control its own ontogenetic process, through many different mechanisms.

At the molecular level, reproductive invariance is related or linked to aspects of the performance of the nucleic acids. Teleonomic processes are related to the functioning of proteins, as basic constituents of teleonomic structures. Autonomous morphogenesis is related to many different types of molecules connected with the morphological differentiation of the organism.

Among the three characteristics of living systems proposed by Monod, the one that seems to be *central* is the occurrence of a teleonomic process. These are physiological aspects, whose orientation has been originated and guided by a program, and depend on the existence of some end point or goal (a structure or function), which in the long run may be regulating the whole program or part of it. The existence of a genetic program in living systems gives the possibility of explaining the occurrence of teleonomic activities in a mechanistic fashion. In this respect it is important that feedback devices oriented to impose the precision of the teleonomic processes exist. In connection with this point, it is important to indicate that each program guiding a biological teleonomic process is the result of natural selection and is constantly adjusted by the selective value of the achieved endpoint. So, it is possible to say that a biological teleonomic process has a proximate cause, but the program guiding it has been acquired through the history of the evolution of living systems.

If we examine how much these characteristics of living matter are applicable to the inanimate world, we find that in this case, there are also processes in which a goal is reached as a consequence of physical laws, such as the fall of a stone, the flow of rivers toward the ocean, etc. What seems to be *unique* in living systems is the existence of a *genetic program,* which has experienced an ancient and continuous adaptation to improve the performance of the teleonomic process.

How much of these living characteristics might be explained by the physical sciences? At the molecular level we have a high degree of complexity in biological macromolecules (nucleic acids, proteins, hormones, antibodies, etc.) with a great deal of specificity in the different functions they perform. Because of this, although the work that some of these molecules perform has a quantitative relevance, it is much more important from the qualitative point of view, because it gives the possibility of change, sometimes with a high degree of variation.

Let us examine one aspect of a teleonomic process, the formation of new genomes through the process of replication. The formation or synthesis of new genomes is an accurate process, based in at least three discriminate steps: The result of the difference in free energy between a correct and an incorrect pairing of nucleotides; the capacity of the replication enzymes to proofread the incorporation of wrong nucleotides (in this respect, the presence of neighbor nucleotides is also important); finally, the system for achieving accuracy rests on the possibility of correcting mistakes after synthesis.

Molecules that are regular constituents of inanimate matter are far less complex and of low molecular weight. They are also present in living matter and it is possible that many of the chemical and physical processes in which they participate follow the general principles of physics, while the biological interactions in which they participate escape these principles. This appears more valid if we consider biological characteristics in an historical perspective.

In biological systems, there are many levels of complexity in the structure of matter, and at each level entirely new properties may appear. For this reason, efforts to explain biological entities in physical terms should be focused on finding structural and dynamic details of biomolecules that are truly primary in biological phenomena.

2. THE GENOME

The genome is made of nucleic acids. These macromolecules code the information for the different morphological and physiological characteristics of organisms. The information coded in the genome is gradually translated to determine the phenotype of the organism through a very complex network of biochemical and developmental reactions. As such, each character is usually affected by many genes and changes affecting one gene usually have consequences for many different characters.

Chemical composition

Nucleic acids, especially ribonucleic acid (RNA) and deoxyribonucleic acid (DNA), are the molecular components of genomes. Ribonucleic acid is the genomic constituent in many viruses and deoxyribonucleic acid constitutes the genomes of bacteria, fungi and higher organisms. In an eukaryotic cell, the genome is located, mainly, in the nucleus, but important genetic information is also localized in mitochondria, plastids, etc. In bacteria, besides the chromosome, we may have transient genomic components in plasmids, bacteriophages or other cytoplasmic structures.

The genome performs many different functions:

1. It replicates
2. It mutates
3. It repairs its own lesions
4. It sends messages (mRNA) for the formation of proteins
5. It recombines
6. It regulates its own work

All these different functions are performed under the instructions coded by sequences of four different nucleotides (Adenine, Guanine, Cytosine and Thymine in the case of DNA; Uracil instead of Thymine in RNA) in the nucleic acid that is the molecular component of the genome. DNA or RNA molecules may occur in nucleotide sequences of infinite variety.

Structural characteristics of DNA

A double helix is the usual representation of the structure of the DNA molecule. For quite a long time, the DNA double helix was looked upon as a very static structure, with very uniform characteristics and a considerable degree of rigidity. This was in accordance with its role of serving as a true blueprint to make new DNA or different types of RNA to serve the different needs of the organism. Today, the new technologies available to study the molecular aspects of genetics have demonstrated that this is not the case. Instead, the DNA double helix is emerging as a structure with a considerable *conformational flexibility* that is the basis for the static and dynamic structural heterogeneity of DNA.

When in 1953, Watson and Crick proposed the double helix model for the DNA molecule, they considered that the two DNA chains were coiled with a clockwise orientation. For that reason, it is called a dextral double helix or B-DNA. During the 1970s it has been possible to synthe-size DNA with a double helix coiled with a sinistral orientation and a zigzag path of the sugarphosphate backbone of the polynucleotide chains and with the highest number of base pairs per turn (twelve instead of ten in B-DNA). This type of DNA molecule, called Z-DNA, is less twisted and more slender than B-DNA. The presence of Z-DNA in nature has been confirmed in *Drosophila polytene* chromosomes. Its coexistence with B-DNA has also been proved in bacterial plasmids, suggesting the occur-rence of variations of DNA structure in particular regions of the same molecule.

Other forms of DNA molecular structure, designated as A-DNA, C-DNA and D-DNA, have been obtained in experimental conditions. The double helix of A-DNA and C-DNA are also dextral and are found in molecules no matter what the sequence of nucleotides is. Although, theo-retically, it is possible that a sinistral double helix exists in these types of DNA, it has not been found in nature yet.

The A-form is observed in DNA fibers maintained at seventy-five percent relative humidity and in presence of sodium, potassium or ce-sium. This is translated into a higher number of base pairs per turn of the double helix than in the standard B-DNA. The C-form appears if DNA fibers are maintained in sixty-six percent relative humidity and in pres-ence of lithium ions. As a consequence, this form has a fewer number of base pairs per turn of the double helix.

These findings indicate that DNA has the possibility of adopting different types of configurations, depending on physical factors (humidity, temperature, ionic strength) that may have an influence upon it. In this way, the DNA double helix is able to experience frequent structural trans-formations, which may be related to different physiological aspects of the genetic material.

In other cases, differences in the structure of DNA molecules may also be related to the sequences of nucleotides. The D-form of DNA is found in polynucleotides lacking guanine, and, as such, is rare. The structure of Z-DNA is favored in nucleotide sequences that have alterna-tions of purines and pyrimidines, such as $C_pG_pC_pG_pC_pG_p$. These situa-tions demonstrate how DNA *codes* its own conformational flexibility and physiological behavior, a very important characteristic of a molecule re-sponsible for the orientation and control of a teleonomic process that starts by making possible the formation of new genetic structures.

The importance of Z-DNA is reflected in a lower degree of stability, as compared with B-DNA, in physiological solutions. This is due to the repulsion of the negatively charged phosphates on opposite strands of the molecule, which in Z-DNA are closer than in B-DNA. Besides, Z-DNA can be stabilized most effectively through the binding of a class of proteins present in higher organisms that bind to Z-DNA and not to B-DNA. Z-

DNA seems to have a role as a regulator of transcription of part of the genetic material. It also may be important for the process of mutation, since this type of conformation of DNA molecule exposes certain atoms that may suffer the impact of mutagenic agents present in the immediate environment.

The DNA molecule is then a rather dynamic structure, and as such, it shows a rich polymorphism that in part reflects the intense interactions with other molecules. B-DNA, in solution or in the form of DNA fibers, is able to undergo internal motions over a wide range of time constants and with significant amplitudes. The fastest change detected in the DNA molecule takes place within one picosecond (10^{-12} second).

Additional structural complexity of the genome is derived from the twisting of DNA molecules around its axis, a characteristic designated as "supercoiling" because it generates other helical structures very important to accommodating the genome in the chromosomes, specially in higher organisms. This new structure has, of course, important consequences for DNA structure and physiology. In fact, different types and degrees of DNA supercoiling affect the physical (hydrodynamic behavior), chemical (enzymological sensitivity, effect of mutagens, etc.) and biological properties (replication, transcription, recombination) of the genome.

A linear DNA molecule in solution, usually adopts the B configuration, with ten nucleotides pairs per turn of the double helix. This is the minimal energy configuration. If the molecule experiences additional coiling, its energy increases. Such an increase may be minimized by adoption of new structural configurations, such as a closed circularization, supercoiling, etc. Many of these configurational changes are made possible by the action of enzymes called topoisomerases and girases, which are synthesized under the control of the genome. This means that DNA is able to adjust the torsional pressure by adjusting the structure of the double helix itself. An extreme situation of this type of molecular structural adjustment would be the local or regional conversion of a right-handed helix into a left-handed helix. Structural fluctuations in the DNA double helix are due to intrinsic conformational preferences derived from its chemical constitution and the *competing* influence of the components of the immediate aqueous ionic environment. It is clear that *the properties or functions of the genome can not be understood in isolation or without consideration of its interdependence with many other molecules of the organism.*

Barbara McClintock[7] has said that "there are 'shocks' that the genome must face repeatedly, and for which it is prepared to respond in a programmed manner." Sensing devices or mechanisms may "alert" the genome of an imminent danger, and the genome starts events to counteract or to mitigate the danger. Such a reaction may even force the genome to restructure itself in order to allow the survival of the cell and itself. This tremendous change in organization of the genetical material may even lead to the formation of individuals with rather different characteristics, perhaps the formation of a new species.

CODING FUNCTIONS

What is the meaning of the genetic code in relation to the control of a teleonomic process? The progress in molecular genetics has demonstrated that there are different aspects for the coding function of the genome. The first coding manifestation is the process of replication to create new genomes with similar structural characteristics. In relation to the formation of other molecules, segments of the genome may control the *structure* of different kinds of RNA (transfer RNAs, ribosomal RNAs) and proteins.

Besides the code to control the structure of other molecules, the genome also contains information for interacting with other molecules. This sort of "recognition code" plays a very important role in the regulation of genomic activities.

Coding for structure

The reading of the genetic code for protein structure is based on the recognition of three letter code words or *codons*. All amino acids, except two, are coded by two or more different triplets of nucleotides. This is especially significant, because it allows a given polypeptide to have many different ways of being written in the DNA. The different possible combinations of the four nucleotides in DNA is equal to sixty-four triplets or code words. Three of them (TAA, TAG and TGA) serve as stop signals. The remaining code words are assigned to the twenty different amino acids. Therefore each amino acid may be coded by an average of three different triplets $^{61}/_{20}$ = 3.

Because of this probability, a polypeptide made of 100 amino acids can be genetically written in $3 \times 3 \times 3 \times \ldots (100)$ different ways. That means $3^{100} = 10^{48}$ different ways—an extraordinary genetic flexibility for controlling a character. This example also gives an idea of the richness of the genetic system in terms of information. It is mainly in this aspect, rather than in the physical complexity, where the genetic system's superiority resides as compared with inanimate matter.

The genome functional order is an essential part of the living system but it is rather difficult to evaluate its biological performance in physical terms. The replacement of one nucleotide, let us say cytosine for thymine, in a gene may maintain the same structural negative entropy of the system, but biologically, such change may have drastic consequences for the physiology of the organism, up to causing its death.

From the physical point of view, genes with equal numbers of different nucleotides may have the same information in terms of negative entropy. For the biologist, of course, this is not true, because in terms of information he may have many different genes depending on the sequence in which the nucleotides are arranged. In this sense, the value of negative entropy or the degree of atomic order of a sequence of nucleotides forming a gene does not give a measure of the efficiency of the system. To evaluate the information contained in the functional order of the genome in terms of entropic units is meaningless from a pure thermodynamic point of view. In the concept of genetic order it is essential to consider the quality or specific value of the information available to perform some biological functions.

But this is not the only aspect of the complexity of the genetic code. Coding for the structure of other molecules (RNA; proteins), very often, does not have a linear and continuous message. On the contrary, it is more and more frequent to find that the gene is interrupted in coding a message for a protein. Only a few segments of the gene have the information necessary to determine the sequence of amino acids in a polypeptide. These segments are called *exons*. Other segments, called *introns,* do not code for amino acids. They may exist in numbers going from one to several dozens in one gene.

In order to control the structure of a protein, a gene with introns requires a processing of its initial product, the pre-messenger RNA (pre-mRNA). Indeed, although the whole gene, exons and introns, is transcribed completely, to form a pre-mRNA, this molecule has to excise the introns (RNA splicing) and then reassociate the exons in the correct order to reconstruct the message in a continuous structure.

So we have an *ordered* coding structure, containing a message in *semi-disorder,* which has to be ordered for the process of translation in the synthesis of a protein. This situation would be in agreement with the postulate of an information theory holding that the transmission of a message is necessarily accompanied by a partial dissipation of the information contained. Other aspects of the genome physiology, like the formation of transfer RNAs and ribosomal RNAs exhibit similar characteristics.

Today, at least three to four mechanisms of excision and reunion of segments of pre-mRNA are known. Some of them are rather interesting because they add new perspectives to the physiology of nucleic acids.

In some genes introns have the capacity to control their own surgery without the intervention of an enzyme and without a clear energy requirement. This has suggested an autocatalytic role for a nucleic acid, a property that in living systems has been reserved for proteins.

In other cases, introns are initiated and terminated by certain combinations of dinucleotides. This characteristic, associated with the structural disposition of other nucleotides in the introns allows the folding of

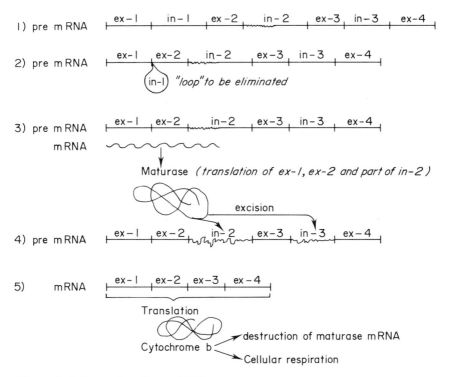

Figure 6-1: Processing of pre mRNA.

the pre-mRNA molecule, forming a "loop" with the intron, to favor its excision by an enzyme.

The mechanism to process primary gene products may be rather more complex and may include a combination of the mechanisms we have seen. Such is the case of a yeast mitochondrial gene, designated as "cob-box." This is a rather complex gene in structure and function, because it codes for the structure of cytochrome *b* and regulates the synthesis of an enzyme, the cytochrome oxidase, that is essential for respiratory metabolism.

Structurally, this gene has several exons and introns. The mechanism to process the transcriptional product of this gene has several steps:

1. One of the introns has the capacity to control its own excision.
2. The reassociation of remaining fragments (exons and introns) allows a *translation* of part of the message, corresponding to two exons and part of an intron, to synthesize a protein, called MA-TURASE of mRNA.
3. This newly synthesized protein is employed in the excision of the remaining introns still present in pre-mRNA.

4. The reassociation of all the remaining exons allows the synthesis of cytochrome *b*, to be used in respiratory metabolism and for the destruction of mRNA coding for maturase.

Fig. 6–1 illustrates the different steps in the processing of the products of the gene "cob-box."

In this way, we have a mechanism for regulating the synthesis of maturase, allowing its existence at very low concentrations and, surprisingly, a rather economic control of the gene activity.

Nevertheless, more important is the fact that a segment of DNA appears being an intron for "cytochrome B" and an exon for maturase. Then, we have the case of a gene contributing to the synthesis of two different proteins as a consequence of regulatory mechanisms of genetic activity.

Single nucleotide sequences coding for more than one polypeptide are called "overlapping" genes, because one gene is part of another gene. This is done by reading the DNA sequence in different ways, and as such, it is possible that the replacement of one nucleotide (a mutation) affects more than one protein.

Overlapping genes are becoming more and more frequent in different organisms indicating that the genetic information along DNA is not arranged in well defined functional units and increasing the difficulties to provide a simple definition of the term gene.'

Nevertheless, it is evident that the coding role of the genome as a basis for specificity and diversity of the characteristics of organisms resides in the sequence of a few small molecules—the nucleotides. In this sequence of nucleotides is where the *stability* and *variability* of organisms apparently reside. This dual function of the genome is perhaps the most important aspect of living matter.

The "recognition code"

The different physiological aspects of the genome require a very rich interaction with different molecules, specially proteins. How do these regulatory proteins recognize specific regions of DNA for binding?

Hydrogen bonds between side chains of amino acids and the edges of base pairs seem to be the basis for a great deal of the specificity in protein-DNA interactions. Other mechanisms of the "recognition code" seem to involve van der Waal interactions between DNA and proteins. These linkages occur between molecules situated close to each other as a result of slight perturbations of electron distributions within the molecules due to interactions among their respective electron clouds. For this purpose it is very important to consider the position and orientation of nucleotides in the DNA strands and of amino acids in the polypeptide and the overall fit of the protein and DNA surface, thus enhancing the importance of the molecular structure and conformation of the genome for the decodification of the information it contains.

The "recognition code" seems to be "degenerate," because each nitrogen base pair can be recognized by several different amino acids and each amino acid may bind to several different nitrogen bases. For example, adenine is recognized by glutamine and serine, and serine binds to adenine and to guanine in different positions.

The aspect of degeneracy of the "recognition code" implies that the meaning of a particular amino acid in a regulatory protein will depend on the conformation and orientation of the protein backbone.

Trying to learn better the coding role of the genome, scientists face a major challenge to elucidate more complex coding principles that may be part of regulatory mechanisms of the genome activity. Until now, it seems clear that coding signals do not reside exclusively in specific DNA sequences. They may also reside in certain aspects of more complex structures of DNA, such as those derived from the supercoiling of the molecule or the different types of DNA structure (B-DNA and Z-DNA). Nevertheless, it is not clear how these structures are recognized by certain proteins. It is also possible that the binding of protein to DNA may produce changes in the fine structure of neighboring regions of the genome, making it accessible to new recognition signals. Besides, there is also the possibility that minor modifications of nitrogen bases, such as methylation, may alter the meaning of the genetic language; changing the message to form a structure, to modulate the activity of the genome; or to mutate and change the information coded. In this respect, it is important to keep in mind the possibility of major changes in evolution as a result of alterations not only of DNA or proteins, but also in other extragenic regulatory elements.

An additional aspect of the complexity of genomic structure and physiology is the ability of certain "genes" to change their positions in the genome, being true "nomad" structures. They have been called "jumping genes," transposable elements or "transposons," "insertion sequences," etc. The process of changing position of some of these genetic elements involves its own duplication, with one copy remaining on site and the other moving to a new location after a break in the DNA sequence to facilitate the insertion of the new genetic material. As a result, DNA rearrangements may take place increasing the capacity of organisms to adapt themselves to different environments, making possible variations and evolution.

It seems clear that the process of transferring genetic information carries in itself *part* of the responsibility to maintain the structure and physiological integrity of the system. The mere maintenance of the system involves a degradation of energy which is taken from the environment.

Evolutionary significance of introns

The existence of introns in the genome of higher organisms was discovered in 1977, and it has been found that very often they are larger than exons. At first it was also considered that introns were present only in higher organisms and not in bacteria or other prokaryotes. Nevertheless, recently, it has been discovered that introns are present in archeobacteria (bacteria living in salt water, methanogenic and thermophilic bacteria). These findings have given rise to many questions about the physiological or evolutionary advantages that a gene with introns may have in relation to a gene without introns. Furthermore, a reconsideration of the main evolutionary lines began to take place. How has this genetic structure evolved?

W. F. Doolittle has suggested that the first unicellular organisms must have had genes with introns and exons, because DNA may not have been very accurate in processing its information.[8] Under these conditions it could have been advantageous to have several exons or DNA segments to code for a protein, in order to secure its synthesis. Besides, it could have been more convenient to have genes organized in segments, giving them the possibility of recombining the products of these segments to synthesize larger or different proteins, helping the organisms in acquiring new properties. Several examples, such as the formation of immunoglobulin proteins, seem to be in accordance with this possibility.

The great significance of this idea is that organisms with genes without segmentation in exons and introns may have appeared lately in evolution. This is the case of many bacteria, which may be a result of a long evolutionary process leading to the elimination of introns that acquire genes with single compact and un-interrupted blocks of information. That means that most bacteria would be extremely highly evolved systems and, as such, they have not preceded higher organisms as we have accepted in the past.

THE "SILENT" GENOME

We have analyzed the coding and regulatory functions of the genome. Nevertheless, in higher organisms, only a fraction of the genome is needed for these functions. In man, it is thought that this fraction is no more than twenty percent of DNA. The other eighty percent of the genome appears to be useless in terms of coding, but is perhaps needed for structural purposes. This DNA has been called the "silent" DNA.

The analysis of the nucleotidic sequences of this "silent" DNA reveals the presence of much repetition of certain sequences, with a scattered distribution in the genome. This "repetitive" or "silent" DNA may be important, not only in maintaining the structure of the genome during the active processes developed during the cell cycle, but also during the evolution of genomes. In fact, the high number of repeated nucleotide sequences available may allow sudden genetic variations produced by the occurrence of translocations within the genome or quantitative changes or by an increase or loss of nucleotides. These events may serve as the basis for "jumps" in the evolution of the genome and, perhaps, of species. This possibility is being tested by comparing gene sequences of different species in order to learn something about the mechanisms by which the DNA evolves.

SATELLITE GENOMES. INTERDEPENDENCE

Until now I have been dealing with aspects characterizing the nuclear genome in eukaryotes. But we should not forget that parts of the genome are also present in other cellular structures (mitochondria, plastids, etc.). These extranuclear genomes may be not so important quantitatively, but their qualitative importance is without question. They may be different in composition and structure as compared with the nuclear genome and they partially control very important functions for life (i.e., photosynthesis in the case of the plastid genome and oxidative phosphorilation by the mito-chondrial genome).

The interactions between the components of the genome localized in different parts of the cell must produce reciprocal flows of information between the different components of the system, enhancing its potential and physiological complexity. As a result of this type of interaction and interdependence important living phenomena, like photosynthesis, take place under the coordinated control of nuclear and chloroplast genomes and external factors such as light. A similar interaction takes place be-tween genomic components residing in the nucleus, in the mitochondria and oxygen to control oxidative phosphorilation.

The interdependence between these different genomic components in a cell results in the cooperative biosynthetic control of the structure of enzymes, like mitochondrial ATPase, or parts of the mechanism for the synthesis of proteins in the cellular organelles. Many very well coordi-nated processes must be necessary to have the genome physiology acting in the way the cell needs. Changes in the nuclear genome affect the mito-chondrial genome and vice-versa. The existence of these interactions or interdependence is in accordance with Peter Medawar's postulate: "At higher levels of organization, new systems properties emerge."

No matter how much information the genome of an organism con-tains, it is possible that it does not store all the information the organism requires for its autonomous morphogenesis and teleonomic process. In the developmental process of an organism it is possible that the interactions among its different parts create the conditions for the input or addition of information not already present. A situation like this is taking the genetic information contained in viruses, plasmids, infective particles, etc., and incorporating it into a bacterium or eukaryotic cell. In this way the genome is also operating as an open system, making it very difficult to explain accurately its historical changes or to predict its behavior for evolutionary perspectives.

A FINAL WORD

The different characteristics, structural or physiological, of the genome I have mentioned are only a few of many other manifestations of complexity that take place in a living organism. Nevertheless, they seem to be sufficient to conclude that the genome, chemically made of only five different elements (C, H, O, N, P) and structured as a sequence of only four different monomers, displays a very rich physiological activity, involving the cooperation of a large number of other different molecules.

Most of the genome activities are physio-chemical transformations taking place in a non-linear chemical system, far from equilibrium. As such, the genome may be considered one of those structures, called "dissipative" by I. Prigogine to designate ordering and function specifics to evolution under non-equilibrium thermodynamics conditions in open systems.[9] This kind of system is able to maintain a spatial-temporal stability thanks to a continuous flow of energy and matter. This condition also allows its continuous renewal, regulated in part by autocatalytic activities and many other processes through which morphogenesis takes place.

The formation of new genomes means the formation of new "dissipative" structures with fluctuations which may force the system to reorganize itself and reach a new state, sometimes with a different spatial-temporal structure at the molecular or at the chromosomal level in the nucleus or in other cellular structures. Under these circumstances, the possibility of a variety of qualitative changes may result in the appearance of new genomic forms and new shapes of living matter.

In this respect, the genome appears as an open system, characterized by non-equilibrium phenomena developed in "order through fluctuations."[10] As such, as I have said, it is rather difficult to reconstruct the past or to predict the evolution of the system.

It is this aspect that makes it difficult to strictly apply the laws of physics to the genomic system, the major success of which seems to be based on the possibility of making predictions about the future behavior of a system once the initial conditions and the interactions among the components are known. In the genome, even with the spectacular achievements of molecular genetics in recent years, this aspect is not clear yet. The genome seems to exhibit certain characteristics that can not be simply explained on the basis of the characteristics of its constituents. As such, the genome is an example of a system that exhibits, to a certain degree, an unexpected behavior that cannot be directly extrapolated from the behavior of smaller systems, as could be done with a single or a few nucleotides. It is another case of a situation in which a larger aggregate of molecules and a high number of interactions with many other molecules makes the system so complex that it is rather difficult to use correlations derived from observations of more simple systems. On the contrary, the genome, as a complex control center for many of the basic functions of living systems, has developed or historically acquired, emergent properties that today are different life forms and shapes.

This condition, associated with a constant variation of the environment, has been and is experiencing continuous changes, which we are not able to predict. What we know about the genome is not yet sufficient to predict the evolution of living systems in a determinate way. Further studies to uncover more details of the macromolecular structure of nucleic acids are necessary in order to understand the forces and principles that govern their behavior, and as a consequence, the functioning of the genomic system.

NOTES

1. E. Wigner. *Proceedings of the Fourth International Conference on the Unity of the Sciences,* New York, 1975, 25.

2. E. Wigner. *Proceedings of the Eleventh International Conference on the Unity of the Sciences,* Philadelphia, 1982, 1367.

3. E. Wigner. Nobel Lectures. Amsterdam: Elsevier, 1972.

4. T. Gerholm. *Proceedings of the Fourth International Conference on the Unity of the Sciences,* New York, 111–117, 1975.

5. E. Mayr. *The Growth of Biological Thought.* The Belknap Press of Harvard University Press, Cambridge, MA. 1982.

6. J. Monod. *Le hasard et la necesitte.* Editons du Seuil, 1970.

7. B. McClintock. *Science* 226:792–801, 1984.

8. W. Doolittle. *Nature* 272:581, 1978.

9. M. Velarde. In "Instability of thermodynamic systems." Edited by J. Casas and G. Lebon. Springer-Verlag: Berlin. 1982, 248–278.

10. I. Prigogine. *Proceedings of the Fourth International Conference on the Unity of the Sciences,* New York, 1975, 216.

REFERENCES

Doolittle, W. 1978. *Nature* 272:581.

Gerholm, T. 1975. *Proceedings of the Fourth International Conference on the Unity of the Sciences,* New York, 111–117.

Mayr, E. 1982. *The growth of biological thought.* The Belknap Press of Harvard University Press: Cambridge, MA.

McClintock, B. 1984. *Science* 226:792–801.

Prigogine, I. 1975. *Proceedings of the Fourth International Conference on the Unity of the Sciences,* New York, 216.

Velarde, M. 1982. In "Instability of thermodynamic systems." Edited by Casas, J. and Lebon, G. Springer-Verlag: Berlin. 248–278.

Wigner, E. 1972. Nobel Lectures. Elsevier: Amsterdam.

———. 1975. *Proceedings of the Fourth International Conference on the Unity of the Sciences,* New York, 25.

———. 1982. *Proceedings of the Eleventh International Conference on the Unity of the Sciences,* Philadelphia, 1367.

7

Complexity and Life

EFRAIM OTERO

In his scholarly paper, Professor Pincheira has undoubtedly confronted the reader with the main problems of modern molecular biology. Firstly, because for many of us it is still difficult to think of the laws of biology as independent of the laws of physics and we keep hoping—as many physicists do today—for a new unifying quantum theory as has been recently suggested.[1] But, as Pincheira accurately observes, this would only be possible if we consider and accept that the distinction between living and nonliving material lies simply in the greater degree of organization of the former.

However, even given the hierarchy demonstrated by the different components of living systems and their increasingly complex interactions, Pincheira points put that biological observations—when considered at the population level—are subject to probability laws and a probabilistic conceptualization. Here, I think, emerges the first dilemma applicable to most biological phenomena, namely, that the laws of physics, together with a lot of sufficiently elaborate instrumentation, could permit us to treat the products of genomic expression in a deterministic manner ("a rose is a rose is a rose," as Gertrude Stein would say); but, given the tremendous amount of interaction and variation in those products, at the usual practical level of analysis their outcome becomes almost a chance matter to be regarded and treated as probabilistic. And this becomes more necessary if we consider the relationships of the genome with the myriad environmental factors experienced throughout the eons of the evolutionary process.

Monod's suggestion of reproductive invariance, teleonomic activities and autonomous morphogenesis as the three main characteristics of living matter is universally accepted. But perhaps the first one, reproductive invariance, is the most outstanding and necessary (I would say indispensable) of genomic expressions and constitutes the basis of all our modern genetic dogma. The capacity for transmission of that reproductive invariance constitutes the essence of teleonomic activity. But, in linking reproductive invariance to the performance of nucleic acids which have coded, in their sequencing and pairing of nucleotide bases, all the information required for the functioning of a living organism, we bring in another dilemma, as Monod himself has pointed out:[2] the genetic code makes sense inasmuch as it is accurately translated; but the translating machine is made of macromolecular products that are themselves coded in the DNA; in other words, the code cannot be translated except by its own translation products. This applies to the structural as well as to the recognition codes. This "closed circle" would explain reproductive invariance (a sort of biological von Neumann machine, given the necessary inputs of building materials and energy) but it would still keep us far from being able to explain the origins of that code out of the primeval "prebiotic" soup. In the same vein, it is also hard to explain—outside purely stereochemical considerations—the affinity of certain amino acids for certain codons.

The processes of excision of introns and reunion of segments are succinctly described, and Prof. Pincheira advances the almost universally accepted hypothesis of the capacity of some introns to regulate their own surgery—without the intervention of an enzyme and without clear energy requirements—which he believes is the demonstration of the autocatalytic role of a nucleic acid. He brings in admirably the sequence of the processing of cytochrome B pre mRNA as an example of this remarkable auto-surgery. What Pincheira fails to mention (perhaps only due to the limitations of space) is the fact that in recent years such surgery has been made possible thanks to the use of restriction endonucleases cleaving specific sequences of DNA, and that this DNA recombination has given rise to the establishment of "genomic libraries" that not only have pushed further the advances in genetic engineering and biotechnology but also have opened the possibility of "genetic surgery" for the treatment of human hereditary disease.[3] Could those "genomic libraries" lead, in future years, to the compilation of more vast dictionaries or encyclopedias of genomic expressions applicable to higher mammals and man?

This artificial manipulation of the gene has helped us to understand the role of introns as carriers of outside information to the genome and thus their evolutionary significance, aptly described by Professor Pincheira in the latter part of his paper. He thinks that the transfer of genetic information carries in itself part of the responsibility for maintaining the structure and physiological integrity of the system; part of that responsibility may also reside in the silent or "useless" DNA which constitutes the vast majority of DNA in higher organisms. But, as he points out, information transfer may also be crucial in the interaction or interdependence of nonnuclear or satellite genomes—such as those present in mitochondria, plastids, etc.—and the nuclear genome. I also think special consideration should be given to the introns that code for the cytoskeleton, particularly for the system of microtubules and microfibrils, seemingly of great importance today for their interaction with prions in the central nervous system.[4] In any case, immunology and immunochemistry shall perhaps play, in the years to come, a greater role in our understanding of the acceptance or rejection of such information. Also, the structure and mechanism of action of nuclear endocrine receptors should be clarified in order to better understand the phenotypic effects of certain hormones.

In describing the complexities of the genome as an open system, Professor Pincheira's provocative paper undoubtedly opens more questions than it resolves. Perhaps, understanding the interactions of the genome with the environment will not only bring us closer to the comprehension of the pathogenesis of disease (oncogenes being one of the most recent and outstanding examples) but to the origin and evolution of life as well.

NOTES

1. M. K. Gaillard. "Toward a Unified Theory of Elementary Particle Interactions." *American Scientist* 70(1982): 506

2. J. Monod, *et al.* "La recherche en biologie moleculaire" (translation). *Biologia Molecular—CONACYT,* Mexico, 1981.

3. C. M. Steele. "DNA in Medicine: The Tools (Part I)" *Lancet* 2-8404(1984): 908.

4. D. C. Gajdusek. "Hypothesis: Interference with Axonal Transport of Microfilament as a Common Pathogenetic Mechanism in Certain Diseases of the Central Nervous System." *New England Journal of Medicine* 312(1985): 714.

8

Organization and Change in Eukaryotic Cells

CLAUDE A. VILLEE, JR.

1. INTRODUCTION. CHANGE AND RESISTANCE TO CHANGE IN LIVING SYSTEMS: HOMEOSTASIS

Living systems represent islands of order, of low entropy, in a vast sea of disorder. This low entropy must be maintained by the constant expenditure of energy by the living system. Moreover, the living system changes with time in defined ways as it undergoes growth, differentiation, maturation, aging and death. Living systems may change in other ways in response to trauma or disease. Both of these types of changes are ultimately regulated by the turning on and turning off of specific genes in specific tissues as time progresses or by differential changes in gene activity in different tissues of the same organism. The programmed ability of an organism to respond to changes in the environment by processes that tend to minimize the effects of these environmental changes, changes that tend to keep a system constant, is termed *homeostasis*. This ability to counteract changes in the environment is one of the prime characteristics of all living things.

Cells of living beings are complex dynamic systems composed of thousands of different molecular compounds, which interact in many different ways as they carry out specific functions in an organized and coherent form. In the first part of this paper the most relevant aspects of this interplay between change and organization at the cellular level are described, concluding with some brief considerations about cell differentiation and the origin of life.

2. CELLULAR AND SUBCELLULAR COMPLEXITY

Microtrabecular Lattice

There have been many surprises as we have learned more and more about the structure and function of living things. The electron microscope and its various improved forms have revealed a dazzling complexity at the sub-cellular level which parallels the remarkable complexity of the atomic nucleus now becoming apparent (Alberts 1983). What originally, by rather primitive light microscopy, appeared to be simply the nucleus and the cytoplasm of the cell has been resolved by electron microscopy to reveal a wealth of subcellular organelles—mitochondria, endoplasmic reticulum, lysosomes, peroxisomes, chloroplasts, and others (Figure 8–1) (Marx 1983). Even the apparently formless background of the cytoplasm of the cell, which had appeared to be structurally homogeneous by conventional electron microscopy, has been shown to have an internal structure when examined by high voltage electron microscopy (Buckley and Porter 1967). The cytoplasmic ground substance contains a microtrabecular lattice, an irregular three-dimensional lattice of very slender protein threads that extend throughout the cytoplasm and are attached to the cell membrane (Wolosewick and Porter 1979). These interlinked filaments form a three-dimensional spider web in which are suspended the several kinds of intracellular organelles. Microtubules and microfilaments are coated with a protein similar to that composing the individual lattice filaments. Microtubules, microfilaments, endoplasmic reticulum and mitochondria are integrated with the lattice and are suspended in it. This microtrabecular lattice links the cellular organelles into a highly organized structural and functional unit which appears to play an important role in cell movement. Enzymes that were previously believed to be simply dissolved in the cytoplasm may in fact be bound to this microtrabecular lattice; indeed, bound in a nonrandom orientation. That is, enzymes that act in sequence may be located on the lattice in a particular spatial orientation so that they can pass substrate molecules from one enzyme to the next. The microtrabecular lattice serves as a sort of intracellular musculature and undergoes local contractions that change its shape and redistribute and reorient the intracellular organelles as the cell goes about its various functions (Goldman and Follett 1970, Goldman et al. 1979). This can be seen most readily in the movement of granules that occurs within the pigment cells in the skin of fishes, frogs and reptiles under hormonal or nervous control. These movements of the pigment granules enable the animal to lighten or darken its skin color rapidly to match the color of its surroundings.

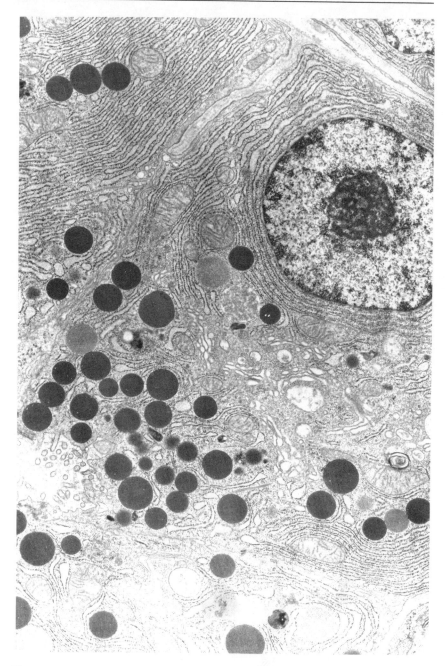

Figure 8-1: Electron micrograph of a cell from the human pancreas showing nucleus and nucleolus, extensive endoplasmic reticulum, some circular mitochondria with cristae, and a large number of secretion granules (solid black), enlarged 55,000 times.

Nuclear Matrix

Just as the cytoplasm of eukaryotic cells has been shown to be permeated by the highly ordered subcellular skeleton of filaments and membranes, the nucleus has also been shown to contain an organized proteinaceous skeleton that probably plays a role in the proper positioning of gene sequences important for replication, transcription and chromosomal integrity (Maul 1982).

This nuclear skeleton, termed the nuclear matrix, makes up about ten percent of the mass of the nucleus. It contains neither lipids nor histones, but is composed of some 20 major proteins (some of which are phosphorylated), together with many minor proteins. The laminar polypeptides with molecular masses of 62, 66 and 69 kilodaltons migrate to the cytoplasm during mitosis.

We can now recognize three clearly different matrix systems—the nuclear matrix, the cytoplasmic matrix, and an extracellular matrix present in tissues such as bone, cartilage, ligaments, tendons and dense connective tissue.

Role in DNA Replication

It is now realized that the double helix of chromosomal DNA is a very long fiber—with a length measured in meters—and that it must be folded and refolded very carefully to fit inside a nucleus only a few micrometers in diameter and yet be able to undergo replication rapidly without getting tangled with adjacent chromosomes (Hoagland 1979). The evidence now suggests that this is achieved by having the ends of the chromosomes attached to the inner edge of the nuclear membrane in specific places.

To obtain a sample of nuclear matrix the tissue or group of cells is homogenized and the nuclei are separated from the remainder of the cell by centrifugation. The nuclei are then treated with nonionic detergents and 2M NaCl to remove lipids and histones and then are digested with deoxyribonuclease. Before being treated with deoxyribonuclease the chromosomes can be shown to be attached to the matrix at multiple sites. This organizes the DNA into topologically independent supercoiled domains. After the nuclei have been digested with deoxyribonuclease the nuclear matrix retains the shape of the nucleus and has three features—an outer lamina, a residual nucleolus, and a fibrillar network. This nuclear matrix may provide a structural support for the replication of DNA. It has been shown experimentally that newly synthesized DNA is tightly associated with the matrix. Other workers have found that the structural genes are preferentially associated with the matrix in those cells in which the genes are activity transcribed. Based on findings such as these, many investigators have concluded that the nuclear matrix serves some crucial role in organizing and regulating nuclear events (Maul 1982). Other investigators suggest that they may be artifacts produced by the isolation process. Comparable structures have been isolated by a different method from both metaphase and nondividing cells.

When nuclei are lysed by a gentle low salt procedure the resulting nuclei have their histones depleted, and then when they are digested with restriction endonucleases, about 70 percent of the DNA is solubilized. Analyses of the solubilized versus the residual DNA shows that one type of DNA appears to be found exclusively associated with the nuclear matrix whereas all other DNA fragments are found primarily in the soluble supernatant. This nuclear matrix-bound fragment is rich in adenine and thymine and is derived from a non-transcribed "spacer" sequence upstream from the histone I gene. A similar adenine- and thymine-rich fragment from the HSP70 heat shock gene has been shown to be associated with the nuclear matrix. Other adenine- and thymine-rich fragments of DNA have also been shown to be bound to the matrix. From these findings it has been inferred that the loops of DNA in interphase nuclei are maintained by way of these sequence specific associations with matrix proteins and that the associations are not changed as a function of transcriptional activity. These results support the hypothesis that the nucleus is indeed highly ordered and organized and that changes in this organization may play a role in controlling nuclear functions.

The average human diploid nucleus with a radius of 2.6 micrometers and a volume of 75 cubic micrometers contains 5.5×10^9 base pairs of DNA, which would extend 1.7×10^6 micrometers, or 1.7 meters. This length is 650,000 times the nuclear radius! Clearly, the replication of DNA must be organized in space in such a way that the resultant daughter chromosomes remain untangled and can segregate properly during mitosis. The replication of DNA in eukaryotes is ordered chronologically; that is, different sections of the genome appear to replicate at specific times during the S phase according to a schedule which is the same for each consecutive cycle of division. The chronological and topological ordering of DNA replication may be a function of the structural components of the nucleus called the nuclear matrix. These ubiquitous proteins, which are not dissolved by salt, are sensitive to proteolysis and hence must be isolated in the presence of protease inhibitors. The nuclear matrix is composed of three major polypeptides of 62, 66 and 69 kilodaltons. These proteins appear by tryptic peptide mapping to be structurally related and perhaps derived from a common precursor or evolved from closely related genes. They are also related immunologically, for they cross-react with monospecific antibodies.

The replication sites of DNA are bound to the nuclear matrix. The transcription of DNA and the synthesis of the several kinds of RNA also appear to be located on the nuclear matrix. Newly synthesized RNA is localized in the nuclear matrix and all of the heterogeneous nuclear RNA (the precursor of messenger RNA) is bound to the nuclear matrix. RNA is transported from the nucleus to the cytoplasm through nuclear pore complexes which are linked by way of the nuclear matrix to the sites of RNA synthesis.

Mechanism of Action of Steroid Hormones

A fascinating problem at present is the question of how steroid hormones control the expression of specific genes in their target tissues. There is experimental evidence to support the belief that this involves specific binding protein receptors and acceptors which take up the steroid hormone and bind the steroid-receptor complex to specific gene locations. For example, estrogens bind to salt insoluble nuclear subfractions in their target tissues which have been shown to be nuclear matrix. Similar studies with other tissues also show the binding of steroid hormones to salt resistant nuclear protein fractions; that is, the androgens bind to the nuclear matrix in the prostate, the glucocorticoids to the nuclear matrix in fibroblasts and liver and so on.

3. INFORMATION FLOW

Introns and Exons

The central dogma of biology states that information flows from DNA (deoxyribonucleic acid) through mRNA (messenger RNA) to proteins. This is substantially true in the relatively simple coliform bacteria, *Escherichia coli,* in which many of the early studies of molecular biology were made. However, when scientists turned to other forms of life, and particularly to eukaryotic organisms, some surprises occurred. One of the first was that most eukaryotic genes were found to contain very long sequences of nucleotides that do not end up in the corresponding mature messenger RNAs. During the processing of messenger RNA after it has been transcribed from DNA in the nucleus, the RNA is split at precise points, certain segments are removed, and the remaining segments are spliced back together again. The sequences that are retained in the mature RNA are called *exons* and the discarded ones are called *introns*. The gene for the globin component of hemoglobin produces a messenger RNA after the deletion of two introns. The gene for ovalbumin (egg white protein) contains seven introns and the gene specifying another egg white protein, conalbumin, contains 16 introns. The apparently unused introns may be collectively much longer than the functional exons. The ovalbumin gene contains about 7700 base pairs despite the fact that its mature messenger

RNA contains only 1859 bases. It remains unclear why a cell should contain 5841 apparently wasted and useless bases in just one of its many genes.

RNA Viruses and Reverse Transcriptase

Another surprise came with the discovery that certain viruses contain only RNA and not DNA. It was then discovered that a class of enzymes called reverse transcriptases can synthesize DNA using RNA as the template. The resulting DNA can then be used in a regular transcription system to produce many copies of RNA which will be available for the multiplying virus.

DNA Codes and Prions

The establishment of the genetic code which assigned each of the possible triplet codons to a specific amino acid appeared to be universal as systems from bacteria to the human were analyzed and all were found to use the same genetic code. However, examination of the details of the coding relationships in the DNA of both yeast mitochondria and human mitochondria led to the unexpected finding that some of the codons are different from the accepted universal code (Grizell 1983). For example, in yeast mitochondria the sequence AUA codes for methionine rather than for isoleucine and the sequence UGA codes for tryptophan instead of serving, as it does in the nucleus, as a terminator code. An even greater shock has come with the recent finding that certain diseases, such as scrapie of sheep, the kuru of New Guinea cannibals and Alzheimer's disease, which originally were thought to be caused by viruses may actually be caused instead by small protein particles called *prions*. Prions have not yet been found to contain any nucleic acid. It is not clear yet how prions cause disease, but they may do it by affecting genetic expression, rather than by actually transmitting genetic information. It is not at all clear how such particles could be self-replicating, which is a condition required of any particle that transmits genetic information.

Thus our understanding of the organization of living systems and of the factors that control changes in the system has grown remarkably in the past few years, but it seems likely that there will be many more surprises in store for us before the final chapter is written.

4. CELL STRUCTURE

Early biologists thought that the inside of a cell was filled with a homogeneous jelly-like material that they called protoplasm. With their primitive microscopes they could recognize only a few structures within the cell such as the nucleus. Our present perception of the world within the cell has been greatly expanded, and we know that each cell is a highly organized, complex structure with its own control center, its own power plants, its own internal transport system, its own factories for synthesizing a variety of needed materials, places for packaging these biosynthetic products and even a "self-destruct" system within the cell (Figure 8-2) (Fawcett 1981). The various subcellular organelles are enclosed by membranes which effectively partition the cytoplasm into specific compartments. These membrane barriers make possible the accumulation of specific chemicals and enzymes in certain compartments. The chemical contents within that compartment may be quite different from the chemical environment in the general cytoplasm or inside other organelles.

Endoplasmic Reticulum

Proteins are synthesized on the ribosomes attached to the rough endoplasmic reticulum (Avers 1981). Since the ribosomes are the site of protein synthesis, the amount of rough endoplasmic reticulum is especially large in those cells that synthesize protein for export from the cell, such as those in the pancreas that secrete digestive enzymes.

Golgi Complex

The Golgi complex consists of layers of platelike membranes which may be distended to form vesicles or sacs which are filled with cell products (Holtzman and Novikoff 1984). The Golgi complex functions as a processing and packaging center and is most highly developed in cells that are specialized to secrete products. As proteins are synthesized in the rough endoplasmic reticulum, they are sealed off in little packets of membrane, forming vesicles. These pass through the endoplasmic reticulum to the Golgi complex and there fuse to form new Golgi complex membranes. Within the Golgi complex the proteins secreted may be concentrated by the action of its membranes or the proteins may undergo modification such as having carbohydrate residues added or having certain amino acid residues removed. The proteins are then packaged within a sac made of Golgi complex membranes and these secretory vesicles are released from the Golgi complex and moved to the cell membrane. They fuse with the cell membrane, releasing their contents to the exterior of the cell. An actively secreting cell, such as a goblet cell in the lining of the digestive system that secretes mucus, may completely renew all of its membranes every 30 minutes.

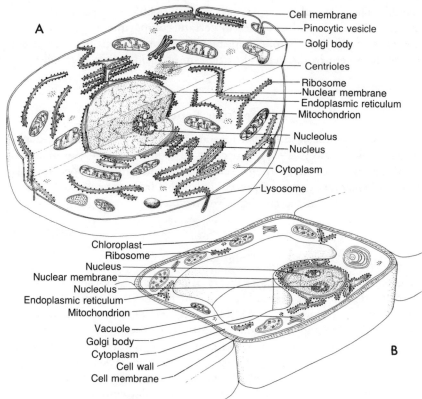

Figure 8-2: Diagrams of a typical animal cell (upper left) and plant cell (lower right) showing the several subcellular organelles.

Lysosomes

Another type of subcellular organelle is the lysosome, which contains intracellular digestive enzymes (DeDuve 1963). These include a variety of hydrolases that can cleave peptides, carbohydrates, lipids or nucleotides. These lysosomes are dispersed throughout the cytoplasm. When a white blood cell eats bacteria, debris or dead cells, the foreign matter is surrounded by a vesicle consisting of part of the cell membrane. One or more of the cell's lysosomes then fuse with the vesicle containing the foreign matter and the enzymes from the lysosomes digest the proteins, polysaccharides, lipids and nucleic acids which make up the dead cell or bacterium. When a cell dies, the lysosomes release their enzymes into the cytoplasm and these enzymes then break down the cell itself. This self-destruct system accounts for the rapid deterioration of cells following the death of the organism. Christine DeDuve, the Belgian biochemist who discovered lysosomes, referred to them as "suicide bags."

Mitochondria

Most of the enzymatic reactions of cellular respiration occur within the mitochondria and, as one might expect, mitochondria are more numerous in cells that are very active (Figure 8–2). Mitochondria may be spherical, rod-shaped, sausage-shaped or thread-like. Each mitochondrion is bounded by a double membrane. The outer membrane forms the smooth, outer boundary, whereas the inner membrane is folded repeatedly into parallel plates or cristae that extend into the center of the mitochondrial cavity. The shelf-like cristae contain many of the enzymes involved in cellular respiration. Other enzymes involved in cellular respiration are located within the semifluid matrix inside the inner compartment (Margulis 1981).

Peroxisomes

Another type of subcellular membrane-bounded organelle is the peroxisome which contains enzymes that utilize oxygen in metabolic reactions. Some reactions produce hydrogen peroxide, but before the cell can be damaged by this potentially lethal compound the hydrogen peroxide is split by the enzyme superoxide dismutase to yield water and oxygen.

Microtubules and Microfilaments

Most cells contain in their cytoplasm hollow cylindrical cytoplasmic subunits called microtubules which are important in maintaining and controlling the shape of the cell (Fawcett 1981). Microtubules also play important roles in cellular movements such as the movement of the chromosomes on the spindle formed during mitosis. Microtubules are also the major structural components of cilia and flagella. They are composed of the protein tubulin made up of two subunits. Microtubules can grow in length by the addition of more subunits or can shorten by the disassembly of subunits. The microtubules present within the axons of nerve cells play an important role in the rapid transport of proteins and other molecules down the axon to its tip where these substances are released.

Microfilaments are solid cytoplasmic strands that are composed of protein molecules. These protein filaments play additional roles in maintaining cell structure and permitting cell movement (Wessels 1971). The cytoplasm of skeletal muscle fibers contain long, thin filaments, the myofibrils of two types—one composed of the protein actin and the other composed of the protein myosin. The interaction of these two is the basis of the process of muscle contraction. Microfilaments made of actin are also associated with such cellular movements as the flowing of cytoplasm in amoebas (Lazarides and Revelle 1978). The assembly of microfilaments and microtubules forms a flexible cellular framework termed the cytoskeleton. Each kind of animal cell contains two centrioles, organelles that play a role in cell division. Each centriole is a hollow cylinder made up of nine triple microtubules.

Within the nucleus and readily visible in a stained cell in the light microscope is the *nucleolus,* a compact, spherical body rich in RNA. It is the site where ribosomal RNA is synthesized.

Cell Membrane

Even with the primitive early microscope, it was possible to recognize that cells have a cell membrane which separates the complex structures within the cell from the surrounding environment. The cell contains a host of specific proteins, lipids, carbohydrates and inorganic ions and the concentrations of these cellular components must be maintained relatively constant if the cell is to continue to remain alive. The cell membrane is not simply an inanimate wall, but rather a complex structure that permits selective interactions between the cell and its environment (Lodish and Rothman 1978). The cell membrane regulates the passage of materials into and out of the cell, enabling the cell to maintain many of its constituents at concentrations different from those in the surrounding environment. The cell membrane prevents the passage of certain substances and permits or even facilitates the passage of others.

Cells can, in a sense, talk to each other. The cell membrane receives information that permits the cell to sense changes in its environment and respond appropriately to these changes. Cell surfaces are equipped with a variety of receptor proteins that receive chemical messages from other cells. These receptor proteins bind specifically with certain hormones, growth factors and neurotransmitters, and the binding triggers the specific response of the cell.

The cell membrane is really thin, about 6 to 10 nanometers in thickness, and is composed of a fluid lipid bilayer in which are imbedded a variety of globular proteins (Singer and Nicholson 1972). The lipid components of the cell membrane include phospholipids, glycolipids and cholesterol, all of which are asymmetrical, elongated molecules with one hydrophilic end and one hydrophobic end. The bilayer is arranged so that the nonpolar hydrophobic ends of the lipids meet, overlap and interdigitate with each other, whereas the polar hydrophilic ends are directed towards the outside of the membrane. The two sheets of the lipid bilayer differ in their chemical composition. The outer layer is especially rich in choline phospholipids and glycolipids, whereas the internal fluid layer is rich in other types of phospholipids. The fatty acids of the outer choline-rich lipid layer are primarily saturated fatty acids whereas the inner layer is rich in polyunsaturated fatty acids.

Embedded in the bilayer lipid fluid matrix are proteins which can move around like "protein icebergs in a lipid sea." The lipids serve as a general permeability barrier to ions and polar molecules, whereas the membrane proteins carry out specific functions such as chemical transport and transmission of messages. The plastic quality of the lipid bilayer permits the cell to respond to a wide variety of external stimuli. The membrane proteins that protrude from the outer surface away from the cytoplasm are largely glycoproteins; that is, proteins to which sugar residues are attached (Unwin and Henderson 1984). Thus nearly all cells are "sugar-coated" like some breakfast cereals. Little or no sugar is attached to the inner surface of the cell membrane or to any of the intracellular membranes. Membrane proteins can move laterally within the membrane and can change their position on the cell surface.

5. CELL DIFFERENTIATION

Organisms such as human beings are composed of an exceedingly large number ($>10^9$) of individualized cells of many different kinds. Each kind of cell is specialized and adapted to carry out certain functions important for the survival and growth of the human being. One of the central questions in biology at the present time concerns the molecular basis of this process of cellular differentiation. Put more simply: what kind of processes occur during development that insure that a single fertilized egg cell will develop into all of these many types of cells, each in the proper place in the organism, each with its appropriate spectrum of enzymes, and each with its characteristic structure, so that the net result is a human being? We now have a good idea of how a single gene can code for the production of a single kind of enzyme and how the activity of the enzyme in the cell can result in the conversion of a precursor molecule into the product, the right kind of product for that cell. However, we have very little idea of how a gene may determine the structural features of a cell or tissue or how the malfunctioning of genes during development may lead to a tremendous alteration in the structure of the body, such as that seen in anencephaly, spina bifida, cleft palate or club foot. What is truly remarkable is that these mistakes in the developmental process happen relatively rarely.

6. THE ORIGIN OF LIFE

Another important problem in present-day biology is the question of how life got started on the planet earth (Ambrose 1982). We now know that living things come only from other living things, but under the very different conditions than those that obtained when the earth was young, living things may indeed have developed from nonliving things. The concept that the first living things evolved from nonliving things and suggestions as to what the sequence of events may have been were put forward by Haldane, Beutner and Oparin in the early 1930's. The earth originated some five billion years ago and was probably very hot and molten when it was first formed. Conditions consistent with life may have appeared on the planet only three billion years ago. Twenty-two different amino acids were isolated from Precambrian rocks from South Africa that are dated at about 3.1 billion years old. It seems likely that in the early period of the earth's development there was essentially no free oxygen in the atmosphere. All of the oxygen atoms were combined as water or as oxides. The primitive atmosphere of the earth would have been strongly reducing and would have included the gases methane, ammonia and water vapor.

Oparin suggested that the carbon atoms in the earth's crust were present as metallic carbides which could react with water to form acetylene. Acetylene can polymerize to form compounds composed of long chains of carbon atoms. High energy radiation, such as cosmic rays, can catalyze the synthesis of organic compounds. This was shown by Melvin Calvin's experiments in which solutions of carbon dioxide and water were irradiated in a cyclotron and formic, oxalic and succinic acids, which contain one, two and four carbon atoms, respectively, were obtained. These compounds are intermediates in the metabolic pathways of living organisms.

Irradiating solutions of inorganic compounds with ultraviolet light or passing electric charges through the solutions to simulate lightning also produces organic compounds. Stanley Miller and Howard Urey (1952) exposed a mixture of water vapor, methane, ammonia and hydrogen gases to electric discharges for a week and demonstrated the production of organic compounds, including D and L amino acids. Other theorists believe that the early atmosphere consisted of water vapor, carbon dioxide, carbon monoxide, nitrogen and some free hydrogen. When this mixture of gases was subjected to electric charges, even greater amounts of organic compounds were formed, including (surprisingly enough) nucleotide bases of DNA and RNA. Amino acids and some other compounds are produced on earth at the present time by lightning discharges or ultraviolet radiation, but any such organic compound produced would be phagocytized by protists or degraded by molds and bacteria that now abound on earth. Under the original presumably sterile and anoxic conditions, the compounds could have persisted.

The details of the chemical reactions that could give rise, without the intervention of living things, to carbohydrates, fats and amino acids have been described by Oparin, Calvin and others. They believe that most, and perhaps all, of the reactions by which organic substances were formed probably occurred in the sea which contained a rich pool of precursors. The sea became a sort of dilute broth in which the molecules collided, reacted and aggregated to form larger molecules. As more has been learned about the role of hydrogen bonds and other weak intramolecular forces in the pairing of specific nucleotide bases and the effectiveness of these processes in the transfer of biological information it has become clear that similar forces could have operated early in evolution before living organisms first appeared. Oparin's theory continues with the suggestion that the forces of intermolecular attraction and the tendency for certain molecules to form liquid crystals might provide an explanation for the spontaneous formation of large, complex, specific molecules. It has now been shown that such reactions can take place with the molecules adhering to particles of clay as well as in free solution in water, and that the particles of clay may help direct reactions in a certain direction (Cairns-Smith 1982). Hence some theorists suggest that life may have begun on a clay beach at the edge of the sea rather than in the sea itself.

Once some of the protein molecules were formed and had achieved the ability to catalyze reactions, that is, once they were enzymes, the rate of formation of additional molecules would have greatly speeded up. Eventually, when they combined with nucleic acids, the complex protein molecules would acquire the ability to catalyze the synthesis of molecules like themselves. Such hypothetical autocatalic particles made of nucleic acids and proteins would have been something like a modern virus, or perhaps a plasmid.

A major step in the evolution of these prebiotic systems was the development of a protein-lipid membrane surrounding the aggregate that permitted the accumulation of some molecules and the exclusion of others from the surrounding medium. Of course, another major evolutionary step was the development of the genetic code. No feature of a living cell could be maintained for more than one generation, if that long, without an informational basis. Thus, any credible theory of the origin of life must suggest ways whereby not only the nucleic acids, but the informational content of the nucleic acids, as well as the read-out mechanisms by which the information is translated into cellular structures, could have originated.

The first living organisms, having arisen in a sea of organic molecules and in contact with an atmosphere lacking oxygen, probably obtained energy by fermenting these organic substances. The first organisms, therefore, were almost certain heterotrophs, organisms unable to synthesize their own food. From these early heterotrophs probably evolved the autotrophs which were able to make their own organic molecules by chemosynthesis or photosynthesis. One of the byproducts of photosynthesis is gaseous oxygen. All of the oxygen in the atmosphere is now produced by photosynthesis and, according to this, it always has been produced by photosynthesis. Other inorganic sources of oxygen, such as the photolysis of water vapor by ultraviolet light, might have contributed some oxygen to the early atmosphere.

Although at one time it was generally believed that living things have some unique "vital force" that governs their existence, there is no doubt at present that living things are subject to the same principles and laws of physics and chemistry as are nonliving things. Living things are typically much more complex in their organization and structure than are nonliving systems. Our understanding of the complexities of the structure of the atomic nucleus had to wait until the appropriate technology was developed—cyclotrons, linear accelerators and other types of atom smashers. Similarly, our understanding of the complex structure of the cell became possible only with the invention and development of electron microscopes and a variety of physical and chemical micromethods. Our understanding of the structure and organization of living things has increased by quantum jumps in recent decades, but much remains to be done to achieve an equivalent understanding of the nature of the processes underlying change in living systems and the factors controlling these changes.

REFERENCES

Alberts, B. 1983. *Molecular Biology of the Cell*. New York: Garland Publishing.

Ambrose, E. 1982. *The Nature and Origin of the Biological World*. New York: John Wiley.

Avers, C. 1981. *Cell Biology*. Second Edition. New York: D. Van Nostrand Company.

Buckley, I. and Porter, K. 1967. "Cytoplasmic Fibrils in Living Cultured Cells." *Protoplasma* 64:349–356.

Cairns-Smith, A. 1982. *Genetic Takeover and the Mineral Origins of Life*. Cambridge: Cambridge University Press.

DeDuve, C. 1963. "The Lysosome." *Scientific American* 208:64–78.

Fawcett, D. 1981. *The Cell*. Second Edition. Philadelphia: W. B. Saunders Company.

Goldman, R. and Follett, E. 1970. "Birefringent Filamentous Organelle in BHK 21 Cells and Its Possible Role in Cell Spreading and Motility." *Science* 169:286–288.

Goldman, R. *et al.* 1979. "Cytoplasmic Fibers in Mammalian Cells: Cytoskeletal and Contractile Elements." *Annual Review of Physiology* 41:703–722.

Grizell, L. 1983. Mitochondrial DNA. *Scientific American* 248:78–88.

Hoagland, M. 1979. *The Roots of Life: A Layman's Guide to Genes, Evolution and the Ways of Cells*. New York: Avon Books.

Holtzman, E. and Novikoff, A. 1984. *Cells and Organelles*. Third Edition. Philadelphia: Saunders College Publishing.

Kornberg, R. and Klung, A. 1981. "The Nucleosome." *Scientific American* 244:52–64.

Lazarides, E. and Revel, J. 1978. "The Molecular Basis of Cell Movements." *Scientific American* 240: 100–112.

Lodish, H. and Rothman, J. 1978. "The Assembly of Cell Membranes." *Scientific American* 240: 48–62.

Margulis, L. 1981. *Symbiosis in Cell Evolution*. San Francisco: W. H. Freeman and Company.

Marx, J. 1983. "Organizing the Cytoplasm." *Science* 222:1109–1111.

Maul, G., ed. 1982. *The Nuclear Envelope and Nuclear Matrix*. New York: Alan Liss.

Singer, S. and Nicholson, G. 1972. "The Fluid Mosaic Model of the Structure of Cell Membranes." *Science* 175:720–731.

Stebbins, G. 1982. *Darwin to DNA, Molecules to Humanity*. San Francisco: W. H. Freeman.

Unwin, N. and Henderson, R. 1984. "The Structure of Proteins in Biological Membranes." *Scientific American* 250:78–94.

Wessels, H. 1971. "How Living Things Change Shape." *Scientific American* 225:76–88.

Wolosewick, J. and Porter, K. 1979. "Microtrabecular Lattice of the Cytoplasmic Ground Substance: Artifact or Reality?" *Journal of Cellular Biology*, 82:114–139.

9

Mind: Mapping and Reconstruction of Reality

PERCY LÖWENHARD

1. SOME ONTOLOGICAL REMARKS ON REALITY AND ORDER

> *Here and elsewhere we shall not obtain the best insight into things until we actually see them growing from the beginning. . .*
>
> ARISTOTLE *vii*

The main title of this paper implies two ontological statements: the existence of an external reality, independent of an observer, and the existence of that function of our brain which constitutes the universe of subjective experience: the mind.

The world as we see it is a world of perpetual change and evolution. At least it appears to us that parts of it show time sequences which alternate between states of chaos and perfect order. Within the realm of changing complex systems, living organisms are the most salient proponents. They are not only the result of a very complex evolutionary process, which has taken place over billions of years, but one of the results of this process, the human brain, is able to transfer the application of organizatory principles outside the boundaries of the organism itself.

The human brain is one of the most marvellous achievements of nature. It is not only the most complex single structure in that part of nature which is known to us, but its complexity includes the existence of functional principles whose details to a large extent are still more or less enigmatic. One may illustrate the meaning of this complexity if one considers the performance of the mammalian eye. The retina of the eye is functionally a part of the brain. If one wants to simulate the real-time information processing of a single retinal nerve cell, this would be equivalent to the simultaneous solution of about 500 non-linear differential equations within a time-span of 10 milliseconds. The very fast Cray supercomputer would demand a computing time of several minutes to perform this task (Stevens 1985). Now, one has to consider that the information processing of the retina involves the simultaneous interaction of several millions of nerve cells. Finally, the cerebral cortex contains on the order of 10^{10} to 10^{11} neurons and 10^{13} to 10^{15} synaptic junctions. Hence, with respect to its integrative potential, the information processing capacity of the brain is truly stupendous. Some further details will be given later on.

Any description of such a system has to take several central concepts into consideration:

1. The notion of *hierarchically organized systems* with dynamic interaction between all levels of their hierarchy.
2. The notion of *self-organizing systems,* which has two aspects:
   a. A phylogenetic aspect, related to the concept of evolution in a Darwinian sense.
   b. An ontogenetic aspect, related to genetically controlled growth and development of an individual organism.
3. The notion that *phylogenetic adaptation represents an information process.* This means an interaction between organisms and their biosphere as well as between living systems and non-living matter or radiation.

Some of the basic principles which are related to the self-organization[1] of lower level systems are dealt with in previous chapters in this volume. With respect to living systems, the above-mentioned aspects are integrated within the relatively new thought model of evolutionary epistemology (see e.g. Campbell 1974, Riedl 1979, Vollmer 1981, Lorenz and Wuketits 1983). While this model is based upon the Darwinian concepts of evolution, selection and individual adaptation (including findings from embryology), it is not identical with the classical theory. Some intermediary steps are Neodarwinian Theory, which also includes genetics and chance mutations as a source of variability and finally "Synthetic Theory," which enhances its sphere to include population genetics and molecular genetics as well. To be precise, one must add that evolutionary theory is not a theory in a strict sense, but rather a bundle of theories from different disciplines within a common frame of reference.

Contemporary theory includes cybernetics and systems theory. Essentially its models are much more complex. While mutations mainly are "blind" processes, survival of the fittest (selection with respect to a given environment) does not seem to follow a long term teleological master plan

either. It may be added that "fitness" can be defined without reference to
survival, which nullifies the allegation of a circularity (cf. Vollmer 1982).
Evolution then must *not* be viewed as the result of a chain of single,
directed factors which influence a given system, but as a multicausal feedback process between interacting systems. The central postulate of molecular biology, the functional order

$$D N A \quad \rightarrow \quad R N A \quad \rightarrow \quad protein$$

must in some cases be modified because there are interactions between
the different elements of the *epigenetic system,* which gives a more complex
picture. The origin and evolution of living systems seems to be the result
of the inherent dynamics of material systems, leading to an optimal adaptation. An excellent survey of these questions has recently been given by
Wuketits (1985).

Phenomena such as "time," "matter," "space," "energy," and
"life," to which "consciousness" might be added, seem to be basic attrib-
utes of our universe. They are, however, of different quality. Within physical theory, the nature of our world is ultimately described in terms of
particles and interactions between them. The term "particle" here must
not be interpreted as something akin to our everyday experience but as a
quantum mechanical entity described by measurable parameters, such as
mass, electric charge, spin, etc. As far as we know today, there are four
different types of interaction (or forces) which in the near future may
perhaps be united within a common theory. An up-to-date survey on this
topic is given by Quigg (1985). Within the framework of our mesocosmic
world, however, the electromagnetic interaction is dominant, with gravitation in second place. The electromagnetic interaction is responsible for
the vast majority of everyday phenomena such as the coherence of matter,
the molecular bond, chemical reactions, electric and magnetic phenomena and their different applications such as the generation and transmission of electric energy, the processing and transmission of information
and so forth.

The phenomena of "life" and "consciousness," however, must be
said to represent a higher ontic level (within the same basic ontology),
where "consciousness" demands the previous existence of "life," while
life in turn demands the existence of matter and energy. Matter reveals a
tremendous variety of properties and potentialities. One may mention its
ability to organize itself into complex structures under suitable conditions, which is a precondition for the emergence of living systems. A
critical factor is the existence of a universe which has a sufficiently low
level of entropy and which allows for local variations in it. Furthermore,
the emergence of life, as we know it, seems to demand the existence of a
large set of favorable conditions: a planet of suitable mass at a critical

distance from a star of suitable spectral class, planetary rotation, a suitable composition of the geosphere etc. It is probable that the creation of order and life on earth has been made possible by the emission of low-entropy (highly ordered) energy from the surface of the sun at 6000 K and a re-radiation of high-entropy energy (infrared radiation) at 300 K (Sexl 1984). Among other critical factors one may mention the homopolar bond of carbon atoms (ensuring the formation of large carbon chains) or the large number of "unusual" properties of common water: its ability to work as a nearly universal solvent, its density maximum at 3.9 °C above its freezing point, its very high dielectric coefficient, its high boiling point and heat capacity etc. These properties, which are due to the marked dipole moment of the water molecule, influence geology, the biosphere and molecular biology in a remarkable way. They also nicely illustrate the variety of effects which relate to a single factor: the molecular distribution of electric charges or in other words, the geometry of electromagnetic interactions.

2. LIVING ORGANISMS: SELF-ORGANIZATION AND COMPLEXITY

In this section I will discuss some general features of living organisms and the notion of life. Since the contributions of Dr. Pincheira and Dr. Villee in this volume deal in more detail with genetic and cellular functions, these are only mentioned cursorily here within contexts to which they relate.

The concept "life" is intuitively well-known but shows a treacherous elusiveness if one tries to define it strictly. This is due not only to the intrinsic complexity of the phenomenon, but also to its wide range of connotations. Generally, the term "life" is a common label which we apply to the totality of systems which constitute the biosphere of earth. The functional properties which are necessary to sustain the continuous existence of living systems may be called their *life functions*. Organisms are a subset of living systems and are characterized by a particularly high degree of autonomy. Thus the term "life" may be used to denote the totality of life functions which characterize a given organism. Meanwhile, one must also consider the characteristics of life as a holistic phenomenon:

a. The *existence* of life is dependent on the *state* of the system (living or dead). This means that life functions are strongly integrated and interdependent. The hierarchical structure of all organisms implies that "life" means partly the same, partly different things at different levels of the organism. Essentially there is a distinct

holistic difference between *any* system in a "living" and a "dead" state. Examples are given by Löwenhard (1981).
  b. The existence of a living organism is limited to a time-span between "birth" and "death."
  c. The system properties of an organism change during *ontogenesis* (evolutionary aspect).
  d. The changes which the organism undergoes during its existence reflect the aspects of life as a *process*.

With respect to more specific features, the following characteristics are now viewed as sufficient conditions for life: 1) Metabolism, 2) Reproduction, 3) Mutability, 4) Interaction between functional elements (e.g. proteins) and carriers of information (DNA;RNA). Living organisms show, furthermore, a variety of additional properties, some of them specific, others common to many organisms. Some further details are given by Löwenhard (1981, 1984) and Wuketits (1982).

Basically, living organisms are very complexly structured chemical systems. With respect to this fact, biology favors a reductionistic view. Nevertheless, reduction then leads to the problem of handling complexities. Also, one has to consider the problem of *emerging properties*. In the sense of General System Theory (Bertalanffy 1952, 1973, Laszlo 1973, Weiss 1969, 1971) living organisms are hierarchically organized, stratified, multi-levelled systems with dynamic interaction between all levels. According to Weiss (1971) this may be illustrated by Figure 9–1.

The model does not only imply an interaction among all levels of the hierarchy, but a simultaneous superposition of their working principles. This means that living systems form *integrated wholes*. The intricate multi-dimensionality of such systems is clearly shown in the excellent work of James Greer Miller (1978), which gives both an extensive and comprehensive treatment of the topic.

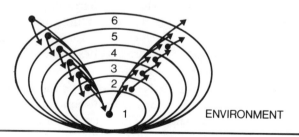

1 = GENE
2 = CHROMOSOME
3 = NUCLEUS
4 = CYTOPLASM
5 = TISSUE
6 = ORGANISM

ENVIRONMENT

Due to the complexity of living systems, the probability of their occurrence by chance is infinitesimally small. While chance events undoubtedly play an essential role in evolution, any unqualified random shuffle theory falls short in accounting for the large variety of organic systems which constitute the biological sphere of earth. One has to introduce additional assumptions:

1. Besides the tendency of matter to organize itself, there exist restrictions which drastically cut down the number of functionally stable combinations of elements. At the atomic level one may think of electronic configurations and the exclusion principle of Pauli (see e.g. Alonso and Valk 1973) and at the biochemical level one may mention the specificity of protein reactions.
2. The development of the life-forms of today must have been critically dependent on the number and distribution of potential intermediate stable forms. Nature seems to conserve successful stages of evolution. These systems then may either be used as building blocks for higher-order systems or be subjected to further adaptive modifications (cf. Laszlo 1973).

During growth and development the complexity of the organism increases steadily. This means that growth implies the occurrence of consecutive states with steadily decreasing probability. In order to maintain structure and keep life functions intact, the organism has to rely on well-established and stable principles of self-organization, homeostasis and self-mend. In a certain sense, mechanisms of defense and the ability to modify the environment so as to fit the needs of the organism may be looked upon as an extension of homeostatic functions outside the physical boundary of the organism. Their task is to prevent any disruption of the organism's life functions and integrity.

Any description of such a system must take all the above-mentioned features into consideration. A supersystem may show emerging properties which cannot be predicted *solely* from the knowledge of its subsystems, since some holistic features of the supersystem may not be reducible. The principle of *superadditivity* (Leinfellner 1984) represents a sophisticated way to describe this fact.

This also holds for the relationship between living systems and the *implicit information* of their genetic determinants. A sequence of codons (triplets of nucleotides) determines the order of amino acids within a protein. However, in order to know the function(s) of this protein in a given biochemical environment, one has also to know the chemical properties of this specific array of amino acids as well as the distribution of hydrogen bonds, which ultimately determine the secondary or tertiary structure of the protein and thus, for example, its enzyme functions.

Generally speaking, any detailed description of living systems makes at least a partial reduction necessary. Essentially this means that such systems cannot be described in terms of concepts from a single science, but elements from "higher order" sciences as well as from more "basic" sciences have to be included. While there is a strong interdependence among sciences with respect to concepts and methodology, each scientific discipline also develops methods, concepts, rules of thumb and theories of its own (some more details are given by Löwenhard (1984). Suppose that one wants to describe the chain of events which ultimately results in a conscious perception; one then has to start with the specific interaction between a receptor and the stimuli which convey physical energy. With respect to vision this means a photochemical excitation of photopigment molecules (rhodopsin or iodopsin) within the retinal receptor elements (rods or cones). The first event is, hence, a quantum-chemical event, the absorption of photons (light energy), followed by a dissociation of the photopigment molecule. In the case of rhodopsin this is accompanied by a cis-trans conversion of retinene (aldehyde of vitamin A) which is the chromophoric (specifically light absorbing) component of the photo pigment molecule. The chain of further events results in a generator potential by interruption of an ion current which normally passes through the plasma membranes of rods or cones (details are given by Gemme and Bernhard (1975) or Zurer (1983).

Concerning hearing, one has to start with the transfer of the complex amplitude-time function of a sound wave to the phonosensitive mechanism of the inner ear. This mechanism works in an aqueous environment. Since the transfer of sound energy between media of different acoustic density is usually very inefficient, the lever system of the middle ear performs the task of conveying the oscillatory movement to the inner ear, faithfully conserving the amplitude and phase relationships. In the next step the hair cells of the inner ear transform the mechanical oscillations into corresponding electrical ones. These microphonic potentials (choclear microphonic, Wever-Bray effect) are essentially the equivalents of piezoelectric potentials which result from a periodic elastic deformation of certain crystals such as quartz or the organic Seignette salt (potassium-sodium tartrate). Further details will be omitted here, since they are not relevant for our analysis (see e.g. Lindsay and Norman 1973).

A common task for all sense mechanisms, then, is to convey both general and specific information from the stimulus to the higher levels of the brain. The information has to be encoded primarily into a common language of nerve signals which allows for a comparison of messages from different receptors. Essentially, there are two known principles of encoding:

1. The information content of nerve signals is related to their spatio-temporal pattern (involving the cooperation of several nerve fibers).
2. The information is identified by the channel through which it arrives. This principle of "specific termination" may be regarded as a modern reformulation of Johannes Miller's famous doctrine of "specific sense energies" from 1826.

Some more details will be given in the next paragraphs. These short examples illustrate the above-mentioned thesis of scientific interdependence in the description of living systems.

3. BRAIN AND CNS: THE PHYSIOLOGICAL BASIS OF INFORMATION TRANSFER

The earlier sections have dealt with some main features of living organisms and have also touched upon the question of how an organism retrieves information from its environment. Within the animal domain the brain and CNS constitute, together with receptors, the information system of the organism. For more details see Löwenhard (1981, 1984).

One has to make a distinction between anatomical structures and functional systems. Essentially, there is no one-to-one relationship between them. Otherwise, one would easily end up in phrenology. The *structural* unit of the Central Nervous System is the *nerve cell* or *neuron,* while *nerve nets* constitute *functional units.* The existence of a certain nerve net may be restricted in time or not, while the structural components are more stable. An analogy may illustrate this. Telephone communication is based on the creation of a temporary communication line by connecting a subset of existing wires into a functional unit. This is done with the aid of relays which are controlled by a coded time sequence of electrical impulses. In a similar way, the brain utilizes associative networks which may be said to connect a set of input channels with corresponding output channels in a manner which optimizes information processing with respect to a given problem (cf. Crick 1979). The brain is both an open system and, in a sense, a cooperative system.

An understanding of the working principles of our brain has been facilitated by computer technology, which in turn has profited from brain research. There are similarities between brains and computers, but also essential differences. Basically both are information processing systems, but one may argue that the brain is primarily an instrument for survival, since sufficiently detailed knowledge about our world makes it somewhat more safe. The brain is the result of an essentially self-sustained evolutionary process, while the computer is designed and presupposes the existence of brains. The computer depends on deterministic principles, components of high reliability and the use of rapid sequences of electromagnetic pulses. The brain uses partly stochastic principles, its design is only roughly deterministic and it is rather insensitive to the failure of single neurons. As a *chemical system* it depends on rather slow processes of ion transport through membranes, but uses many lines in parallel. It has a high degree of economic flexibility and performs sophisticated processing of information at the synapses. Its partly digital, partly analog mechanisms have lately revealed a capacity which still today surpasses that of computers by many magnitudes. An illustrative example has been given in the first section of this paper.

Animal organisms use two types of information systems in parallel:

1. The nervous system which starts its activity rapidly, but mainly has effects of short duration. There exist, however, mechanisms (neural loops, for example) which may ensure more enduring actions. There are two types of information processing:
   a. Long-range transfer of information is based on the mediation of action potentials (nerve impulses) in conducting fibers (neural axons) and may essentially be compared to telegraph lines, utilizing a digital (all or none) code.
   b. Local information processing is based on the intricate interplay of graded slow potentials and chemical processes. The local synaptic junctions may use chemical transmitter molecules (neurotransmitters) or the effects of local electric fields (electrotonic synapses). There also seem to exist mechanisms which perform analog-digital-analog conversions (John 1968).
2. The endocrine system starts its activity slowly, but has an enduring action. It utilizes signal molecules (hormones) which are injected into the bloodstream and in this way are distributed all over the organism. They affect, however, only specific receptors, which chemically respond to a certain hormone. Receptor sites may be located at glands (which allows for hormonal feedback mechanisms), at other organs such as the heart or at the synaptic junctions between neurons. The transfer of nerve signals from a presynaptic to a postsynaptic neuron is mediated by neurotransmitters, which in some cases are identical with hormones. In this way the nervous system and the endocrine system are able to interact at the synaptic junctions between neurons.

This interactive duplicity of information processing is the reason why a change in the *biochemical environment* of a synaptic system may change the information content of a message which passes through the system. The action of psychotropic drugs may be viewed in this way. Their medical use aims at a renormalization of a distorted message. The use of different neurotransmitters in different subsystems of the CNS makes it possible to have a local web of functionally different nerve nets which are functionally separated from each other and do not interfere. They may, however, be engaged in an independent control of the same higher-order function.

Long range information transmission is not solely strictly linear, but convergence and divergence of information seem to occur simultaneously (schematically illustrated by figure 9-2).

Divergence may be illustrated by the mediation of pain signals:

1. A single train of nerve impulses may originate from a small group of "pain receptors" (possibly nerve endings).
2. After having passed several relay stations, the signals already engage five different pathways at the spinal level.
3. Several cortical and subcortical structures are activated and perform a partial analysis of the incoming message. They then contribute to the pattern of signals.
4. The final *brain state*,[3] corresponding to the perception of pain, represents complex information about the *site* and *type* of injury, the *intensity* of pain, its *emotional* aspects in relation to *knowledge* about the danger of the injury, the *attitude* of the person towards pain within a social context, etc. (Melzack 1961).

The second example shall illustrate both the principle of convergence and some aspects of synaptic functions with respect to *quantitative* information processing. The eye receives on the order of 10^8 bits of information each second, while only about 50 bits/s are recorded at the highest levels. What happens to the rest? One may assume that each nerve impulse corresponds to one bit. In order to trigger a postsynaptic nerve impulse, a minimum number of input impulses have to summarize their effects at a given synapse. This includes a superposition of both excitatory and inhibitory effects within a limited period of time.

Suppose that the equivalent of N excitatory input impulses is needed in order to trigger a postsynaptic neuron within a critical time period Δt (the effects of input signals are of short duration). If N is a large number, the probability is very small that the postsynaptic neuron is triggered by spurious "dark noise" signals. Hormones may change the threshold value

of the synapse, i.e. the number N (or alternatively the period Δt). This means that the synapse works as a coincidence detector with an independently controlled time constant. The synapse however, reduces the number of bits which pass the synapse by a factor $1/N$. This "degradation" of information in a *quantitative* sense means that the system loses information in order to gain certainty whether something at the output really corresponds to something at the input (McCulloch 1951). But this also reflects a change in quality: a large amount of raw information at the input emerges as a small amount of refined information at the highest levels of the CNS.

This may be the place to make some remarks on information, entropy and order. The aspect of entropy which is relevant here appeared first in statistical mechanics. States of high entropy have high probability. The same is true for systems with low degree of order. The thermodynamical entropy S of a physical system (of molecules) is, according to Boltzmann, a logarithmic function of the thermodynamic probability P of its occurrence:

$$S = k \ln P$$

(k = Boltzmann's constant = 1.38×0^{-23} J/K. Strictly speaking, P is not a probability in a statistical sense, but a large number denoting the amount of possible microstates that correspond to a given macrostate. However, the thermodynamical probability is proportional to the statistical; see e.g. Fermi (1956).

In a similar way the concept of entropy appears in *The Mathematical Theory of Communication* (Shannon and Weaver 1959). The information content H of a message (information theoretical entropy) is a negative logarithmic function of the probability P_a of its elements.

$$H(A) = - \Sigma P_a \log_2 P_a$$

(a are the elements of an ensemble A (a message), H is expressed in bits if binary logarithms are used.) H then denotes the *average* number of bits which are necessary to identify an element of the ensemble. It may be added that the concept H is not limited to discrete functions or stochastic processes, but may be related to any probability density function $\varphi(x)$ of a stochastic variable x:

$$H = - \int_{-\infty}^{+\infty} \varphi(x) \log_2 \varphi(x) \, dx$$

(the integral denotes essentially an infinite summation with respect to a continuous function). Thus both types of entropy and the concept of information are related to the probability of the state of a system. The main formal difference is the minus sign. The relationship between the concepts has been interpreted so that information theoretical entropy (information content) can be viewed as a negative function of thermodynamical entropy, which means that H increases as S decreases. This gives rise to Brillouin's and Wiener's characterization of information as negative entropy or negentropy (Wiener 1961, Brillouin 1962). The deeper implications of this relationship have, however, been the object of different interpretations.

The transfer of information to a living system means essentially the transfer of organizational or structuring principles which increase the order of the receiving system. Living organisms receive a vast store of basic information through genetic instructions, which are encoded in the DNA of genes (order through order). Later on, the organism receives information through sensory processes and stores it in different types of memory.

Meanwhile, one has to be careful with respect to some differences. Shannon's theory is formulated for *closed* systems, which presuppose the existence of established channels, transmitters and receivers; no net energy is transferred to the receiving system, only information. All living systems, however, are open systems, exchanging energy and information with their environment. Hence, one may assume that information is gained by different processes at different stages of ontogenetic development and by different processes at different levels of the hierarchy. Transfer of information in the sense of Shannon's theory starts in connection with learning and feedback processes, when the necessary mechanisms have been developed. The transfer of information is then restricted to certain structures, which at the *given hierarchical level*[2] of the organism behave as closed subsystems. The transferred information then is encoded in a way which confines it to the boundaries of these subsystems. It must be assumed that the internally coded information is comparatively stable to the distorting influence of metabolic processes which always bring about a change of thermodynamic entropy.

4. CONSCIOUS INFORMATION PROCESSING: CONTROL AND CREATION OF INTERNAL ORDER

An essential feature of the brain is its ability to detect and record its own states. The brain works as an *autoanalytical* instrument. Nevertheless, it is possible to accomplish certain autoanalytical functions with the aid of a computer, if a suitable hierarchy of analyzing programs is available, where higher level programs evaluate and change lower level programs with respect to external criteria of efficiency. But the brain has an advantage in that it is endowed with the superior principle of *conscious* information processing; this means that certain nerve nets seem to be able to sense their own states within the realm of their *own* functional level, but *may* simultaneously have access to other levels as well. This reflects both the peculiar self-referring or reflexive property of such systems and the holistic nature of the phenomenon of consciousness.

The brain is self-organizing with respect to its handling of information. The really marvellous accomplishment, however, is its ability to create by itself the programs which perform this task, even if one has to assume that the necessary prerequisites are genetically determined. The brain runs without anyone telling it how to run. This does not, however, preclude programs acquired later.

Since the term *consciousness* is used in a variety of ways, it is necessary to clarify the terminology within this paper. Due to the limitation of space, only some main features of the phenomenon can be treated here. For further details see Löwenhard (1981, 1984).

Consciousness is used as a technical term to denote what in subjective language is called *awareness* or *subjective experience.*

Sensation is used as a general term to denote the effects in terms of subjective experience of the activation of receptors. A clear distinction is made between the *phenomenon* of consciousness as such and *mental objects* (symbols, images) which represent the *information content* of the conscious brain process.

Perception is defined as the conscious interpretation of *sensory messages* in terms of earlier experience.

Feelings is an ambiguous term which is used to denote unspecified qualities of awareness which are neither related to mental objects nor to specific emotions, acts of will or motivational states (hunger, thirst, etc.). One should note, however, that *feelings* in everyday language include moods, emotional and motivational states as well as sensations such as pain (Jaspers 1948, Zethraeus 1962).

Mind is used as a label to denote the "non-material universe of mental phenomena", i.e. *World 2* in the terminology of Karl Popper (Popper and Eccles 1977). It is the conceptual framework to which all phenomena of conscious experience are related. One should note, however, that the term in this paper does not imply an internal homunculus (see Crick 1979) nor any dualistic ontology in the sense of Descartes (cf. Eccles 1970).

The following statements are either speculative hypotheses or descriptions of observable phenomena, related to consciousness. While some people want to restrict the use of the term to the human level, it is used here in a much wider sense. *Life* and *consciousness* are analogous phenomena, but there is an essential difference: life can, at least principally, be explained in terms of earlier known principles, even if many details are still obscure. Contrary to this, consciousness has features which presently are outside the realm of a strict scientific treatment. This does not mean that they will be so in the future.

Consciousness seems to be restricted to a certain class of living organisms which are equipped with nervous systems. It is a *phenomenon* which accompanies certain modes of information processing, characterized by the above-mentioned ability of nerve nets to "sense" their own states. Subjectively, we speak of a direction of attention onto the information content of the ongoing process. It is essential to distinguish among a) participation in an immediate act of experience, i.e. "to be aware"; b) the actual information content of the ongoing process (object of awareness); and c) knowledge about the principles which underly the emergence of consciousness as such, distinct from the coding principles of internal information. Both, however, may be the object of (b) and of conscious experience.

Consciousness seems to arise as a result of system properties which contemporary computers lack. It probably is not *solely* a consequence of the system complexity as such, but reflects inherent properties of the neurons to which the phenomenon is related. The critical system parameters are, as yet, not known. They may be related to the cellular level, to the subcellular level or to both, but consciousness seems to manifest itself only clearly in sufficiently complex systems. Nevertheless, the genetic instructions which govern the development of conscious nerve nets have to be encoded into the genome as part of the explicit and implicit genetic information.

While the brain is a physical object which has a *spatial structure* and a limited existence in time as a living system, *mind* seems to be a holistic phenomenon, which somehow reflects a non-locality, but has a definite extension in time. This indicates the intimate relationship of consciousness to *brain-processes*. The conscious brain state may be dependent on patterns of slow potentials and discrete pulses (bioelectric fields) which are related to aggregates of nerve cells and which fulfil certain (yet not known) conditions with respect to spatial and temporal continuity ("world lines"). A model of this kind has been proposed by Culbertson (1963, 1982); it contains the above-mentioned features under the heading of *historical causality*.

Conscious information processing probably involves large parts of the entire brain, although *specialized* processing of information largely is related to different parts of the *cerebral cortex,* which covers a total area of about 20 dm.[2] The cortex is functionally divided into several millions of modules (or columns), each containing many thousands of neurons, which are arranged in the well-known six layers of the cortex.

Each module may be compared to an integrated circuit (IC "chip") of a computer and takes care of a certain type of local information proc-

essing. One should note, however, that all neurons are engaged simultaneously in the performance of different tasks. Memory functions, for
example, may be common to all neurons. There exists an extensive web of
interconnections, which comprises virtually all of the cortex and subcortical structures as well. In this way each part of the cortex is able to contribute in a specific way to the total conscious experience. The interconnected
network renders it possible for the brain to perform the functions of a
cooperative system, thus creating the impression of an *integrated mind*. Notwithstanding lateralization of some brain functions such as speech (hemispheric specialization), each hemisphere is a brain in itself, although the
two normally act together as a unit. There are two types of clinical observations, which show that each hemisphere is capable of producing its own
conscious experience:

1. Observations on split-brain patients, where the corpus callosum
   (the great cerebral commissure) has been surgically dissected in
   connection with severe epilepsia.
2. Total *hemispheric anesthesia,* produced by unilateral injection of a
   hypnotic drug (e.g. amylobarbital) in connection with cerebral
   angiography (X-ray contrast mapping of cerebral blood vessels).

Further experimental evidence has been gained from the animal domain
(Sperry 1964, Gazzaniga and LeDoux 1978).

Consciousness seems to change with respect to both quantitative and
qualitative features as a function of the complexity of the nerve net to
which it is related. Thus, in analogy to life, consciousness means partly
the same, partly different things in relation to different brains. One may
assume that consciousness has developed alongside new system properties
of living organisms; it means an increase of both quality and scope from
primitive awareness at lower phylogenetic levels to abstract thinking and
self-consciousness in man. Elementary mental functions have been shown
to exist in very simple organisms and systems of neurons (Kandel 1979,
Sokolov 1981). One should, however, be careful not to project *human*
modes of experience onto other animals. There is reason to believe that
the perception of the external world shows species-bound variations,
which reflect the adaptation to a certain ecological niche. As early as
1928, von Uexküll stated that "it would be a very naive sort of dogmatism
to assume that there exists an absolute reality of things which is the same
for all living beings. Reality is not a homogeneous thing, having as many
different schemes and patterns as there are different organisms."

Conscious information processing seems to represent a principle
which combines high efficiency regarding sensory discrimination with
economy regarding the necessary number of neural elements (Culbertson
1963). A principle which represents superior qualities is likely to be pre-

served in evolution and will probably be "adopted" by all organisms which can make use of it. "Human consciousness, like learning, is the product of evolutionary bias towards life forms with superior *negentropic flexibility*, for conscious life forms excel in their ability to receive information and to apply it under a wide variety of living conditions." (Sayre 1976, p. 139).

The term negentropic flexibility is coined by Sayre: "In speaking of flexibility in the assimilation of negentropy I refer to the capacity of an organism to establish efficient couplings with its environment under a range of different conditions, through which negentropy can be obtained to support growth and metabolism and to control its response to environmental contingencies." (Sayre 1976, p. 117).

Any organism which is confronted with the task of coping with its adaptation to a very complex environment not only has to integrate a large amount of information, but has to do it in a way which makes it possible to optimize a holistic response. Such a task includes, for example, the probability matching of different sensory messages in space and time in order to reveal their possible causal relationship. An appropriate behavior within a given context has to be based on a processing of information which includes an internal representation of the organism itself together with elements of its environment. An animal which successfully wants to jump over a cliff has to judge its own trajectory in relation to distance and initial acceleration (a more detailed discussion is given by Jerison (1978).

Cybernetic self-regulation is a universal system property. While homeostasis may be defined as adaptive self-stabilization, *adaptive self-organization* characterizes a selective progression towards better-adapted species. The brain is mainly an instrument for survival. Its capacity and way of information processing are determined by the needs of the particular organism to which it belongs. The behavioral repertoire of phylogenetically lower organisms (such as invertebrates) is to a high extent predetermined. This includes the structure of their nervous systems and their way of retrieving and processing information. During the course of phylogenetic evolution there have been changes alongside the development of new species. Meanwhile, some basic properties of the nervous system must have been preserved during evolution. Simple and complex nervous systems alike, for example, show both short-term and long-term habituation, i.e. the ability to learn and to modify behavior (Kandel 1979). The evolution of new species often implies the emergence of new modes of behavior. This demands a change in existing brain structures or the development of new ones. In order to adapt and to increase its behavior efficiency the organism may be dependent on new types of stimuli and an increased range of information, which has to be processed appropriately. New additional brain functions, however, brings about an increased specialization ("division of labor") and a more complex organization (Luria 1970).

Nature seems to preserve successful stages of evolution. One therefore finds a superposition of phylogenetically newer structures on older ones. A model of this import has been proposed by McLean (1973) in his Triune concept of the brain. From the very basic structures of the spinal cord and *medulla oblongata,* the R-complex (reptile complex) has evolved stepwise. Its main functions are related to the survival of the species and the individual (reproduction, struggle for the establishment of a social hierarchy). The R-complex has been supposed to be the brain of the dinosaurs, but it is still a part of our own "ancient" brain—modified, however. Reproduction as one of the main characteristics of living organisms may illustrate some steps of evolution. Reptiles lay eggs which then are hatched by the sun. Birds lay also eggs, but they sit on them and feed their offspring. This more extensive caretaking demanded new brain structures and appropriate programs. Both are related to the "new" structures of the limbic system (rhinencephalon). Carl Sagan, in his charming epic *The Dragons of Eden* (1978), makes the remark that the development of the limbic system meant the birth of altruism. Mammals, finally, give birth to living offsprings, which demands a still more complex repertoire of caretaking. Mammals then are dominated by the neocortex, the complex "new brain." Nevertheless, all the earlier structures remain; what has changed is their relative dominance and the details of their functions. They have become part of a more complex, integrated brain.

The brain uses both conscious and non-conscious modes of information processing. Strictly speaking, one has to make a distinction between *unconscious* processes (information not retrievable except by inference), *subconscious* processes (information retrievable under appropriate circumstances) and non-conscious processes (information not stored in memory) (Hilgard 1980). Normally different modes of information processing are used simultaneously.

Our conscious experience is characterized by *content, modes of consciousness, states of consciousness* and *sense modalities.* Different modes of consciousness seem to be related to different processes, e.g. different stages of information processing. A model of this import has been proposen by Aurell (1979, 1983). It is well known that the vivid and clear experiences during sensory perception are different from the pale reproductions of past memories. Actual perception demands both cortical *arousal* (defined in terms of phasic physiological responses to sensory input) and *activation* through subcortical mechanisms (reticular activation system), defined as a tonic physiological readiness to respond (Pribram and McGuinness 1975). Nevertheless, there exist conditions during which images may gain the qualities of actual perceptions: hallucinatory states, hypnotic states or intoxications.

Different *states* of consciousness correspond to different neurophysiological brain states. One makes a difference between normal state (NSC) and altered states of consciousness (ASC). ASC occur naturally during sleep; there are also *transitory* states, such as the hypnagogic state, the transition from wakefulness to sleep.

Sense modalities are known from experience. Seeing and hearing are different sensations. A given modality cannot be transformed into another. Sense modalities are distinct sensations which contribute to the stability of our perceptual world. Even if a person suffers from a grave intoxication, he is normally able to tell whether he *hears* or *sees* something, independent of the possible hallucinatory nature of the experience.

The *content* of conscious experience may broadly be divided into two classes: *mental objects,* which represent sensory information from the external world and *feelings, emotions* or *motivational states,* which represent changes in the physiological state of the organism. The latter have their importance as manifestations of mechanisms which control, organize and direct behavior. One should note that any conscious experience always represents a mixture of cognitive, emotional and other elements. This is a subjective equivalent of the earlier-stated principle of superposition of different systemic functions.

Mental objects correspond to an internal mapping of the external world. They are not simple projections of external objects, but sophisticated *cognitive constructs,* based on selected information from the environment. One has to remind oneself that only a fraction of existing information is directly available to our senses. Our visual world consists of three-dimensional moving objects which change their distance and position, but nevertheless are perceived as constant objects. Also there is an integration of *temporal sequences* of information into a single momentary sensation, which represents the elementary time span of conscious experience.

Innate brain mechanisms largely determine the way in which we perceive our world. They are part of the basic setup of automatically working mechanisms on which the organism has to rely. Perceptually controlled behavior depends on the action of triggers and filters, which activate innate programs under appropriate circumstances. Examples are:

Instinctive behavior which is elicited by a specific stimulus pattern and mainly consists of a predetermined, rather stereotypical chain of actions.

Imprinting, which means an act of learning during a critical period of an organism's life. Essentially, the process means that an innate program which governs a certain behavior is coupled to an external stimulus object, which selectively activates the associated trigger mechanism.

Mechanisms of perception determine the way in which stimuli are analyzed and they contribute by means of given principles of analysis to the perceptual stability of our world. One may mention depth perception and the tendency to perceive certain two-dimensional figures as three-dimensional objects (figure 9-3A). In spite of the continuous change of retinal images, we perceive corresponding objects as being constant (figure 9-3B illustrates size constancy). We normally analyze complex figures in terms of simple harmonic elements, called *gestalts* (figure 9-3C). This also applies to auditory perception with respect to *temporal gestalts*. Elements of human speech may be an example. The brain shows an innate expectation that three-dimensional objects are solid. All the above-mentioned features have been shown to exist at a very early age (Bower 1966, 1971).

If we look at a set of moving elements, e.g. dots, we perceive a *spontaneous organization* in that all elements which share a common motion form a group. This group may or may not constitute a known figure. Subgroups are formed by elements which show a motion in relation to the common group, but simultaneously share the motion of the latter. The movement of arms and legs in relation to a walking person may be an example. Essentially, the sensory mechanism in question seems to determine the degree of coupling between the spatial velocity vectors of the moving elements. Shape and size constancy may be explained in terms of this mechanism (Johansson 1964, 1975). The consecutive retinal images of moving objects then may be viewed as a geometrical transformation group.

A final word may be said about *self-consciousness*, which is often confused with consciousness as such. Any organism must be able to make a distinction between itself and its environment. Higher organisms have developed the ability to create an internal cognitive representation of themselves *in toto*. Probably there exist different levels of this ability. A cat or dog may react to their mirror image as a signal which indicates the presence of another animal, while at least humans recognize the image as

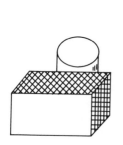  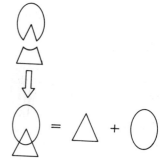

Figure 9-3

a *symbol,* representing themselves. Humans also have an abstract awareness of being aware. This seems to be the essence of Descarte's dictum
"cogito, ergo sum."
  This short treatment of conscious information processing has shown

  • some of the given prerequisites on which an active control and
    handling of information must rely,
  • the restrictions which any given mechanism by necessity imposes
    on the system,
  • the fact that these mechanisms nevertheless are the result of a long
    lasting adaptive and organizational evolution, which ensures an
    optimal choice and retrieval of information from the environ-
    ment.

The term "optimal" here means that the organism fits into its environment 1) as to its adaptation to those sources of information, which are
most pertinent to the ecological role of the organism, and 2) as to its
ability to use these sources with high efficiency. An example would be the
close correspondence between the spectral sensitivity curve of the human
eye during photopic vision and the spectral intensity distribution of the
sunlight.

5. CONSCIOUS RECONSTRUCTION OF EXTERNAL REALITY: INTENTIONAL ORDER AND CREATIVE THOUGHT

The brain performs some essential tasks:

  1. Mapping and reconstruction of external reality in terms of cogni-
     tive constructs, which means the creation of internal order.
  2. Extension of this order by an *active* manipulation of thought ob-
     jects and the creation of entirely new concepts.
  3. Interpretation of information and storage in memory as knowl-
     edge.
  4. Intentional control of behavior, aiming at a manipulation of the
     organism's physical environment.

These processes are not independent and pose some profound problems.
As early as 1949, the Cambridge psychologist Kenneth Craik made the
assumption that perception means the creation of a model about our
world, presupposing the categories of space and motion (Craik 1967,
Blakemore 1977). Cognitive constructs are based on a process of *reconstruction* where lost or otherwise missing sensory information may be regained
in a hypothetical way. This demands access to earlier stored knowledge. If
the available sensory information is insufficient, the reconstruction may
gain the features of an *illusion.*

There are essentially three levels of knowledge (the German word *Erkenntnis* (insight into) would have been more appropriate here). The *process* which leads to *perceptual knowledge* is generally *unconscious, uncritical* and *non-revisable,* but the result is instead *visualizeable.* The brain, however, has the ability to transcend these limitations stepwise. One crucial ability is the handling and transformation of mental objects. One may imagine the movement or rotation of a thought object in mental space. This task can essentially be simulated by a computer which controls the visual display of an object on a monitor screen. In a similar way *knowledge by experience* is created and mediated with the aid of concept formation, language and logic. This process is *consciously controlled,* but still *uncritical. Scientific knowledge,* finally, is based on highly abstract and formalized models (atoms, quarks, particle-wave duality, neutron stars, black holes, etc.); the process of construction is *critical,* but its results are often no longer *visualizable.* (Vollmer 1982, 1984).

The working principles of the brain seem to demand a random access memory with unique features. Recognition of visual patterns, for example faces, occurs very rapidly and demands the simultaneous comparison of a very large number of stored "templates" (Lindsay and Norman 1973). Experimental results (e.g. Lashley 1960) seem to indicate a non-locality or very diffuse localization of the memory content. Furthermore, there is the demand for a very high memory capacity within a limited space. These features promoted the idea of a *holographic* memory, which essentially constitutes an *analogon* to the three-dimensional forms of holograms (Pribram 1966, 1969, 1971, 1981). While the basic elements of the stored information (including some indices of their order) must be very stable, there also has to exist random access to minor or major blocks of them, since this is necessary for a recombination of elements. This supports the idea of a hierarchical order of memory content.

By means of a Fourier transform, sensory messages can be expressed in a way which makes them compatible with a holographic memory. There exist some observations which support this assumption. The ear is normally able to recognize the composition of complex sounds in terms of their harmonic components, which essentially amounts to a Fourier analysis. This performance of the ear enables us to perceive polyphonic music.

In a sense, the eye and the ear work in opposite ways. While the visual mechanism integrates a composite stimulus into a single perception (a mixture of light is perceived as a single color), the auditory mechanism analyzes a complex sound with respect to its harmonic components. Two or more different sound stimuli are perceived separately (notwithstanding certain exceptions such as human speech). This fact is known as Ohm's Acoustic Law.

The discovery that the retina contains a large number of so called receptive fields, each one related to a set of higher order neurons, gave a clue to the functional architecture of the visual cortex (cf. Hubel 1963, Hubel and Wiesel 1979). The partial overlapping of receptive fields (using common receptor elements) illustrates the parsimony of the system. Receptive fields, which are related to cortical neurons or modules, react to the presence on the retina of linear stimuli (bars or edges) with "correct" orientation. Hence, this mechanism was initially interpreted as a line-orientation detector. But it was shown later on that cortical neurons cannot be classified with respect to single properties, and that their receptive fields represent transfer functions which express multiple feature selectivities (Pribram et al., 1981). DeValois had earlier proposed a multi-channel spatial filter model, where retinal fields of different orientation are regarded as narrow windows to the external world. The mechanism essentially may be viewed as a set of spatial frequency filters which perform a total Fourier analysis across strips of the visual world (DeValois and DeValois 1980).

The multi-levelled intricacy of human memory may be illustrated by the phenomenon of multiple personalities. During certain phases of her life, a person may show quite different personalities, comparable to a naturally occurring "Dr. Jekyl–Mr. Hyde" syndrome. This implies that complete programs have to be stored in memory which represent the different personalities, but which probably utilize common subprograms and memory elements. The actual emergence of these specific patterns of behavior, which constitute the "personalities," seems to be *state-dependent*. While both sets of programs are stored in the same substrate, they are only activated under appropriate states. The fact that one "personality" is not even aware of the other gives an extra dimension to the relationship between memory and conscious experience (Hilgard 1977).

Another tough problem is the fact that the internal kind of order is not necessarily identical with the external one. This problem was already stated nearly 35 years ago by Friedrich von Hayek in a very profound analysis of the subject. The author distinguishes between "1) the physical order of the external world. . . . 2) the neural order of fibers and impulses proceeding in these fibers. . . . 3) the mental or phenomenal order of sensations (and other mental qualities), directly known although our knowledge is largely a 'knowing how' and not a 'knowing what'. . . . Our problem is determined partly by the fact that the first and third of these orders are *not* ismorphous." (von Hayek 1952). The author recognizes that one main problem relates to the multiple classification of the external world in terms of single subjective experiences.

In fact, one should note, that there exist correlations between neurophysiological brain states[3] and mental events, but only weak or partial correlations between physical stimuli and experiences (notwithstanding very simple cases). One may illustrate this by the fact that "color stimuli" are defined in terms of *quantitative* properties of light (wavelength or photon energy), while color experiences are purely subjective phenomena, which are described in terms of *qualitative* features. The equivalent could be said about the pitch discrimination of auditory stimuli. Colors are not properties of the physical world and there is no one-to-one relationship between physical stimuli and their conscious representation. (For details see Löwenhard 1981, 1984).

This leads to the meaning of the concept information. The problem has already been touched upon in connection with the "degradation" of information which occurs at the synaptic junctions. Heelan (1983) points out that one has to make a distinction between *information 1* in the technical sense of Shannon's theory and *information 2* which corresponds to a communicated content about the world. A stimulus really conveys a dual system information (1) + information (2). The whole problem arises, of course, because the brain has access to *two* partly different sources of information. One is represented by recordings of electrophysiological or biochemical brain states (a subject may record its own electroencephalogram [EEG]). The other is related to the earlier-mentioned autoanalytical principle, which allows for experimental introspections.

Heelan illustrates this dual information well in the construction of an elaborate model about visual perception. The author shows that perceived visual space may be described in terms of a hyperbolic (non-Euclidean) metric space, which by means of specific transformation laws is linked to physical space (in terms of Cartesian coordinates). The model explains in a natural way a majority of visual illusions and other optical phenomena related to the eye.

The nature of information (2) is somehow related to *meaning*, which has both cognitive and emotional aspects. The cognitive aspect has to do with recognition, the ability to identify a pattern as a *known* symbol. The emotional aspect has to do with an experience of something familiar, essential or important, independent of the cognitive content of the symbol(s). It defines the *subjective* difference between signals and noise. Warren Weaver speaks of three levels of communication problems. The first level is related to the technical problem of how accurately a message is transmitted. The second level deals with the semantic problem of how accurately the transmitted symbols convey the desired meaning. The third level, finally, deals with the problem of efficiency: how effectively does the received message change the conduct? The first level, however, overlaps the second and third ones, which means that the technical theory significantly influences any higher-level theory (Shannon and Weaver 1959).

Hofstadter (1979) takes a different approach in his conception of "the three layers of a message":

1. The *frame message* evokes the recognition that a set of (non-random) symbols may represent a message; also, there may be the need for a "decoding mechanism."
2. The *outer message* gives the necessary information about "how to build the correct decoding mechanism" or where aids to decipher the message can be found. An example would be the recognition of the language in which the message is written.
3. The *inner message,* finally, represents the meaning which the sender intended to convey.

An aspect of brain functions which as yet defies detailed analysis is the phenomenon of *intention* or *will.* In a general physiological sense, the terms are used to denote the initiation of nerve activity which controls striate muscles and causes "voluntary" movements. At the level of the CNS, however, the problem is similar to the one which lies behind the notions of the *self* or the *ego.* In essence, *intention* denotes the subjective correlate to brain processes which start a controlled and guided nerve activity. But *what* exerts the control? *What* is controlled? Part of the answer lies in the functional hierarchy of the brain, but another part lies in the reflexive nature of consciousness. Conscious brain processes are not only characterized by the ability of the participating nerve nets to recognize their own states, but these processes work as *organizing agents* which are controlled by the information content of the ongoing process.

An *act of will* comprises a complex chain of events, both internal ones and observable actions:

1. The formation of a program (thought process) which works as an internal prototype (model) of the intended action.
2. The formation of executive master programs, which in turn use numbers of well-established subroutines.
3. The more or less conscious decision to start the execution of the program.
4. The actual initiation of the chain of actions.
5. Continuous control and supervision of the performance through sensory feedback and comparison of the real actions with the internal model program.

Alexander Luria (1970) has given a very elaborated model of the functional organization of our brain with respect to the different levels of its hierarchy.

In all probability the human brain has changed very little since the stone age. The only difference lies in our factual knowledge about the world. one may speculate whether or not a phylogenetic "hardware" evolution of the nervous system has been succeeded by an accelerated "software" evolution after a critical stage of phylogenetic evolution had been reached. The complexity and plasticity of the brain as a physiological system makes, however, any distinction between "software" and "hardware" rather subtle. There exists an interesting reciprocal feedback process between the brain and its environment. In a sense one may view the brain as a universal Turing machine, i.e. a machine which is able to simulate the function of any other machine. *Programs* may in this context be viewed as *virtual* machines. Their actions primarily result in cognitive constructs which, with the aid of directly controlled tools (arms, hands, legs, feet) are then transformed into physical constructs (artifacts, physical tools, machines). As known, this process has resulted in substantial changes of our environment, which in turn has created the preconditions for the evolution and realization of new ideas, inventions and discoveries.

One can thus recognize certain levels of development of human technology. The first one is related to force: manpower, means of transportation, tools, simple machines. The next level is determined by the availability of energy and raw materials: the search for new materials, more advanced and sophisticated machines, new sources of energy, miniaturization and growing emphasis on security. The third level is characterized by entropy (or information). Systems and states of higher order become more important than an increased range of technology. Key concepts are synergetics, bionics, automatic control. Systems of this type show a dynamics of their own. Their demand is on intellectual rather than manual skill or muscular strength (Schopper 1982). This development has radically changed man's relation to his own technology.

At the dawn of civilization, this process started when questions were asked by magicians, priests and scientists alike. They all aimed at an understanding of the rules of nature in order to predict future events and to control the environment. Science slowly has adapted its models according to the growing knowledge and empirical evidence, while magicians tried to impose their thought models onto nature. The difference reveals itself in the continuously increasing efficiency of science: it works.

Some years ago, Abdus Salam, Nobel Laureate in physics, gave an interesting illustration of the efficiency of scientific thinking. During a lecture given in Stockholm in 1975, he presented the following example: One may remind oneself that 300 years ago, in about 1660, two of the greatest monuments in modern history were created, one in a western country, the other in an eastern. I am speaking of St. Paul's Cathedral in London and The Taj Mahal in Agra. Both symbolize better than words the comparable level of craftsmanship, art and sophistication that both cultures had reached at this epoch of history. At the same time, however, a third monument was created, and this time only in the west—a monument whose importance to mankind should be still more overwhelming: Newton's *Principia,* published in 1687. Newton's great work had no equivalent in the India of Moguls. Salam pointed out that this difference has only existed for about 300 years, but it gave rise to the rapid development of western civilization, built on its mastering of the rules of nature. This development, in turn, created the broadening gulf between industrialized and underdeveloped countries with respect to technological standards (cf. Pietschmann 1980). There were, of course, other factors which contributed to this result, such as economic and cultural circumstances. Some of them will be treated in the contributions of Dr. Radnitzky and Dr. Ayres.

The future development and destiny of mankind, however, is critically linked to those brain functions which have been the topic of this paper.

NOTES

1. The term "organizing" has for some decades been applied to inorganic matter in order to denote its tendency to arrange itself into complex molecular structures. It may, however, (as pointed out by Dr. Scuricini) be more adequate to restrict the use of this term to the level of living systems (organisms).

2. The concept of hierarchical level is difficult to define strictly in a general sense (see e.g. Bunge 1973, Kanitscheider 1974). Here, the term refers to a functional system of receptors, mediating neural pathways and analyzing nerve nets. The final stage, storage of information in memory, is still an open question since the physiological basis of memory is not known in detail (cf. John 1968).

3. Neurophysiological brain states may be defined in terms of specific patterns of electric and metabolic activities in brain structures which consistently participate in a given type of experience or mental event. Technically the information which indicates a certain brain state may be obtained from analysis of EEG recordings and the selective distribution of blood flow, indicating local metabolic activities. Detailed correlates are only known in certain specific cases.

REFERENCES

Alonso, M. and Valk, H. 1973. *Quantum Mechanics.* Reading: Addison-Wesley.

Bertalanffy, L. 1952. *Problems of Life: An Evaluation of Modern Biological Thought.* New York: Wiley.

Bertalanffy, L. 1973. *General System Theory.* Middlesex: Penguin University Books.

Blakemore, C. 1977. *The Mechanics of the Mind.* London: Cambridge University Press.

Bower, T. 1966. "The Visual World of Infants." *Scientific American* 215(4):80.

Bower, T. 1971. "The Object in the World of Infants." *Scientific American* 225(4):30.

Bunge, M. 1973. "The Metaphysics, Epistemology and Methodology of Levels." In *Model, Matter and Method.* Dordrecht: Reidel, p. 160.

Brillouin, L. 1962. *Science and Information Theory.* New York: Academic Press.

Campbell, D. 1974. "Evolutionary Epistemology." Edited by Schilpp, P. in *Philosophy of Karl Popper,* Volume I. Lasalle: Open Court, p. 413.

Craik, K. 1967. *The Nature of Explanation.* London: Cambridge University Press.

Crick, F. 1979. "Thinking about the Brain." *Scientific American* 241(3):181.

Culbertson, J. T. 1963. *The Mind of Robots.* Urbana: University of Illinois Press.

Culbertson, J. T. 1982. *Consciousness: Natural and Artificial. The Physiological Basis and Influence on Behavior of Sensations, Percepts, Memory Images and other Mental Images Experienced by Humans, Animals and Machines.* Roslyn Heights: Libra Publishers.

DeValois, R. and DeValois, K. 1980. "Spatial Vision." *Annual Review of Psychology* 31:309.

Eccles, J. 1980. *Facing Reality.* Edition Roche. Basel/Heidelberg/Berlin: Springer.

Fermi, E. 1956. *Thermodynamics.* New York: Dover Publications.

Fulton, J. 1956. *A Textbook of Physiology.* Philadelphia/London: B. W. Sounders.

Gazzaniga, M. and LeDoux, J. 1978. *The Integrated Mind.* New York/London: Plenum Press.

Gemme, G. and Bernhard, C. 1975. *Ögats funktion hos djur och människa.* Stockholm: AWE/Gebers.

Hayek, F. von. 1952. *The Sensory Order.* London: Routledge and Kegan Paul Ltd.

Heelan, P. 1983. *Space Perception and the Philosophy of Science.* Berkeley/Los Angeles: University of California Press.

Hilgard, E. 1977. *Divided Consciousness: Multiple Controls in Human Thought and Action.* New York: Wiley.

Hilgard, E. 1980. "Consciousness in Contemporary Psychology." *Annual Review of Psychology* 31:1.

Hofstadter, D. 1979. *Gödel, Escher, Bach. An Eternal Golden Braid.* Harmodsworth: Penguin Books.

Hubel, D. 1963. "The Visual Cortex of the Brain." *Scientific American* 209(5):54.

Hubel, D. and Wiesel, T. 1979. "Brain Mechanisms of Vision." *Scientific American* 241(3):150.

Jaspers, K. 1948. *Allgemeine Psychopathologie.* Berlin: Springer.

Jerison, H. 1978 "The Evolution of Consciousness." *Proceedings of the Seventh International Conference on the Unity of the Sciences.* Boston: November 1978:711.

Johansson, G. 1964. "Perception of Motion and Changing Forms." *Scandinavian Journal of Psychology* 5:181.

Johansson, G. 1975. "Visual Motion Perception." *Scientific American* 131(6):76.

John, E. 1968. *Mechanisms of Memory.* New York/London: Academic Press.

Kandel, E. 1979. "Small Systems of Neurons." *Scientific American,* 24(3):66.

Kanitscheider, B. 1984. "Reduction and Emergence in the Unified Theories of Physics." *Communication to the Thirteenth International Conference on the Unity of the Sciences.* Washington, D.C.

Lashley, K. 1960. "In Search for the Engram." Edited by Beach *et al.* in *The Neuropsychology of Lashley: Selected Papers of K. S. Lashley.* London: McGraw Hill.

Laszlo, E. 1973. *Introduction to Systems Philosophy.* New York: Harper and Row.

Leinfellner, W. 1984. "Reductionism in Biology and the Social Sciences." *Communication to the Thirteenth International Conference on the Unity of the Sciences.* Washington, D.C.

Lindsay, P. and Norman, D. 1973. *Human Information Processing.* New York/London: Academic Press.

Lorenz, K. and Wuketits, F., editors. 1983. *Die Evolutiondes Denkes.* München/Zürich: Piper and Co.

Löwenhard, P. 1981. "Consciousness. A Biological View." *Göteborg Psychological Reports,* 11(10).

Löwenhard, P. 1984. "Mind and Brain-Reduction or Correlation?" *Communication to the Thirteenth International Conference on the Unity of the Sciences.* Washington, D.C.

Luria, A. 1970. "The Functional Organization of the Brain." *Scientific American* 222(3):66.

McCulloch, W. 1951. "Why the Mind is in the Head." Edited by Jeffres, L. in *Cerebral Mechanisms in Behaviour.* New York: Wiley, p. 42.

McLean, P. 1973. *A Triune Concept of the Brain and Behaviour.* Toronto: University of Toronto Press.

Melzack, R. 1961. "The Perception of Pain." *Scientific American* 204(2):41.

Miller, J. 1978. *Living Systems.* New York: McGraw Hill.

Pietschmann, H. 1980. *Das Ende des naturwissenschaftlichen Zeitalters.* Wien: Paul Szolnay.

Popper, K. and Eccles, J. 1977. *The Self and Its Brain.* New York: Springer.

Pribram, K. 1966. "Some Dimensions of Remembering: Steps towards a Neurobiological Model of Memory." Edited by Gaite, J. in *Macromolecules and Behaviour.* New York: Academic Press, p. 165.

Pribram, K., editor. 1969. *On the Biology of Learning.* New York/Chicago: Harcourt, Brace and World.

Pribram, K. 1971. *Languages of the Brain.* Englewood Cliffs: Prentice Hall.

Pribram, K. 1981. "Non-Locality and Localization: A Review of the Place of the Holographic Hypothesis of Brain Functions in Perception and Memory." *Proceedings of the Tenth International Conference on the Unity of the Sciences.* Seoul, Korea, November 1981, p. 1373.

Pribram, K. and McGuinness, D. 1975. "Arousal, Activation and Effort in the Control of Attention." *Psychological Review* 82(2):116.

Pribram, K., et al. 1981. "Classification of Receptive Field Properties in the Cat Visual Cortex." *Experimental Brain Research* 43:119.

Quigg, C. 1985. "Elementary Particles and Forces." *Scientific American* 252(4):64.

Riedl, R. 1979. *Biologie der Erkenntnis.* Berlin/Hamburg: Parey.

Sagan, C. 1978. *The Dragons of Eden.* Coronet Edition. London: Hodder and Stoughton Ltd.

Sayre, K. 1976. *Cybernetics and the Philosophy of Mind.* London: Routledge and Kegan Paul Ltd.

Schopper, E. 1982. *Communication to the Conference on Technology Transfer.* Rome, March 1982, unpublished.

Sexl, R. 1984. "Order and Chaos." *Communication to the Thirteenth International Conference on the Unity of the Sciences.* Washington, D.C.

Shannon, C. and Weaver, W. 1959. *The Mathematical Theory of Communication.* Urbana: University of Illinois Press.

Sokolov, E. 1981. "Introduction to Learning in Isolated Neural Structures (Intracellular Mechanisms of the Associated Learning)." Edited by Adam, G. *et al.* in *Advances of Physiological Science 17. Brain and Behaviour.* Budapest: Pergamon Press/Akadamiai Kido.

Sperry, R. 1964. "The Great Cerebral Commissure." *Scientific American* 270(1):42.

Stevens, J. 1985. "Reverse Engineering the Brain." *BYTE,* April 1985:282.

Uexküll, J. 1928. *Theoretische Biologie.* Berlin: Springer.

Vollmer, G. 1981. *Evolutionäre Erkenntnistheorie.* Stuttgart: Hirzel.

Vollmer, G. 1982. "On Supposed Circularities in Empirically Oriented Epistemology." *Proceedings of the Eleventh International Conference on the Unity of the Sciences.* Philadelphia, November 1982, p. 783.

Vollmer, G. 1982. "Das alte Gehirn und neue Probleme. Aspekte und Folgerungen einer evolutionaren Erkenntnistheorie." Darwin Symposium *"Das Phänomen der Evolution."* Vienna: Technische Universitat.

Vollmer, G. 1984. "New Problems for an Old Brain. Synergetics, Cognition and Evolutionary Epistemology." Edited by Frehland, E. in *Synergetics—From Microscopic to Macroscopic Order.* Berlin: Springer, p. 250.

Weiss, P. 1969. "The Living System: Determinism Stratified" *Studium Generale* 22:361.

Weiss, P. 1971. *Hierarchically Organized Systems in Theory and Practice.* New York: Hafner.

Wiener, N. 1961. *Cybernetics or Control and Communication in the Animal and the Machine.* Second Edition. New York: MIT Press and John Wiley, Inc.

Wuketits, F. 1982. "Das Phänomen der Zweckmässigkeit im Bereich der lebenden Systeme." *Biologie unserer Zeit,* 12(5):139.

Wuketits, F. 1985. "Die Systemtheoretische Innovation der Evolutionslehre." Edited by Ott, J. *et al. Evolution, Ordnung und Erkenntnis.* Berlin/Hamburg: Paul Parey.

Zethraeus, S. 1962. *Känslan.* Stockholm: Natur och Kultur.

Zurer, P. 1983. "The Chemistry of Vision." *Chemical and Engineering News* 61(48):24.

III

ORGANIZATION AND
COMPLEXITY IN SOCIAL SYSTEMS

10

The Evolution of The Extended Order: Reflections on Hayek's Theory and its Political Implications

GERARD RADNITZKY

1. INTRODUCTION

The idea of *evolution* originated in the early studies of language and law; biology imported the concept from the cultural sciences. While theories of biological evolution and theories of cultural evolution differ with respect to details, they also exhibit striking similarities: both rely on the general schema of variation-and-selection followed by retention/transmission; neither of them contains laws of historical development, and neither can make forecasts; each theory describes a singular development. In spite of these limitations, the theory of cultural evolution can help us to explain the origins of social patterns and their spread over societies by showing how highly complex structures possess a built-in mechanism for self-correction that leads to further development. Both theories help us to improve our image of man and our image of society. The disciplines that, recently, have made the most important contributions to this improvement are biology and economics. From *evolutionary biology* we learn that the human capacity for developing is itself of genetic origin; the economic approach powered the imperialist expansion of economics into the traditional domains of various disciplines, including biology.[1] It did so because the key concepts of economics: scarcity, costs, opportunities, preferences, etc., are of universal application; they apply not only to all cultural phenomena but to all of life (Hishleifer 1985, Radnitzky and Beruholz, eds. 1987).

All of life is problem solving, and, at all levels, practical problems include *knowledge problems*. Hence, a theory of action can succeed in analyzing social organization only if it is embedded in an adequate epistemological framework, i.e., in a theory about the generation, improvement and transmission of knowledge (Albert 1985). At the same time, epistemology and the methodology of research can profit from applying the economic approach, since solving knowledge problems involves action.[2] *Thus, unlimited competition—i.e., criticism—in the world of ideas is the intellectual counterpart to the market order; and dogmatizing,* i.e., the protection of certain ideas from critical examination, *is the intellectual counterpart of economic protectionism,* which is an attempt to impair or even to eliminate the selection mechanisms.[3] Competition functions both as discovery process and as constraint, but, above all, it functions as a selection mechanism. It is, as Hayek points out, a process in which a small number of people makes it necessary for a large number to make a greater effort than they otherwise would have made.

In an important sense *internal criticism* is relatively unproblematic. There is a good reason for it whenever one discovers a particular inconsistency in a norm system. The problem of criticism becomes very delicate when the issue is one of *external criticism*. In such cases the critic has to reply to the question of whether his criticism is more than simply an objection from a different point of view, and genuine value issues may have to be faced. Hayek's social and political philosophy posits the priority of liberty, of the autonomy of the individual. From this value standpoint, the crucial test for any system of rules is whether it maximizes the chances of an individual chosen at random to achieve his unknown purposes, which makes it necessary that equal freedom is conferred upon all, i.e., provided only that the individual's aims are compatible with the prevention of infringement onto the protected domain of one's fellow men.[4] The main argument for individual choice is not based on considerations of the creativity or efficiency of the ensuing social order; it is a moral argument. An image of humanity that acknowledges the unique individuality of each human being—genetic individuality, uniqueness of experience and life history, and, hence, uniqueness of the self—strongly suggests the desirability of leaving the reins of each person's destiny so far as possible in the individual's own hands. It is the task of the philosophy of classical liberalism to make the value position explicit and to produce arguments in favor of the priority of freedom.[5] In our century no one has undertaken this task with more success than Hayek.[6] Before attending to Hayek's theories I propose to use as a *foil* a brief outline of the routes to sociality that biological evolution has developed.

2. BIOLOGICAL EVOLUTION HAS DEVELOPED TWO ROUTES TO SOCIALITY THAT GO BEYOND KIN SELECTION AND STRUCTURED DEMES.[7]

It may happen that a species is trapped in an ecological niche wherein it is no longer possible for an isolated individual or for a single family to survive. In this case the species either solves the problem of how to develop a sociality or it disappears. Biological evolution has made possible the non-human primates' route to the semi-sociality of the small horde; social insects (termites, ants, bees, and some wasps) have achieved ultrasociality. By "ultrasociality" is meant that state of social organization where the division of labor is so far advanced that not only the survival of the group depends upon it, but that almost all of the population would perish if the division of labor broke down.

The semi-sociality achieved by non-human primates: chimpanzee politics

The key to the semi-sociality of primate hordes is the dominance principle. The horde evolves clear-cut, facultative polymorphisms of dominance and submission.[8] That means the hierarchy is not fixed; if it were, the incentive to cooperate would be reduced. *Dominance and submission hierarchy* thus makes relatively peaceful group life possible. Ranks are more or less formalized. A division of labor is associated with the dominance structure. The second important organizing principle is *sharing*. Chimpanzees share information about food location and food, and, of course, they also share risks. Ethological studies suggest to me that a protoform of norms of possession is also recognizable in the chimpanzee horde. Certain behavior patterns are readily interpreted as an "as-if" recognition of private property. For instance, the dominant male will beg meat from a subordinate. Frans de Waal reports that the human economic system, with its reciprocal transactions, is recognizable in the group life of chimpanzees.[9] He convincingly argues that what is fascinating about chimpanzees is their acumen as practical politicians; he is able to show that they intelligently manipulate others, that they can plan their strategies of dominance in advance; and that they form coalitions just as good human politicians do. All parties strive after social significance. This too is a trait common to chimpanzees and man: the desire for status pervades all human activities. The hierarchy is cohesive, since it keeps competition and conflict within boundaries, and makes cooperative behavior possible. For there ensue stability and clear-cut expectations about the reactions of others. In sum, *chimpanzee politics appears to be not only a precursor of, but even similar to the norm system or moral system that brings cohesion to and makes possible life in the human hunter-gatherer horde and the tribal society.* Humans have developed a profound need for significant participation in face-to-face groups. This is understandable considering that man has lived for at least one and a half million years, perhaps much longer, mainly as a hunter. However, this craving for the life in a small, intimate group, this craving for face-to-face interaction, appears to be grounded in a much longer prehistory: it may very well be a craving for a return to primate politics.[10]

The social insects' route to ultrasociality

The social insects succeeded in removing genetic competition among co-operating males through the mechanism of caste sterility. They carried the division of labor beyond the functional level to the extreme of anatomical specialization. If castes are sterile, not only is competition among individuals removed and perfect equality between caste members realized, but individuals cease to be individuals and become tokens of a species-being. Thus, the realities of the social insects have great affinity with the ideal of National Socialists and Marxist Socialists.[11] Incidentally, there is also a mammal called the "mole rat" whose social life is almost identical to that of the social insects. It too would be a model for the Marxists.

3. CULTURAL EVOLUTION: THE HUMAN ROUTE TO ULTRASOCIALITY

What we have learned from ethology

A sociality can come into being and be maintained only if there exist workable expectancies concerning the behavior of others. This can only be achieved if much of the behavior is rule-following behavior, and this in turn is possible only if there are incentives to follow-rules.[12] If the norms have become psychologically internalized, the costs of rule-breaking behavior also include remorse, pangs of conscience, and the like.

Man's dispositional preference for life in a face-to-face group

The evolution of parental behavior, of a stable mother-child relationship, *constitutes the turning point in the evolution of sociality,* both in animals and in humans. Once mechanisms of individual bonding had evolved, they could be extended beyond the family, but only to a small group. At the age of six to eight months the child develops the well-known "fear of stranger" response, which is an innate disposition that develops independently of culture.[13] When the infant develops personal bonds with a few reference persons, behavior is shifted towards trust. As a result humans have an *innate disposition for life in a face-to-face-group*, a *closed* group demarcated from strangers. Thus, individual bonding combined with xenophobia form a preadaption for group selection.[14]

Respect for norms of property is a precondition of sharing and group cohesion.

In mammals and birds, patterns that have evolved from parental feeding have become rituals of bonding. In all vertebrates, and very clearly in primates, there is an "as if" recognition of norms of property. Not even the leading animal will attempt simply to take a bit of food from the animal that happens to be in possession of it. These inhibitions, innate dispositions, have adaptive value; they have been selected because without them quarrels over objects and partners would lead to the group's disintegration. In humans, the mutual respect for ownership of tools, weapons, etc., obviously has survival value. In animals and humans, the party requesting something must, in order to be given, first show that he respects the norms of property. Here, as elsewhere, non-verbal and verbal behavior may substitute each other as functional equivalents. Moreover, in humans, *sharing and gift-giving are the most important bonding devices, and they themselves presuppose ownership*. Cross-cultural comparison reveals that norms of possession are found in all cultures, and also that very young children are ready to share, but only after the partner has signaled that he is respecting the norms of possession.[15] However, gift-giving and sharing with other gene-pools can be adaptive only if reciprocity is ensured. In sum, ethological studies have shown that ownership and norms of possession must be a pre-cultural factor, and that respect for these norms is an innate disposition not only in man and the great apes, but also in many other species, e.g., in the form of territoriality even in fish. This disposition as well as the predispositions for ranking have an integrative function, i.e., without them the formation of a sociality would not be possible. In the primordial human face-to-face group these dispositions become institutionalized in the articulated and unarticulated norms that govern behavior. The norms function to strengthen the innate inhibitions, to reinforce the suppression of greedy impulses. Even on this level, Hayek's dictum holds that man has been civilized much against his will. The few remaining tribes that still hunt and gather at the level of the Stone Age, such as the bushmen of the Kalahari, live in face-to-face groups that show clear-cut ranking orders of various kinds, whereby status is mostly accorded on the basis of relevant achievement. The claim that primordial human groups were egalitarian is a myth, if it refers to an egalitarian distribution of wealth or status. Whenever a group is egalitarian—of course, with the exception of the headman—this equality has been enforced. Egalitarianism never develops as a spontaneous order. Various cultures may attempt to indoctrinate the governed according to their ideals, e.g., egalitarian or heroic ideals, but certain tendencies crop up again and again. They have been selected because of their adaptive value. They can be suppressed, but only temporarily. A totalitarian regime that wishes to enforce egalitarianism for the masses of the population has continuously to use force in order to suppress up-coming dispositions that are partly our heritage and even go back to our primate ancestors.[16]

Spontaneous order as the prime motor of cultural evolution

The decisive breakthrough on the route from the chimpanzee horde to the human hunter-gatherer horde is the emergence of *language*. Only when language in the full sense has evolved, i.e., with descriptive and argumentative functions, is it appropriate to speak of *cultural* evolution. *Language is the best example of a spontaneous order,* i.e., of an order that evolved in a gradual and decentralized process, that constitutes an unintended effect of the deliberate actions of many interacting individuals and that, therefore, is the product of human action but not of human design.[17] No individual or collective could have deliberately designed it. With language emerge also abstract entities: the contents of linguistically formulated statements (true and false statements), theories, problems, rules, criteria, i.e., the entities that shape and occupy our intellectual life. They are man-made but have a certain autonomy, and *our intellect (and our brain) have developed in a give-and-take relationship with them.*[18] (Hayek rightly criticizes the myth that the intellect developed first and then constructed language, morals, etc.) Popper calls the step that allows us to dissociate ourselves from our hypotheses and to look upon them critically the *human step.*[19] This step brings an enormous advantage and economy, since thereby risks and costs are reduced, and rational decision becomes possible. Now the individual can compare descriptions (representations) of possible situations with expected payoffs, i.e., he can compare states of affairs which he imagines, but does not perceive, since they do not exist or do not yet exist.[20] Linguistically formulated expectations can, if falsified, be eliminated, while the believer, the carrier of that expectation, can survive. In this way deliberate selection can complement and, in some areas such as scientific research, supersede natural selection and cultural selection in form of spontaneous orders. The testing of theories is an example of a specialized deliberate selection procedure that can be operated only within the framework of certain spontaneous orders, such as language and the criticist tradition. The transmission of knowledge made possible through language is in turn a precondition of the rapid tempo of cultural evolution compared with biological evolution. Cultural evolution also provides differentiation within the species that has no biological counterpart, by making possible innumerably subdivided skills and role specialization.

According to Hayek the history of cultural development, the rise of civilization that took at least 1.5 million years, is essentially a *self-accelerating process*. An increased population density makes possible a greater division of labor; this provides the possibility for higher productivity, which in turn may help the group to further population increase. This self-accelerating process is nothing more than a possibility; whether or not it is realized depends upon the constraints that obtain in the particular historical situation. Those groups that grow faster than others supplant other groups. Thus, for the long period of human development ending when technology based upon science began to acquire decisive importance, the criterion of "success" has been that of growing faster in number than the competing groups—not so much through biological reproduction as from attracting outsiders (Hayek 1973, *LLL,* p. 107; 1976, p. 159; 1952, p. 107). Given a particular state of technology and the natural resources of the region, a certain population density will constitute a problem situation that may stimulate creativity and induce people to "gamble on new ideas" in order to overcome the pressing problem. Eventually, this feedback process will meet with definite limiting conditions. The process under consideration has accelerated enormously for the past 100 or 60 years because of the rapidly increasing importance of technological change: inventions followed by innovations (Brunner 1984, p. 25). Because of the negative external effects of an uncontrolled increase in population density—in the last resort even on the liberty of others (whose consumption set is supposed to include also a bit of "unspoiled nature")—Hayek's above-mentioned criterion of "success" will have to be redefined for our age (see the final section below).

Hayek's theory jibes with the analyses made with the economic approach, e.g., work on the environmental selection of firms and their business routines, and it also harmonizes with evolutionary anthropology, which produces "*as-if*" rational explanations of the cultural selection of social patterns, traditions, i.e., which model the situation *as if* the group's aim were to optimize the chances of "evolutionary success."

The main mechanism of cultural evolution is the *selection of competing rules of perception and action,* the whittling away of those cultural practices (rule systems, institutions, etc.) that, on balance, bring the group which partakes in them more costs than benefits. *Cultural selection proceeds through group selection.* A rule system or social pattern that has evolved spontaneously, i.e., that has come into existence as an unintended effect of the actions of individuals who were pursuing their own purposes (whatever those may have been) but did not intend to produce this effect, has thereby passed the test of daily experience. It has survived the selection process of competing rules or social practices. The problem solutions we see in the world around us tend to be adapted at least to a certain extent, because otherwise they would hardly have survived.

Some words of caution may, however, be in order.[21]

1. The fact that a particular norm or social pattern has evolved spontaneously is no guarantee that it is optimal, that it could not be improved—even if we assume that the environment remains constant.

2. Although a spontaneous order represents a successful evolutionary solution in the past, from this follows no guarantee that it will continue to succeed.[22]

3. From the statement describing the structure and functioning of a spontaneous order or explaining its origins, no value judgment about that order can be deduced. No amount of empirical knowledge can decide a genuine, i.e., a non-instrumental value issue. Evaluating a particular social practice as preferable to others that compete with it means asking whether or not that social practice helps us to realize those values that we wish to realize more efficiently than any of the rival social practices would do. This evaluation can be made rationally only if we first have made explicit the values to be used as criteria.

4. Natural selection selects for survivability pure and simple, and a trait *may* survive that is bad for the ecology or for the species or even for its individual bearer.[23] *Nature is not always wise, nor is culture.* Similarly, in cultural evolution, a trait or social practice has been selected because, on balance, it brings the group partaking in it more benefits than costs. That it has remained in existence is no guarantee that it contains no dysfunctional characteristics. Yet, whoever proposes a change must produce good reasons for his conjecture that the institution in question will function better after the change. *In dubio pro traditione* holds for spontaneous orders even more than for social patterns which are the result of design. It is a rational maxim if only because risks and costs are always associated with a change, costs that have to be compensated by its expected marginal benefits.

The norm system that is fitted to the hunter-gatherer group and the tribal horde, to groups with small and relatively stable populations

On the basis of the ethological finding one can attempt to reconstruct the norm system that underlies behavior in the small hunter-gatherer group or tribal horde, underlies behavior because it is adapted to life in an identifiable group of limited size, in a visible community. I follow Hirshleifer[24] in proposing that any system of norms can be interpreted as a mixture of three main organizing principles: the principles of dominance, communal sharing, and private rights. The combination of these three organizing principles that is most propitious will vary with the type of ecological niche in question. *The norm system underlying social life in the face-to-face group has much in common with the chimpanzee politics;* early man and chimpanzees shared the same ecological niche, and they have common roots.

Dominance is the central organizing principle in the chimpanzee horde, and it is the first and deepest layer of human sociality. Primates lacking biological weaponry could initially survive only by banding in groups. Dominance had to be the governing rule holding the band together; it made possible a hierarchy that in turn made possible the social stability of the group. Among the emotions that support the dominance principle are the instinctive drive for leadership and the complementary quality of willing followership.

No social order can be maintained without the dominance principle, because any sociality requires organization and organization breeds control. However, the fact that every collective brings with it coercion is one of the arguments for the minimal state, for the principle of the subsidiarity of the state. On the other hand, the creation of a legal framework and the enforcement of the law is a public good, which only the state can provide. "The worm of domination lies at the heart of what it is to be human, and the conclusion faces us that the attempt to overthrow domination, as that idea is metaphysically understood in ideology, is the attempt to destroy humanity" (Minogue 1985, p. 226). Leftist utopians attempting to replace the principle experience by the principle of hope would, if successful, inevitably destroy what we in the free world have got. It is relevant to note that the coercive order, the rule by fear, that is characteristic of socialist countries is in its functioning similar to a spontaneous order: it arises from or is reinforced by innumerable transactions, such as, e.g., preemptive informing on neighbors, transactions, which, in themselves are not devoted to bringing about the rule of fear.

The second important principle is *sharing* in the sense of a give-and-take relationship. For the continued efficiency of a face-to-face group a certain amount of sharing is indispensable; and under conditions of resource variability, sharing may also serve a mutual insurance function. In face-to-face groups there is typically an investing in others, a reciprocation of gifts, etc.[25] Among the supportive emotions for the organizing principle of "sharing" are, of course, also envy and fear of envy. Anger may provide the needed commitment to retaliate and is hence useful in the small group. The psychological "loss of control" which leads one to punish aggression even when to do so is not to one's short-run material advantage may just be what is needed to deter future invasions into the realm of one's "private rights."[26] On the other hand, behavior which is ostensibly "altruistic" (in the everyday speech sense) or follows the "sharing principle," such as, e.g., willingness to share gains even if one is not required to do so, may be materially rewarding later on when cooperation on the part of others is elicited thereby. In short, emotional responses such as anger and generosity can enforce implicit contracts between two parties and thus be useful in social situations where the parties are in *personal* contact and expect to continue to interact on future occasions.

The role of *war* in the selection of rule systems can hardly be overestimated. Warfare as an economic activity is characterized by an economy of scale leading to larger group size.[27] In warfare, the environment also selects for loyalty and dedication, properties that appear to result from combining the dominance and the sharing principles. Anthropologists stress the importance of group struggle (combined with polygyny for the most "successful" males) for the rapid development of the human brain, because intergroup warfare imposes rigorous selection for inventiveness and cunning. For the success of the group, particularly in warfare, a *common* perception of reality and *common* concrete purpose will be favorable. This is probably the most striking characteristic of the norm system adapted to the hunter-gatherer group or tribal horde: that *no alternatives are visible* to the group members and that, hence, criticism of the common goal is not possible. The injunction to trust and obey covers everything.[28] Each member of a tribal community is subordinated to the common ranking order of needs. The politics of the tribal horde is necessarily a politics of goals. (In our times we witness attempts to return to this stage of human development by all those ideologues who operate with an end-state principle of justice (Brunner 1983, Brunner and Meckling 1977, note 17; Bartley 1962, pp. 34f). A tribal horde cannot afford the luxury of holding its central myth or ideology open to criticism, because such criticism would erode the cement of its social structure. Hence, the central myth has to be dogmatized, immunized against criticism. Incidentally, this situation appears to have been the normal condition of mankind—the free society being an improbable, rare and fragile species. Morality in the tribal horde is effected through social control, the feeling of the group, and such control is effective where private life is scarcely known and men can watch each other's behavior. Hence, the so-called "communist fiction," which plays a prominent role in the thought of many contemporary economists, i.e., the idea of a uniform preference structure in a society, is appropriate for the tribal horde and *only* for it. From the viewpoint of methodological individualism (i.e., the view that social patterns can, in the last resort, be explained by reference to the action of individuals) it is clear that in an anonymous society there cannot be any such thing as a collective evaluation of the result of the economic activities of a nation (by whatever statistical measure it may be expressed), if only because of the presence of conflicting interests among individuals and interest groups. However, *for life in the tribal horde the "communist fiction" is well-chosen.* There is no room for independent action, no place for privacy.[29] Primitive man is collectivist and cannot help being so. The practical recognition of the moral system, the emotion-supported moral system fitted to the face-to-face group—we could call it the "moral system of the horde"—by all members of the horde is indispensable for the success of the group in the process of group selection through group struggle. Hence, this norm system will be selected by the cultural whittling process. Since the individual depends upon his fellow group members and, with few exceptions, can survive only as a member of the group, the "free-rider" problem, which besets any moral system, does not loom large. The expected cost of violating the norms—expulsion from the group—is too high. Although individual selection ("free riders") and group selection may operate in opposite directions, group selection through group warfare in combination with the ability to deter or punish "free riders" have led to the evolution of a degree of group-oriented benevolence, to a sense of responsibility to a *visible* community.[30] Cultural evolution will select the emotion-supported moral system because it brings the horde that adopts it advantages in intergroup warfare. The moral system of the face-to-face group has obviously xenophobic implications. This should caution those moral philosophers who preach a return to the coziness of the *Gemeinschaft*.

The mechanisms for maintaining social order are personal; trust, kin, and custom. The reciprocity in rights and duties have their origins in and are modeled on the family. One of the main functions of the moral system is to suppress instinctive aggressiveness, to curb greedy impulses, which, if given free reign, would hinder the formation and preservation of a group as a group, and to channel aggressiveness towards rival groups. This trait is also similar to chimpanzee politics.

In the tribal horde, what is the role of the third organizing principle, the principle of *private rights?* I already mentioned that in the chimpanzee horde there is an as-if recognition of private property, and that all known primitive communities have been found to possess relatively elaborate structures for property rights. In animal hordes there is an exchange of interpersonal cooperative services, and hence an investment in others. Exchange of material goods may be uniquely human. Trade preceded the so-called agricultural revolution, and very likely it was more important for the dawn of civilization than agriculture. The possibility of personal exchange required a mutual recognition of property, and so does sharing and gift-giving. It seems likely that with increasing specialization an increasing respect for private property evolved.

To summarize: The moral system of the horde evolved in the era when man lived in small face-to-face groups. It was indispensable for the survival of mankind. It fits life in groups that are so small that trust and personal ties can function as mechanisms that keep the group together. Hence, it is fitted also to the various face-to-face groups that are interspersed in the anonymous society, to groupings where one can touch one's fellow both literally and metaphorically, i.e., in our anonymous society it is appropriate for the private sphere.

The tribal horde is collectivist and conformist; its population size is stable and its norm system conservative. Hence, it is to be expected that institutional innovations will occur only when the problem situation changes. An institutional innovation is likely to occur only if there is some disequilibrium in the system that adds weight to the profit side in the judgment of the decision-making individuals or groups, i.e., if the perceived benefits of innovation have risen or the perceived costs fallen.

The shift to pastoralism[31] modified the relative importance of the three organizing principles: dominance, sharing and private rights. Property rights became even more important, because pastoralism requires private ownership of flocks and agriculture, private ownership of crops and, in particular, the efficiency of the peasant working his own soil is unmatched by any form of group farming.[32] The strengthening of property rights also helped to clarify the distinction between the public and the private sphere and, hence, contributed to the development of individuality. However, the moral system fitted to life in the tribal horde can be replaced by another norm system—i.e., replaced in the public sphere, including professional and business activity—only if population size has increased so much that the group has turned into an anonymous society; only then is it to the group's advantage to adopt—in the public arena—a norm system composed of abstract rules.

From the tribal horde to the anonymous sociality governed by abstract rules

From personal exchange to impersonal market

Gift-giving and give-and-take relationships (presupposing norms of property) were the mechanisms that made it possible to *extend* social bondings beyond the family so that the tribal horde could evolve. Trade made peaceful intergroup contacts possible. When, through the above-mentioned self-accelerating process—division of labor, trade (presupposing property rights), and further increase in population—the size of the grouping had become so large that an anonymous society had come into existence, personal exchange was successively replaced by impersonal market. The development of the market order constitutes the second main step on the human route to ultrasociality: it made it possible to *extend* the peaceful order beyond the face-to-face group to the anonymous society. The *extended order* came into being. How did it happen?

In order to make voluntary exchange possible, the rule system governing exchange has to be adapted to the size of the population. In small tribal hordes property rights are identified through personal acquaintance with an owner. Exchange in small economies is based on trust; being honest is not only moral but also rational, because one expects repeated dealings with the same people in the future; and disputes are settled by trust, kin, and custom. Personal exchange minimizes the need for formal rules, because of the continuous reciprocity of dealings. Trust is an investment in another human being, and in the face-to-face group each individual has a certain debt towards the group that has invested in him. Expectation of less frequent exchange between any two individuals leads to a lowering of rule-following behavior and successively undermines the norm system fitted to the face-to-face group. Increase in population must sooner or later lead to an anonymous society.[33] This will make new institutional arrangements necessary. The most important adaptive response to population increase is the gradual transition from personal exchange to successively more anonymous exchange. In impersonal markets, formal rules replace trust, and competition constrains behavior. In some circumstances, competition brings out extremely intelligent behavior on the part of some people which is adaptive and makes them more inventive, prosperous, etc. Moralists often denigrate competition, because they do not understand that it not only functions as selection mechanism but may also increase average wealth. In the words of Georg Simmel: "Modern competition is described as the fight of all against all, but at the same time it is the fight of all *for* all."[34]

The concept of a private sphere, and with it the distinction between public and private and the concept of private rights in the full sense, can emerge only with anonymous exchange—exchange where, moreover, it is to be expected that at least sometimes, the individual's behavior has no significant effect on others. Hence, population increase—up to a certain level—has paved the way towards a society of free men. However, from a certain population density onwards, any *further* increase must not only lower freedom but eventually abolish it. There must be boundary conditions for the self-accelerating process described by von Hayek (see text before note 21).

The functions of an economic system

An economic system functions properly if and only if it solves the following problems 1) providing *information* about people's desires, preferences, skills, etc., and also handling this information in such a way that creative entrepreneurial activity becomes possible; 2) creating *incentives* for people to act on such information, i.e., if it provides a system of reward and punishment that makes the decision makers accountable. It must help to *control* behavior. 3) In this way it can coordinate the activities of millions of individuals, households and firms.

Hayek demonstrated that *only* the market order is capable of meeting these requirements. He has shown that the market order is basically a discovery system, which tells man how to serve the needs of people whom he does not know in order to serve his *own* interest. The relevant knowledge for market operations is "local" knowledge: knowledge about fleeting circumstances, about occasions, i.e., knowledge that is dispersed over millions of market participants, knowledge about one's own resources, capabilities and aims, and, moreover, knowledge that is "tacit" knowledge in the sense that one could not articulate it, even if one wished to do so. For instance, a sensitivity for what the ancient Greeks called *kairós*— the propitious, non-recurring moment for action.

Already these considerations unmask the constructivist hubris of central planning. Centralized planning is unable to simulate the efficiency of the market order because of *epistemic* reasons. Since it is impossible to transfer "local" knowledge to a central planning board, the only efficient way of collocating the relevant knowledge and decision rights is to transfer the decision rights to the individuals who possess the relevant local knowledge.[35]

The market order not only functions as a discovery system, but also controls human behavior by collocating decision rights with the rights to the proceeds of the exchange in such a way that the consequences of decisions are imposed on the decision-makers themselves; it makes them accountable for their actions. It establishes a firm link between benefit and individual contribution. By contrast with the non-market or collective provision of goods and services, in the market order the individual, typically, gets what he pays for and pays for what he gets. In non-market provision the link between benefit and contribution applies only to aggregates, not to individuals—hence overconsumption and freeriding will follow. The market prices not only tell the individual what to do in the *future* in order to be better off than before the deal; they also function as a measure of the performance of the parties and determine reward and punishment on the basis of performance (Meckling and Jensen 1984). The prices indicate what is scarce in the sense of being "wanted" by the many people willing to pay for it and they basically represent the present value of rights to future flows of revenue or to future consumption service. Their constellation provides the basis for entrepreneurial creativity, for conjectures about possibilities for gains—competition functions also as a discovery process.

The market order presupposes an institutional framework.

1. Since the assignment of decision-making rights is a matter of law, it presupposes a legal system. In any economy, exchange refers not to physical articles or services *per se,* but to bundles of rights attached to those articles or services. The relevant decision rights comprise essentially the right to sell whatever rights the person has in the resource and the

right to capture the proceeds of the sale; i.e., it is a system of *alienable* rights.[36]

2. Every sociality is faced with the problem of the enforcement of individuals' rights to property. In the anonymous or abstract society an individual possesses property rights or, in general, decision rights with respect to specific objects or actions, to the extent that he can use the police powers of a state to help him ensure his ability to take a particular action. Hence, the market order presupposes also an apparatus of law enforcement. Otherwise, the Prisoner's Dilemma, which arises from the non-enforceability of contracts, cannot be eliminated.[37]

3. Since not all of the rules governing business transactions can be codified by law, the market order also presupposes a certain basis of trust and honesty. Honesty, in particular, the norm of *pacta sunt servanda*, has a central place in the rule system governing activities in the public arena. It constitutes a part of the human capital. To the extent that the abstract rules of the extended order become internalized, contract uncertainty diminishes and the costs of exchange in the economy are lowered. If we wish to attach watch-words to the two norm systems, the norm system fitted to life in the face-to-face group might be called the *"solidarity system"* and the system fitted to activities in the public arena of the anonymous society might be labeled the *"honesty system"*.

In view of these preconditions, the market can only constitute a part of a social order; not all of public activity can be left to the marketplace. The example of the lighthouse, which provides benefits for which, at a certain stage of technology, no charge can be made, has been in the textbooks for two centuries. The example may not be ideal. But there are a few inherently indivisible goods. The non-market provision of such goods may be organized either on the basis of state coercion or on voluntary contribution. Hobbe's famous dilemma of "public goods" may not be a genuine dilemma after all (Jasay 1989).

Most of the institutions in an exchange economy are concerned with property rights. The classical function of the *state* is to protect and secure the possessions of individuals, i.e., private rights to body, time, material possessions, etc., against intruders from the outside (national defense) and against intruders from inside (internal security, equality before the law, etc.). The modern state evolved from the monopolization of violence, and places it in the service of these functions. Nozick's invisible-hand explanation of the rise of the "ultraminimal state" is suggestive even if it is speculative.[38] He sketches the evolution of more and more efficient solutions to the problem of the enforcement of individuals' rights: from inefficient mutual-protection associations to more professional private protective agencies and eventually to the single protective agency that emerges as dominating a geographical area: the ultraminimal state.

If priority is given to the value of individual freedom and it is acknowledged that the constraints include the fact that any collective brings with it coercion (even in democratic systems minorities may be overruled, and even majorities may not be able to hold their own because of information problems), then the principle of the subsidiarity of the state will be insisted upon. This insight has obvious implications for the problem where the boundary line should be drawn between the private and the public sector, and, in particular, between market processes and governmental decision processes. It, moreover, suggests that in the realm of state activity *federalism* is indispensable: thus the principle not to allow more state than absolutely necessary is complemented by the principle, within state institutions, not to allow more central government than absolutely necessary. The classical functions of the state are: 1) To provide a framework of laws and institutions of law enforcement, i.e. institutions to prevent the rule of force and fraud. This may itself be regarded as a public good, which only the state can provide in an efficient way. Required is a system of general law that safeguards private rights and does not confer privileges on any politically-favored groups. 2) To provide certain true public goods such as national defense and law and order. 3) To provide a minimum income for people who, through no fault of their own, cannot maintain a civilized standard in the market economy, e.g., by reverse income tax. (However, such a schema may too have unintended effects.)

Function 2 requires comment. The concept of public good is a contested concept. When proposing an explication of it, it should be stated what role the explicatum, the improved concept, is intended to play in which theory. The two main properties of a public good are: a) Its privacy or "privatizability": does the consumption of the good by one person diminish the possibility of other people consuming it? Scientific knowledge is a textbook example of a good whose possession by one person does not diminish the possibility that others may also possess it, enjoy it, etc. b) The degree in which it is possible or economically viable (or, sometimes, considered socially desirable) to exclude people from its consumptions. Can people be prevented from benefiting from the good, and, if so, at what cost? For instance, national defense is a good from which each citizen benefits, even those who engage in sabotaging it.

To the category of goods that are not "privatizable" also corresponds the class of rights that Karl Brunner calls *non-scarce* rights, i.e., rights such that granting the right to one person in no way limits the opportunity to offer the same rights to others (Brunner 1983, p. 340). Examples are freedom of speech and freedom of exchange. On the other hand, when a scarce right—scarce, because of the constraints operating in the situation—is exercised by one person, certain options are eliminated from the opportunity sets of others. Hence, there must be legal provisions for regulating the allocation of scarce rights. From Brunner's reflections follow two injunctions for the free society under the rule of law: a) Since non-scarce rights can be given to everyone, it would be morally wrong to deny any individual those rights; b) Scarce rights cannot be given to everyone, and, hence, there must be some institutions resolving conflicts about such rights; but it would be morally wrong to deny a scarce right to everyone (e.g., on the egalitarian, or better Procrustean, principle that none must possess what not everyone possesses) or to deny it to anyone.

The system of abstract rules that is fitted to the public arena in the anonymous sociality is scarcely supported by our emotional reactions. These are tied with the "solidarity" system of the tribal horde that is fitted to the form of life in which man lived at least for one and a half million years. However, since norms of possession exist already in the primordial group and even in the non-human primate horde, emotions that support private rights are deeply ingrained in our emotional make-up. The desire for private property is most intense insofar as it concerns control of one's own person and one's own time; possessions, or more accurately, property rights with respect to material things, are valued also because they are guarantors of our autonomy from particular other persons. This is one of the advantages of the anonymous society.

To sum up, the argument for the market order is based on epistemological considerations. For *epistemic* reasons it is impossible for a central planning agency to match the efficiency of the market order, and, in an important sense, socialism is impossible.[39] Without stealing a glance at prices in the world market, central planning faces calculational chaos, since one never knows what it costs to produce anything. Hayek's thesis that "all our efforts to improve things must operate within a working whole which we cannot entirely control"[40] finds ample exemplification: In the legal system the authority of legislator and state derives from pre-existing conceptions of justice of individual conduct (negatively defined);[41] the order of management hierarchy in a business corporation depends upon a larger spontaneous order; and the same holds for an army unit, an army, a school, a business corporation, etc.[42] The reasons why a command economy is dependent upon an existing framework that constitutes a spontaneous order are clearly epistemic: a) the complexity of the relevant information, b) the difficulty of handling information centrally, if only because it tends to be modified in the transferring process, and c) the difficulty of getting honest information, since it may not be in the interest of the parties concerned to provide such information.

The market order presupposes property rights and, hence, also the argument for private rights rests on epistemic reasons: that without private rights the market order is not possible and, hence, an efficient use of the relevant knowledge is not possible. Since, therefore, a change of the problem situation is not feasible, this argument is decisive. For the institution of the family, the situation is different. The adaptive value of that institution (be it in the form of monogamy, polygamy, etc.) is mainly due to the inability to conduct efficient birth control.[43] With the emergence of new technologies the situation has changed, and, hence, the case for the family appears to be less strong than that for private rights or for the market order. The best arguments for the family—although they can never be so strong as epistemic arguments—are the following: first, pointing out that the family provides a focus for personal responsibility and altruism, and that people are likely to be more enterprising if they are concerned with the welfare of their family. (Swedish social democrats have denigrated this altruistic behavior and coined a special derogative label for it: *familjeegoism:* a good socialist should not prefer his family to other people or groups, rather his first loyalty should be the collective, to *the* society, to the *folkshem* [a term and idea derived from the German *Volksheim* of the 1930's].) A second argument for the family is that very likely the moral education of the child can be provided best, and perhaps only, by the family.

Man as self-interested actor: Two cheers for self-interest

The model of man that underlies the description of how the market order functions and the explanation of its origins, treats man as a *self-interested* actor. The model assumes that all evaluations are located in the individual's conscientiousness and that every individual has a preference for making his *own* decision according to his *own* assessment.[44] Behavior is non-self-interested to the extent that the actor attaches utility to the impact of events upon others—on a spectrum from benevolence to malevolence.[45] Of course, this does not tell us anything about the arguments referring to others that are included in the utility function of the actor. The evaluation of an outcome as "increasing the well-being of the other person" or as being to his or her "best" remains purely subjective. Hence, there will be conflicts, which have to be resolved by market processes or by other decision mechanisms. Nonetheless, the common objection that the model disregards altruistic behavior (as the expression "altruistic" is understood in everyday speech) is mistaken. The model by no means denies the overwhelming role of non-self-interested behavior, for instance, in the family. The work of A. A. Alchian, Gary Becker, Karl Brunner, and Jack Hirshleifer have shown the basic irrelevance of the traditional distinction between altruistic and egotistical behavior for economic analysis or for an understanding of social patterns. The Adam Smith "Invisible Hand" doctrine claims that we will do others more good if we behave *as if* we are following our self-interest rather than by pursuing "altruistic" purposes. Hayek's argument for the market order makes it perfectly clear that *even in a community (sic) of pure altruists, provided that it is larger than a face-to-face group, people would produce the best situation for ALL by behaving AS IF they were following their self-interest—for epistemic reasons.* Since prices signal relative scarcity at the moment and have a role in allocating resources, there is no such thing as a "just price"—no more than a gratis lunch. However, a free lunch is only an *economic* impossibility: it is not *empirically* impossible since, after all, manna might again fall from heaven. This may be an exceptional case, but we understand what is meant by the phrase "a free lunch." On the other hand, "just price" (the quotes are scare quotes) is a category mistake: the economic theory of prices and markets and the philosophical attempts to explicate the intuitive idea of justice—which is expressed in a single Latin tag, *suum cuique tribuere*—are incommensurable. The predicate "just" cannot meaningfully be predicated of a price.

In addition, the idea of self-interested behavior helps us to make a clear distinction between behavior governed by the individuals' *own* (unknown) interests and behavior governed by the *common* aim of the tribal horde or by the concrete *national goals* of states. According to the economic approach to decisionmaking the individual agents try to follow their own interest, which may or may not coincide with what they perceive to be the public interest; their behavior is self-interested in this important sense and, hence, invariant under changes of institution so that such variations effect only the specific expressions of self-interested behavior. Economic analysis and social science studies have shown that the public interest view of government, i.e., the hypothesis that persons in the role of bureaucrats can be expected to act in the "public interest," is as false as the "benevolent dictator" (or benevolent commissar) hypothesis of government or the "political man" assumption.[46] Adam Smith, as usual, said it best. He asserts that a (private) capitalist, always seeking the safest and highest return on his capital,

"neither intends to promote the public interest, nor knows how much he is promoting it . . . (that) he is in this, as in many other cases, led by an invisible hand to promote an end which was no part of his intention. . . . Nor is it always the worst for society that it was no part of it. . . I have never known much good done by those who affected to trade for the public good."[47]

"Public choice" economics, or perhaps more aptly expressed, the economic theory of politics, has convincingly argued that the rational politician will conduct policies that yield payoffs prior to the next election while generating costs that are observable only after the election, and that he will support positions favored by identifiable special interest groups while generating costs that are spread widely and not readily observable.[48] A cynic has, therefore, proposed the apothegm that a general election is basically a futures market in stolen property.

4. THE "CATALLAXY" AS A PRECONDITION OF THE EXTENDED ORDER

Extending peaceful cooperation beyond the small group

A sociality can exist only if there are reliable expectations about the behavior of others, which presupposes that a large part of this behavior follows rules. In his *Treatise* (1740), Hume argued that a society that offers individual *freedom* can exist only if the principle of property rights plays a key role in the governing rule system.[49] Hayek showed that the market order, based on property rights, is a precondition of an "extended order," i.e., an order that makes it possible to *extend* peaceful cooperation beyond the boundaries of the small group or the tribal horde, an order that *transcends* what we perceive, transcends our experience of people and circumstances with which we are acquainted, and also transcends our personal knowledge. Hayek proposes for the market order the term *catallaxy*, derived from the Greek verb *katallattein*, which "meant, significantly, not only 'to exchange' but also 'to admit into the community' and 'to change from enemy to friend.' "[50]

Hayek's classic account can be summarized as follows. Barter or exchange is a first step towards a peaceful cooperation in the absence of a concrete common purpose of the parties engaging in the cooperation. When the personal exchange has been replaced by impersonal markets, a special order has been brought about by many individuals, who need not, and, normally, do not, know each other, and who, nonetheless, adjust to each other through the barter or market process within the rules of the law of property, tort and contract. It not only reconciles different purposes, but also enables members of the large, anonymous society to benefit from each other's effort in spite of differences in their several aims and often even *because* of such differences.[51] People can now cooperate peacefully *without* having any *common* purpose, apart from the purely instrumental aim of securing the formation of an abstract order that will enhance for all the prospects of achieving their *own* purposes. In a large, anonymous society the mechanisms of social control must be impersonal and the rules governing the public sphere must be abstract rules. The legal framework required for the market order made it possible to restrict coercion to observance of *negative* rules of just conduct—"just" being predicated of *individual* conduct, never of society—and thereby it enabled individuals in groups who pursued different ends to be integrated into an extended order.[52]

"Man has been civilized much against his will" (Hayek, e.g., 1979 *Epilogue*).

The evolution of the market order and with it of the extended order was a gradual and decentralized process. It could not have been designed; it was the unintended effect of innumerable actions of individuals pursuing their own aims. The groups that partook in the rule system which focused on private rights and honesty were more successful than those groups that followed other rule systems, and they supplanted them. They did not understand why they were more successful than these others, and to be successful, it was not necessary that they understand. Yet a cultural practice could continue to be transmitted only it if was provided with some theory about the causal connection between the practice and the effects (worldly or otherworldly) that people evaluated as beneficial. This theory may be a rationalization, for instance, when the effects are explained in terms of the intervention of a supernatural power. Von Hayek claims that civilization is the result of religions teaching a morality of property, honesty and family, and that in the competition of religions only those have survived that support property and the family, thereby endorsing the ethos of individual responsibility and prudent housekeeping, the classical moral and political virtues. Thus he holds that Christianity played a decisive role by giving certain cultural practices supernatural legitimization. Incidentally, Hayek's theory also implies that Christianity now has lost that particular social function, thanks to that theory which enables us, at least in retrospect, to understand the mechanisms involved.

According to his theory, Communism, which is both anti-property and anti-family (as were the great heretical movements, from the Gnostics and Manichaens to the Cathars, Hussites, etc.) is a pseudo-religion, a "religion séculaire," which, in the long run, should be whittled away by cultural selection, since it makes the groups partaking in it less successful than those that have adopted the market order. The testimony of the Communist societies such as Russia is that they would be starving today if their populations were not kept alive by the western world. Ethologists know of no tribes that are egalitarian and tell us that an egalitarian-distributional order can be upheld only by continuous use of force. Egalitarian ideology is a modern phenomenon that emerged with mass society and the modern means of controlling the populace. (There is, however, one classic case of non-European egalitarian totalitarianism: Incan Empire.) It, too, is a European phenomenon. As is highlighted by the three great socialist revolutions: the French of 1789, the Russian of 1917, and

the German of 1933 (Kuehnelt-Leddihn 1985). It succeeded in destroying, or almost destroying, Europe and in enslaving a large part of present
humanity.

Since the tribal horde is held together by a common perception of
reality and a common goal, and since its politics of goals is legitimized by
a central myth, it cannot afford the luxury of holding that myth open to
criticism. The myth provides much of the cement that holds the sociality
together, and, of course, it will contain any amount of errors. Hence, it
would not be rational to expose it to critical examination; it has to be
dogmatized and protected from competition in ideas. The same holds,
mutatis mutandis, for the totalitarian state. The only difference is that in a
theocracy like contemporary Iran, heretics in spirit are persecuted, while
in the Soviet Empire—even if the KGB is the Russian counterpart to the
Holy Inquisition—the authorities are satisfied with lip service or even
with silence, with what may be called "dissident assent" (Shtromas 1983).
*The extended order under the rule of law is the rare and only sociality that can afford
the luxury of critical discussion,* of not exempting any position from critical
examination (Munz 1985, p. 303, Bartley in Radnitzky and Bartley, eds.,
1987.) Hence, it has no use either for such idealized absolutes as the
"ideal, symmetric discourse" of the Frankfurt School, which aims at arriving at a consensus about the aims of the society. In the doctrines of the
New Left it is again the society that has an aim, not the individual. The
tribal horde appears to inspire the vision of the New Left.

5. THE EXTENDED ORDER AS A PRECONDITION FOR A SOCIETY OF FREE MEN

Social patterns such as traditions, cultural practices, institutions, and so
forth, can be appraised with reference to the efficiency with which they
help us to realize or approximate particular substantive values. To assess
efficiency is a scientific problem. It is a peculiarity of the social sciences
that they can easily have political implications since value standpoints
often are tacitly assumed. However, the value positions adopted cannot be
criticized unless they have been made explicit.

Hayek's explanation of the origins of the extended order and of the
prevalence over societies of the market order is purely descriptive, and so
is, in my opinion, his theory of spontaneous order. In his political and
moral philosophy he gives priority to individual freedom; in the tradition
of classical liberalism he sees it as the central value of the public sphere.
As is well-known, the key problem of the political philosophy of classical
liberalism is the problem of how to defend autonomous private rights
against the organized professional guardians of those rights.[53] From these

considerations follows, not a categorical, but a hypothetical imperative: If you want to live in a free society, you ought to insist on your own claims to inviolability of persons and property while being prepared to concede corresponding rights to others and even be willing to participate as a disinterested third-party enforcer against violators.[54]

Since the relationship between individual households and government is game-theoretical, and since not only market procedures but the whole public sphere is governed by abstract, impersonal rules, those who proceed to govern their conduct by a Kantian principle of universalizability, in spite of the fact that they have no security that others will do likewise, are likely to be injured and even have their moral goals thwarted.[55] So long as the actions of many dispersed individuals are not so coordinated as to produce reliable expectations among them (anticipation functioning as a substitute for the enforceability of agreements), each individual will have reason to act in a way illustrated by the Prisoner's Dilemma.[56]

The "privacy ethic" has proved to be a powerful device for creating wealth. Only those nations are rich in which property rights are protected. A command economy does not create much wealth and it precludes freedom, eventually even in the market of ideas. Hayek sees the success of a rule system in the increase in the size of the group that has adopted it. However, he would apply this criterion only for rules that constitute spontaneous orders, i.e., that have been selected in cultural evolution, and not to rules or institutions that have been deliberately constructed. How is increase in size related to increase in the wealth of a nation? The statistical measures that have been developed help little to solve the problem of what exactly to include in estimating wealth. However, there is little doubt that today the most important resource of a nation is not the size of its population but its *human capital*. The moral system of the tribal society protects the parents' investment in children. Hence, they invest in a large number of children. When family ties are weakened, the family-supported system is replaced by legal institutions. People will tend to invest more in their own education and health, and, instead of in a maximum number of children, in a small number of high quality children and in their education. However, to the human capital belongs not only creative talent, diligence and professional ethics, but also honesty.

The development from the tribal horde to the anonymous society does not guarantee an increase in freedom. As the socialist states demonstrate, a large anonymous society can practice an internal command economy together with dictatorship. It cannot be said too often that in no socialist country are even the most fundamental civil liberties guaranteed and respected. The market order under the rule of law opens the way to the *possibility* of a society of free men, which for the ordinary citizen has brought a measure of personal freedom unimaginable in all other known forms of society. This means that this type of sociality is a rare and endangered species. "Law and property, and thus the possibility for peaceful exchange, can only persist where individuals are ultimately willing to use violence in their defense."[57]

Moreover, free society can survive only if individuals are working continuously to adapt it to changing situations and to improve it. What role can piecemeal social technologies play? Popper, who coined the label, emphasizes (probably under the influence of Hayek in London in 1936) that the piecemeal technologist "recognizes that only a minority of social institutions are consciously designed while the vast majority has just 'grown' as the undesigned result of human actions."[58] Hayek distinguishes between organizations which are open to human design and spontaneous orders which are not. However, his ideas of constitutional reforms leave ample room for improvements through deliberate efforts.[59] (I will return to this in the last two sections) Even interventionist policies in the economy may be beneficial provided they are intended to improve the generic rules required for the proper functioning of the market order by removing impediments to its normal functioning. However, any kind of intervention designed to alter the consequences of the normal functioning of the market system is bound to disrupt and eventually to destroy it—and with it also the free society.

6. THE THEORY OF CULTURAL EVOLUTION AND VALUE ISSUES

Hayek argues convincingly that without capitalism the enormous population increase would not have been possible. Ours has been the only species that found it possible to change its way of life without speciating, and to occupy new niches at will. In this way our new way of life has been inevitably hostile to the interest of almost all other species.[60] Today the rate of population increase is falling in all developed countries,[61] while in many Third World countries, having too many children imposes a negative externality on the total population, because the number is too large for the carrying capacity of the environment. In general, in breeding the principle of the commons has not been abandoned. To answer the question of what population density is desirable, one needs a statement of the values to be used in the evaluation. Size can no longer be a criterion for success.

Thanks to Hayek's work we *know* what mankind must do in order to support the world's present population. However, an attempt to deduce a genuine normative statement from a *descriptive* theory such as Hayek's would be an instance of the so-called naturalistic fallacy. If an individual or an organization (and only these entities can entertain aims) desires to preserve mankind at its present level or even at an increased level, then it is rational for this individual or organization to do the things considered necessary to realize this aim. Indeed, if they did not, they would *eo ipso* incur the reproach of irrationality. Hayek's theory tells them what these things are. The theory is descriptive, and so is the hypothetical imperative that is based on it.

Ought one desire that mankind be maintained at its present level? This is a genuine, i.e., a non-instrumental value issue, an issue which individuals have to decide for themselves. It appears doubtful—and this is a descriptive statement of psychology—that an average individual can identify with an abstract concept like "future humanity." Our emotions are tied to concrete people, to persons and things we know, and they cannot readily be attached to a general concept such as, mankind *n*-hundred or *n*-thousand years from now. Moreover, the value of a high density of population or of an increasing density, perhaps in combination with the value of an increase in average wealth,[62] compete with other values such as unspoiled nature, privacy,[63] space, and so forth. These amenities of life cannot be stretched by any technology. From a certain population density onward these resources will have to be rationed, and their control will lead to more bureaucracy, and, hence, to greater restrictions on individual freedom. Liberty will fall progressively as the numbers rise.[64] Thus, there will be a conflict of values. What combination of the competing values is regarded as an optimal balance is also a genuine value issue, a question that cannot be decided by any amount of scientific knowledge. From the value position of classical liberalism one will commend the maxim: *in dubio pro libertate.*

The concept of a spontaneous order and the need to examine such orders critically

The fact that the origins of a particular tradition can be invisible-handedly explained is irrelevant for the evaluation of that tradition from a particular value position (cf. text after note 21). The result of the evaluation will depend not only on the value system but also on the sphere of activity considered. If an order has evolved spontaneously, the probability that it will be evaluated positively from the viewpoint of a value system that gives priority to individual freedom will be greater than the probability that an order that has been introduced by a ukase will be so evaluated. The extended order, which is a choice example of a spontaneous order, is the only one in which individual freedom may be guaranteed by the constitution. An autocratic regime may afford as much liberty, but the tolerance exercised by the rulers may be withdrawn at any moment. The extended order, through offering more freedom than any other order, is more innovative, and, in the long run, will create more epistemic resources. However, it is a fragile order. Exactly because of the openness of the free world, totalitarian regimes can import technological innovations from it, partly by legal and partly by illegal technology transfer. The resulting international system qualifies as a spontaneous order—yet from the value position that accords priority to individual freedom, it has to be evaluated negatively.

Also with respect to foreign policy, liberal democracy is at a disadvantage in comparison with the totalitarian state. The totalitarian state controls all of its mass media, and it can infiltrate the mass media of a liberal democracy; its sympathizers can, by spreading systematic disinformation, successfully carry on psychological warfare in times of peace and in the name of peace (cf., e.g., Radnitzky 1985). The totalitarian state can easily maintain the secrecy necessary for an efficient conduct of foreign policy, while democracies are prone to the hysteria of disclosures. Hence, the extended order and, in particular, the free society is enormously improbable, and in the history of mankind it has been the rare exception. Today, only a tiny fraction of the member states of the United Nations are states that approximate a free order; the great majority are despotisms, which practice rule by fear instead of the rule of law. How important foreign policy is for a state will depend upon its might. When a state has become unimportant in the international game of power, it will automatically become peaceful. A superpower, on the other hand, cannot refrain from giving much attention to its foreign policy and its military strength, if it wishes to hold its own. The pattern of relationships between the states constitutes a spontaneous order. From the viewpoint of the free world the development in international relations has not been favorable; it reached its nadir at the time of the Carterization of American politics, and only recently has the tide begun to turn. Likewise in domestic policy creeping socialism has evolved spontaneously, even if many politicians have deliberately worked for it. (Tocqueville has analyzed that phenomenon, as well as Mancur Olson 1982, Bernholz 1985, just to mention a few of the most important analyses). Creeping socialism in the western democracies appears to qualify as a spontaneous order. It too is an example of a spontaneous order that, from a value position that gives priority to individual freedom, has to be evaluated negatively.

The epistemological basis of the free society (freiheitlicher Rechtsstaat)

An epistemological basis for a free society can be provided only when the dilemma of justificationist philosophy has been dissolved. Justificationism is still the dominant philosophical tradition. It claims that the following dilemma is inescapable: either truth claims can be ultimately justified, i.e., statements can be proven to be true, or genuine knowledge is impossible—in short, either justificationism works or skepticism. In the justificationist context this dilemma is, indeed, inescapable. It was overcome by making critical rationalism self-applicable, by "pancritical rationalism," as Bartley calls this approach. Pancritical rationalism is based on the insight that the ideal of knowledge underlying justification is utopian and, hence, cannot inspire a regulative principle for intellectual activity; in particular, it is based on the insight that there are no logical reasons that would force us to dogmatize anything—that no semantical paradoxes need to arise if the maxim "Hold all your positions (hypotheses, viewpoints, criteria, etc.) open to criticism!" is made self-applicable (Bartley 1962/84, Bartley 1987, Radnitzky 1987a).

The justificationist dilemma in epistemology has an offshoot in ethics in the alleged dilemma: either certain substantive moral judgments and norms can be ultimately justified or nihilism, i.e., arbitrary decisions or discretionary conventions can. This dilemma can be overcome with the help of two insights: 1) A corollary of self-applicable critical rationalism is that an ultimate foundation (*Letztbegründung*) of value judgments or moral norms is impossible, for logical reasons. 2) With respect to value judgments or norms, critical discussion is not only possible, but necessary if we are to act morally. After the dilemma was shown to be spurious, the ethic of individual freedom can stress that it is the individual that adopts values and sets himself aims, not society. The ultimate values adopted by an individual are solely his business and his responsibility, not that of society.

The justificationist dilemma also has an offshoot in political philosophy in the alleged dilemma: either we create institutions for realizing a politics of goals (goals about which a consensus has been reached) or anarchism will reign. In this view, it is society that has a goal; the citizens have a common goal, and the common goal of all "well-meaning" citizens is identical with the goal of society. The politics of goals is typical of the Left; the New Left usually takes the goal of society to be "social justice," interpreted under the egalitarian, or better Procrustian, paradigm. This dilemma, too, is spurious. It is dissolved by the following three insights: 1) In history spontaneous evolution of order has been by far more important than "instinct" and design taken together, i.e., the most important of the social patterns we see around us can be invisible-handedly explained. 2) There is an epistemological primacy of spontaneous order over design; and 3) It is the individuals who set themselves aims, who follow their own purposes; society has no aim. If one gives priority to individual freedom, then given the constraints implicit in social organizations and human motivation, the third alternative (which shows that the dilemma is spurious) is minimal government controlled by severe constitutional limitations.

An indispensable regulative principle for the constitution of a free society

Self-applicable critical rationalism used as a foil

The model situation for the application of pancritical rationalism is intellectual activity, and in particular, research. In this context the *immediate* aim of the individual is the improvement of knowledge (whether scientific progress is evaluated instrumentally or intrinsically is irrelevant). The constraints are given by the fact that all life is problem solving and that successful problem solving proceeds through creativity and criticism (cf., e.g., Radnitzky and Bartley, eds. 1987, Part I). From this value premise and the statements describing the relevant constraints can be derived the maxim: Hold all your positions open to criticism—*including this maxim!* (An infinite regress need not arise, because no attempt is made to justify any proposition.) Without this way of proceeding, systematic error elimination, the main selection mechanism, would not work properly. From the constraints given in social organization it follows that in order to realize the aim of cognitive progress it is necessary to create institutions that facilitate creativity, criticism and the free competition in ideas. It also follows that one has to make an effort to prevent dogmatization, immunization against criticism—which is the intellectual counterpart to protectionism in economy—and to prevent cartelization in the academia. The extended order is the only one that can afford the luxury of pancritical rationalism, and this attitude accounts for its being more innovative than any other order. The evolution of the criticist tradition (probably with the Pre-Socratics) was, in turn, the precondition of the evolution of the extended order. The two have progressed *pari passu*, in a give-and-take relationship. *Unlimited* criticism is rational only in intellectual life. In *praxi*, the question of whether or not to embark on a particular discussion, whether or not to re-check a particular statement, etc., is a risky investment decision (cf., e.g., Radnitzky 1987b).

A regulative principle for the constitution of the free society

In contradistinction to what applies in intellectual activity, in politics it is rational to set limits to criticism. In the extended order people can peacefully cooperate without having any common purpose—apart from the purely instrumental aim to secure the maintenance of an abstract order that will enhance for all the prospects of achieving their *own* purposes. In order to preserve that framework it is necessary to protect it. From Voltaire to Popper philosophers and others have pointed out that those who practice tolerance against those working to destroy the free society by force share the responsibility for the destruction of the free society. The question is whether this is enough. (The free society guarantees to everybody the freedom of speech and the freedom to criticize. Granting these non-scarce rights to everybody is one of its definitorial characteristics.) Yet it may also be necessary to protect the constitution of liberty against all those who, without resorting to violence, form organized groups that work for abolishing the constitution of liberty. For instance, the constitution must contain provisions against the possibility that, by means of a majority decision, the democratic system is converted into an unlimited, totalitarian democracy. Already this reflection shows that the democratic decision-making method can only be subsidiary; it is a formal method and it alone cannot guarantee freedom. Only the constitution can do this.

From the value judgment giving priority to individual freedom, in combination with the statements describing the constraints implicit in social organization and human motivation, the following regulative principle can be derived: The constitution of liberty, the legal framework of the free society under the rule of law (*freiheitlicher Rechtsstaat*) *must not allow the absolutization of any principle—except the absolutization of this principle,* i.e., the principle that no principle may be absolutized (Bernholz and Faber 1986). Thus the exemption refers to a metaprinciple. This distinguishes this absolutization from the absolutization of substantive contents in religions or *"religions séculaires,"* in the various monisms that can be characterized by a single Latin expression *extra ecclesiam nulla salus.* The maxim constitutes a regulative principle for any constitution of liberty; in *praxi,* the metaprinciple entails that any proposal for constitutional reform should first meet the test of whether or not it entails the absolutization of a principle or system *other* than the metaprinciple under consideration. To make the metaprinciple that prohibits the absolutization of any principle self-applicable would leave the constitution of liberty without defense.

A comment on the democratic decision-making method

The main advantage of the democratic method is that it affords a non-violent procedure for getting rid of a government. What method of decisionmaking it is rational to adopt in a particular situation depends, in a large measure, on the sort of problem situation at hand. Hence, the main question appears to be: Which sort of democratic decision-making method is it rational to adopt in which sort of problem situation? The first task is to make explicit the *costs* of political democracy (as opposed to the open-ended democracy of the market) with a view to controlling those costs and to preventing the extension of democratic coercion to activities that can be better conducted by consent in the market and regulated by competition (Harris 1985). Proposals that have been made include the following: 1) Problems of redistribution of income must not be left to the democratic method; they should be tackled by constitutional means. For instance, the parliament may increase taxation only across the board so that the decision makers themselves are subjected to the effects of the change to the same extent as other citizens are. 2) Finance ministers should be obliged to make explicit a supplementary budget statement listing the polices that impose implicit taxation. 3) Or, preferably, governments should be required to balance the national budget and to cover all expenditures by explicit taxation. 4) Public spending and taxation should be limited, in the constitution, to a proportion of national income—a well-known proposal of the "public choice" school. The key principle of Hayek's new constitutional settlement is to confine the sovereign rule of law to what he calls "general rules of just conduct," i.e., prohibiting arbitrary legislation, in particular, special-interest legislation.

These constitutional reforms are urgent, because as long as politicians have the power to enrich sectional interest groups, it will be rational for them—and even indispensable for their survival in the next election—to buy votes with others people's money and freedom. The progressive extension of government and the creeping socialism in rent-seeking societies will gradually diminish the everyday freedom of the individual. It will also reduce the relative power of the private sector to maintain that independence and diversity which is likewise indispensable for the preservation of individual freedom.

On the future of the free society

Today, state intervention leads to increasing dysfunctions, which undermine the value which the interventions are designed to secure; many of the state interventions offer choice examples of unintended consequences. Whether the privacy ethics will win the competition is an open question. Much may depend upon educating the public by promoting a better understanding of the rise of civilization and the functioning of a modern society. As Hayek has often pointed out, the attacks on capitalism are due to the fact that its critics do not understand that it is not the result of intentional design, but a spontaneous order that has been selected in cultural evolution by means of group selection. Lacking this knowledge, Leftist intellectuals attack the moral tradition, the privacy ethic, to which we owe the extended order and the free society.

What about the *costs* of the free society? Everything in life has costs or, more accurately speaking, by acting in a certain way or investing in a particular project we necessarily incur opportunity costs, benefits that would have accrued to us if we had opted for another one of the available alternatives. Neither the open society nor the privacy ethic can satisfy the "instincts" fitted to the tribal horde and the emotions and moral intuitions associated with the moral system that fit the horde. Those who cannot fill the emotional vacuum left by the abstract and even by the free society will long for group membership and for the elation which one may sometimes feel by identifying with a group or with a "cause." Of course, in the abstract society face-to-face groups are interspersed: the family, the circle of friends, and so forth. Apparently, for many this is not enough, and this is, perhaps, understandable considering that the moral system of the tribal horde is not only embodied in the emotions internalized in early childhood, but may, perhaps, to some extent be genetically implanted through man's hunter-gatherer life and may even have its roots in man's primate heritage. The strength of this longing for the emotional atmosphere of the tribal horde is beautifully expressed by Hayek: "It shows itself conspicuously when sometimes even the outbreak of war is felt as satisfying a craving for such a common purpose; and it manifests itself most clearly in modern times in the two greatest threats to a free civilization: nationalism and socialism." (Hayek 1979, *LLL,* III, p. 111). Both represent atavistic impulses and embody the desire to reverse the cultural evolution that extended the order of peace beyond the small groups pursuing the same ends, and the desire to return to a state where a common purpose is required for establishing and maintaining a peaceful order, and consensus is founded upon a common perception of reality. Hence, both nationalists and socialists are susceptible to the *"tentation totalitaire"* (J. -F. Revel's watch-word). Socialism can thus be seen as a paradoxical combination of constructivist rationalism (the belief that design is the best way to solve all societal problems) and romanticism. The first view is an expression of constructivist hubris, a fatal overestimation of the power of reason. The second is a romantic plea for a return, even in the public-political sphere, to the warmth of the face-to-face group, to reintroduce into the public-political sphere the norm-system that fit the tribal horde and still fits our "natural instincts which are the instincts of the savage" (Hayek 1979, *LLL,* III, p. 174, see also p. 165). Socialists can make these reactionary proposals with a good conscience because firstly, they do not understand the rise of civilization and, hence, do not recognize that man was civilized much against his will, secondly, they do not understand the functioning of modern society and economy and, hence, do not recognize that reintroducing into the public sphere the moral system that fitted the tribal horde would destroy the extended order, thirdly, they do not understand that it is impossible—for epistemic reasons—to simulate the efficiency of the market order by a centralized planning board, and fourthly, they do not understand that capitalism is one of the preconditions of a free market of ideas.

NOTES

I wish to acknowledge my debt to graditude to Professor Friedrich von Hayek, who kindly discussed a previous version of the MS with me, and to thank Professors W. W. Bartley, III, Jack Hirshleifer, Angelo Petroni, and Gunnar Andersson, for constructive criticism. Special thanks go to Professor Antony Flew, whose critique of an earlier draft helped me to improve the paper. It has been completely rewritten and undergone considerable changes.

1. See, e.g., Radnitzky and Bernholz (1987) and Hirshleifer (1987).
2. An attempt to apply the economic approach to methodology is made, e.g., in Radnitzky (1987).
3. Bartley (1985), Olson (1982).
4. Hayek (1967), *Studies,* p. 173; Hayek (1979) *LLL* III:168; Gray (1984), pp. 60, 66, 67.
5. Cf., e.g., Radnitzky (1985b), pp. 21–25, for a brief survey.
6. For an overview see, e.g., Butler (1983), Chapters 5 and 6, and Gray (1984), Chapter 3.
7. Campbell (1983).
8. Campbell (1983), p. 27.
9. Waal (1982), p. 210, cf. also Willhoite (1976), p. 1115.
10. Willhoite (1976), p. 1123. Again, a well-known passage from Adam Smith (*The Wealth of Nations,* 1776) comes to mind: "that insidious and crafty animal, vulgarly called a statesman or politician, whose councils are directed by the momentary fluctuations of affairs."
11. John Rawls too—though he repudiates the socialist name—wants all the differentiating characteristics of the individuals in his supposedly "just society" to be treated as a collective asset, or presumably, as the case may be, a collective liability. Cf. the analysis in Flew (1981), Chapter IV and Flew (1980).
12. With the help of the "rational choice" model (the REMM-model: *r*esourceful-*e*valuating *m*aximizing-*m*an. (See, e.g., Brunner and Meckling (1977)) one can see how the rule-following model of man can be used to explain conduct in certain situations, in particular, in tribal society, which is governed by tradition.
13. "Innate" means that a neural network that underlies a certain capacity grows to functional maturity (like any organ) according to the blueprint in the genome, independently of child rearing, and that the disposition, pattern or trait constitutes a universal for the species.
14. Eibl-Eibesfeldt (1982) p. 179.
15. Cf., e.g., Eibl-Eibesfeldt (1967, 1978⁵, 1985) for a brief survey see, e.g., Eibl-Eibesfeldt (1982), pp. 183–188.
16. For instance, in Mao's empire the so-called cultural revolutions were needed in order to prevent emerging new elites from becoming serious rivals to the power-holders.
17. Hayek (1967) *Studies* Chapter 6 is the *locus classicus.*

18. Popper (1972) Chapters 3 and 4.

19. Cf. Popper's contribution in Radnitzky and Bartley (1987). Some misguided philosophers called this dissociation "alienation"; cf. Bartley (1985).

20. Hence, benefits and costs (benefits foregone) are subjective. Cf., e.g., Radnitzky's contribution (section 0.3) in Radnitzky and Bernholz (1987).

21. I am following Hirshleifer (1980) here, pp. 653 f.

22. The same holds good on the biological level: the fact that a species has survived so far is no guarantee that it will do so in the future; it also holds good in science. There is no guarantee that a highly successful theory may not be falsified later on.

23. Hirshleifer (1980), p. 653. An example of a trait that has survived although it appears to be on the way of becoming detrimental to a large part of mankind is the Darwinian breeding strategy. See, e.g., Colinvaux (1978), last chapter, and Hardin (1968).

24. Hirshleifer (1980).

25. Reciprocal giving approximates self-interested exchange among equals, while one-sided giving may have various motivations, e.g., to enhance status (as in "potlatch") or to avoid "excessive differences in wealth among members of the tribe.

26. Hirshleifer (1985).

27. Hirshleifer (1980), p. 662.

28. Knight (1955), p. 176.

29. The National Socialists made an explicit effort to return to this stage, and so do all socialist states today, at least in their rhetorics. Even the neo-Marxist Frankfurt school (Habermas, e.g.) use *privacy* and *privatization* as disparaging terms.

30. Hirshleifer (1987).

31. In the beginning, the primitive agricultural techniques reduced protein consumption, health, life-span, leisure, etc. Apparently, it was adopted because, when hunting grounds had been depleted, agriculture provided the means of surviving at least at a lower material level. Its only advantage over hunting and gathering was that of providing more calories per unit of land and hence of supporting denser populations.

32. Although in the Soviet Union the private plots constitute only about one percent of the land under cultivation, the Soviet press reports that approximately one-quarter of the total value of agricultural output is generated on these plots. Cf. e.g., Gwartney (1985), p. 45.

33. A large increase will, moreover, lower the average income—typically by adding to the population new people with low income, people who (like Marx's "proletariat") owe their very existence to capitalism. It will produce changes in average wealth, in the distribution of wealth, and so forth.

34. Simmel (1955), p. 62. (German original 1908, 1923, p. 217.) I am indebted to Jack Hirshleifer for drawing my attention to Simmel's work on conflict and competition.

35. Hayek has introduced these ideas in a seminal 1954 *American Economic Review* article entitled "The use of knowledge in society," and previously in the paper

"Economics and knowledge," which was published in 1937 in *Economia*. The problem of the collocation of knowledge and decision rights has been developed in Meckling and Jensen (1984) for the theory of the firm.

36. Meckling and Jensen (1984).

37. The Prisoner's Dilemma is eliminated only in a sociality governed by the rule of law. In a system characterized by totalitarian state power uncontrolled by the rule of law, both privileges and necessities of life (as well as tolerance) are instantly revocable by the political process. Hence, everybody is constrained as a matter of survival to collaborate with the authorities and also to sustain practices that harm themselves as well as others, such as, e.g., pre-emptive informing on neighbors. Hence, in a totalitarian state social life is "a vast, generalized Prisoner's Dilemma whose outcome is a stable political state of nature." Cf. Gray (1987).

38. Cf. Nozick (1974), Part I and Ullmann-Margalit (1978), p. 264.

39. Cf., e.g., Gray (1984), p. 35.

40. Hayek (1967), *Studies,* p. 102.

41. Hayek insists that the concept of justice is applicable only to *individual* conduct. This comment is important in view of the currently fashionable, socialist identification of justice—the idea of a "Just Society"—with a Procrustian enforcement of equality. Cf., e.g., the penetrating critique of Rawls in Flew (1980, 1981).

42. A striking illustration of Hayek's thesis is the relationship between constructed formal language systems and natural language. Formal systems are designed for very limited and well-defined tasks (primarily, for checking whether an argument is valid); the last metalanguage must be a natural language, and designers of a formal language could not even begin their construction unless they already had another language in which to work. A *chracteristica universalis* would mean the end of intellectual progress.

43. Incidentally, if one assumes that individuals behave as if they were attempting to maximize their reproductive success, then it would be a rational strategy for the male to invest resources in many wives (or, if paternity is very uncertain, in matrilineal inheritance), while for the female it would be rational to see to it that the family's resources are inherited by their sons in order to enable them to have many wives. Hence, there would be a conflict of interest between the father on one side and the mother with son(s) on the other side: an alternative explanation to the psychoanalytic explanation of the "Oedipus conflict."

44. Brunner (1984), p. 198.

45. Hirshleifer (1987).

46. Brunner and Meckling (1977), Vaubel (1985).

47. *The Wealth of Nations,* 1776, IV.II.9. Cf. also Ullmann-Margalit (1978), p. 278, which mentions an early occurrence of the idea of invisible-hand-explanation in Adam Smith's *The Theory of Moral Sentiments,* IV.1.10., which appeared in 1759. Incidentally, altruism in market transactions is an *inefficient* way to produce psychic income (Gary Becker 1977).

48. For a concise outline see, e.g., Gwartney (1985).

49. According to Hume there are three organizing principles, "three fundamental laws of nature," that make society possible: "Stability of possession, of its trans-

ference by consent, and of the performance of promises." Hume gives absolute priority of property rights: "No one can doubt, that the convention of the distinction of property, and for the stability of possessions is of all circumstances the most necessary to the establishment of human society." (*Treatise of Human Nature,* book III, part II, paragraph II; Hayek (1967), p. 43).

50. Cf., e.g. Hayek (1976), *LLL*:II, pp. 108 ff.

51. Hayek (1976), p. 110.

52. Real markets in capitalist countries exemplify a free market order only to a certain extent. Hayek has dealt extensively with the problem of the denationalization of *money,* but we still appear to be far from practical applications. The medieval doctrine of the "just price" has lingered on longest in the labor market, although, when relative demands for different types of skill are changing, the need for flexibility of relative as well as absolute wages should be obvious.

53. Hirshleifer (1980), p. 651.

54. Hirshleifer (1980), pp. 653, 663.

55. Gray (1986), MS p. 7.

56. This does not preclude that in some situations characterized by the non-enforceability of agreements the best-paying long-term strategy may be a willingness to cooperate combined with a robust determination to penalize non-loyal moves. What the best strategy is depends on the situation. If there are no *defect* players in the population, the *loyal* and *tit for tat* strategies are indistinguishable; if loyal becomes sufficiently numerous, defect becomes profitable again. Moreover, loyal and defect are easier to play than tit for tat, which is a demanding strategy. (Hirshleifer 1987).

57. Hirshleifer (1985), p. 68.

58. Popper (1944), *Poverty of Historicism* 1963 ed., pp. 61 f., 65, 67; the *locus classicus* is Hayek (1967), ch. 6; cf., especially pp. 96, 99.

59. E.g., Hayek (1979), *LLL,* Vol. III, p. 100; Moldofsky (1984), p. 41.

60. Colinvaux (1978), p. 219 f., Erben (1981). Two laws of nature govern the animal way of doing things: every species is constrained to a fixed niche and thereby the size of its population is fixed, and each mated couple behaves as if their aim was maximizing the number of offspring. As to the breeding strategy, man opted for the "large-young gambit," which can be successful only if an accurate choice of the optimum number of children is made; but to this day the necessity of abandoning the commons in breeding has scarcely been recognized (Hardin 1968, p. 1248).

61. From the economic point of view the situation appears as follows. In a tradition-governed society a family-supported system dominates. The family internalizes the problem of raising children as an investment good, because children are supposed to pay back the marginal cost for raising each child. This expectancy holds good only so long as the moral institution of filial obligations is effective. In this situation a Pareto-optimal allocation is likely: each family chooses the "right" number of children. With the transaction to the anonymous society the family-supported pension system is eroded and is replaced by a saving system, a private insurance system or a coercive social security system (with the ensuing free rider

problem). It is not unlikely that the politically-supported pension system may have been a factor contributing to the erosion of the family. Incidentally, for industrialized countries immigration rather than procreation is a new, and perhaps the most important, factor for endogenous population size; it may in turn be a function of the social security system. In affluent Western societies people perceive the opportunity costs of investing time in the education of children as high (servants who would reduce the influence of limited time being no longer available), and hence small families become the rule.

62. At least for certain regions, in particular in South America, it may be expected that the extended division of labor and trade made possible by an even higher population density would lead to an increase in material wealth.

63. Cf., e.g., Eibl-Eibesfeldt (1985), p. 438 ff on the importance of "privacy," "distance," etc., in various social and historical contexts.

64. Colinvaux (1978) p. 233.

REFERENCES

Andersson, G., ed. 1984. *Rationality in Science and Politics*. (*Boston Studies in the Philosophy of Science* Vol. 79), Dordrecht: Reidel.

Bartley, W. W., III. 1962. *The Retreat to Commitment*. New York, NY: Alfred A. Knopf; 2nd ed. Appendix, LaSalle, IL: Open Court 1984.

Bartley, W. W., III. 1985. "Knowledge is a Product Not Fully Known to its Producer," in Leube and Zlabinger 1985, pp. 17–45.

Bartz, S. 1979. "Evolution of Eusociality in Termites," *Proceedings of the National Academy of Sciences,* U.S.A. 76:5764–5768. (Corrections 1980, 77:3070).

Bernholz, P. 1985. *The International Game of Power.* Berlin/New York, NY: Mouton Publishers.

Bonner, J. 1980. *The Evolution of Culture in Animals*. Princeton, NJ: Princeton University Press.

Brenner, R. 1983. *History: The Human Gamble*. Chicago, IL: Chicago University Press.

Bridgeman, D., ed. 1983. *The Nature of Prosocial Development: Interdisciplinary Theories and Strategies*. New York, NY: Academic Press.

———. 1983. "The Perception of Man and Justice and the Conception of Political Institutions," in Machlup 1983, pp. 327–355.

Brunner, K. 1984. *Technological Change: Challenge and Consequences*. (*Working Paper Series,* No. GPB-84-4). Rochester, NY: Center for Research in Government Policy and Business.

Butler, E. and Pirie, M., eds. 1987. *Hayek on the Fabric of Human Society.* London: Adam Smith Institute.

Campbell, D. 1974. "Evolutionary Epistemology," in Schilpp 1974, pp. 413–463.

———. 1975. "On the Conflicts between Biological and Social Evolution," *American Psychologist,* December 30, 1975, p. 1120 (Presidential address).

———. 1983. "The Two Distinct Routes Beyond Kin Selection to Ultrasociality: Implications for the Humanities and Social Sciences," in Bridgeman 1983, pp. 11-42.

Cappelletti, V., B. Luiselli, G. Radnitzky, and E. Urbani, eds. 1983. *Saggi di storia del pensiero scientifico dedicati a Valerio Tonini.* Roma: Società Editoriale Jouvence.

Cohen, M. N. 1977. *Food Crisis in Pre-History.* New Haven, CT: Yale University Press.

Colinvaux, P. 1978. *Why Big Fierce Animals Are Rare: An Ecologist's Perspective.* Princeton, NJ: Princeton University Press.

Eibl-Eibesfeldt, I. 1982. "Warfare, Man's Indoctrinability and Group Selection," *Zeitschrift für Tierpsychologie* 60:177-198.

Eibl-Eibesfeldt, I. 1985. *Biologie des menschlichen Verhaltens.* München: Piper.

Erben, H. 1981. *Leben heißt Sterben. Der Tod des Einzelnen und das Aussterben der Arten.* Hamburg: Hoffman und Campe.

Flew, A. 1980a. "Who Are the Equals?" *Philosophia* (Israel) 9:131-153.

———. 1980b. "Justice: Real or Social?" *Social Philosophy & Policy* 1:151-171.

———. 1981. *The Politics of Procrustes. Contradictions of Enforced Equality.* Buffalo, NY: Prometheus Books; London: Temple Smith.

Goodall, J. 1976. "Continuities Between Chimpanzee and Human Behavior," in Isaac and McCown 1976, pp. 81-95.

Gray, J. 1984. *Hayek on Liberty.* Oxford: Basil Blackwell.

Gruter, M. 1982. "Biologically Based Behavioral Research and the Facts of Law," *Journal of Social and Biological Structures* 5:315-323.

Gwartney, J. 1985. "Private Property, Freedom and the West," *The Intercollegiate Review* 20:39-51.

Hardin, G. 1968. "The Tragedy of the Commons," *Science* 162:1243-48.

Hayek, F. V. 1944. *The Road to Serfdom.* Chicago, IL: University of Chicago Press.

———. 1945. "The Use of Knowledge in Society," *American Economic Review* Vol. 35, No. 4 (Sept.), repr. as pamphlet, Menlo Park, CA: Institute for Humane Studies, 1977.

———. 1960. *The Constitution of Liberty.* Chicago, IL: University of Chicago Press.

———. 1967. "The Result of Human Action but Not of Human Design," in his *Studies in Philosophy, Politics and Economics.* London: Routledge & Kegan Paul, pp. 96-105.

———. 1973. *Economic Freedom and Representative Government.* London: Institute of Economic Affairs.

———. 1973, 1976, 1979. *Law, Legislation and Liberty.* 3 vols. London: Routledge & Kegan Paul.

———. 1978. *New Studies in Philosophy, Politics and Economics.* London: Routledge & Kegan Paul.

———. 1985. "Le regole della morale non sono le conclusioni della nostra ragione" in Ricossa e di Robilant 1985, pp. 1-18.

Heinrich, B. 1979. *Bumblebee Economics*. Cambridge, MA: Harvard University Press.

Hirshleifer, J. 1978. "Natural Economy Versus Political Economy," *Journal of Social and Biological Structures* 1:319–337.

———. 1980. "Privacy: Its Origin, Function, and Future," *The Journal of Legal Studies* 9:649–664.

———. 1982. "Evolutionary Models in Economics and Law," *Research in Law and Economics* 4:1–60 (followed by commentary by various authors).

———. 1985. "The Expanding Domain of Economics," *The American Economic Review*, 75:53–68.

———. 1987. "The Economic Approach to Conflict," in Radnitzky and Bernholz 1987, 335–364.

Isaac, G. and E. McCown, eds. 1976. *Human Origins: Louis Leakey and the East African Evidence*. Menlo Park, CA: Benjamin Cummings.

Knight, F. 1947. *Freedom and Reform: Essays in Economics and Social Philosophy*. New York, NY: Harper & Brothers.

———. 1955. "Knowledge and its Methods in the Social Sciences," in Leary 1955, pp. 165–188.

Kuehnelt-Leddihn, D. 1985. *Die falsch gestellten Weichen. Der rote Faden 1789–1984*. Wien: Böhlau.

Lacy, R. C. 1980. "The Evolution of Eurosociality in Termites: A Haplodiploid Analogy," *American Naturalist* 116:449–451.

Lepage, H. 1985. *Pourquoi la propriété?* Paris: Hachette.

Leube, K. and Zlabinger, A., eds. 1985. *The Political Economy of Freedom: Essays in Honor of F. A. Hayek*. München/Wien: Philosophia Verlag.

Meckling, W. and M. Jensen, 1984. "Knowledge, Control and Organizational Structure," MS for the 11th Interlaken Seminar on Analysis and Ideology, 1984.

Moldofsky, N. 1985. "Open Society: Hayek vs. Popper?" *Economic Affairs* 5:38–43.

Nisbet, R. 1976. "The Fatal Ambivalence of an idea: Equal Freemen or Equal Serfs," *Encounter* 47:10–27.

North, D. 1981. *Structure and Change in Economic History*. New York, NY: Norton.

Nozick, R. 1974. *Anarchy, State, and Utopia*. New York, NY: Basic Books.

Olson, M. 1982. *The Rise and Decline of Nations*. New Haven, CT: Yale University Press.

Popper, K. 1945. *The Open Society and its Enemies*. 2 vols., London: Routledge & Kegan Paul, 11th ed., 1977.

———. 1957. *The Poverty of Historicism*. London: Routledge & Kegan Paul 9th ed., 1976 (first published in *Economica* 1944 and 1945).

———. 1972. *Objective Knowledge: An Evolutionary Approach*. London: Oxford University Press (5th rev. ed. 1979).

Radnitzky, G. 1983b. "The Science of man: Biological, Mental, and Cultural Evolution," in Cappelletti *et al.* 1983, pp. 369–401.

———. 1985a. "Réflexions sur Popper. Le savior, conjectural mais objectif, et indépendent de toute question: Qui y croit? Qui est à son origine?" Paris: *Archives de Philosophie* 48–79–108.

———. 1985b. "Sul fondamento epistemologico della filosofia della società aperta," in Ricossa e di Robilant 1985, pp. 21–49.

———. 1987a. "Cost-Benefit Thinking in the Methodology of Research: The 'Economic Approach' Applied to Key Problems of the Philosophy of Science," in Radnitzky and Bernholz 1987, pp. 283–331.

———. 1987b. "The Constitutional Protection of Liberty," in Butler and Pirie 1987, pp. 17–46.

———. 1987c. "Erkenntnistheoretische Probleme im Lichte von Evolutionstheorie und Ökonomie: Die Entwicklung von Erkenntnis-apparaten und epistemischen Ressourcen," in Riedl und Wuketits 1987, pp. 115–132.

———. and W. W. Bartley, III, eds. 1987. *Evolutionary Epistemology, Theory of Rationality, and the Sociology of Knowledge*. LaSalle, IL: Open Court.

———. and P. Bernholz, eds. 1987. *Economic Imperialism: The Economic Approach Applied Outside the Field of Economics*. New York, NY: Paragon House Publishers.

Ricossa, S. and E. di Robilant, eds. 1985. *Libertà, giustizia e persona nella società tecnologica*. Milano: A Giuffrà Editore.

Riedl, R. and F. Wuketits, eds. 1987. *Die evolutionäre Erkenntnistheorie*. Hamburg-Berlin: Parey Verlag.

Schilpp, P. A., ed. 1974. *The Philosophy of Karl Popper*. LaSalle, IL: Open Court.

Simmel, G. 1955. *Conflict and the Web of Group-Affiliations* (tr. R. Bendix). New York, NY: Free Press, (original: *Soziologie*. Berlin: Duncker & Humblot 1908, 2nd ed., 1923).

Smith, A. 1759. *The Theory of Moral Sentiment*. (Reprint: West, E., ed. Indianapolis: Liberty Classics 1976.)

———. 1776. *An Inquiry into the Nature and Causes of the Wealth of Nations*. (Reprint: Chicago, IL: University of Chicago Press, 1976.)

Tiger, L. R. Fox, 1971. *The Imperial Animal*. New York, NY: Dell.

Trivers, R. and H. Hare, 1976. "Haplodiploidy and the Evolution of Social Insects," *Science* 191:249–263.

Ullmann-Margalit, E. 1978. "Invisible-Hand Explanations," *Synthese* 39:263–291.

Vaubel, R. 1985 "A Public Choice Approach to International Organization," MS for the 12th Interlaken Seminar on Analysis and Ideology.

Waal, F. de. 1982. *Chimpanzee Politics*. London: J. Cape.

Willhoite, F. 1976. "Primates and Political Authority," *The American Political Science Review* 70:1110–1126.

Wilson, E. 1979. "The Evolution of Caste Systems in Social Insects," *Proceedings of the American Philosophical Society* 129 (4).

Winter, S. 1964. "Economic 'Natural Selection' and The theory of the Firm," *Yale Economic Essays* 4:225–272.

11

Note on von Hayek's Theory

ANGELO M. PETRONI

In this chapter I shall restrict my comments to certain points of Hayek's theory that have also been touched upon in Radnitzky's chapter in this volume. In particular, I shall criticize some of the fundamental ideas of Friedrich von Hayek about spontaneous order, whose work I greatly respect and admire. I wish to stress that the critical theses I shall put forward (and which are far from being original) do not concern those that have to be considered as the fundamental achievements of Hayek's political theory and political philosophy. It would be not too difficult to demonstrate that they are completely independent of his more recent—and, in my opinion quite dubious—social evolutionism.

Radnitzky's paper is not just a penetrating exposition of Hayek's ideas on social evolution and spontaneous order. In my opinion, it contains ideas which constitute a deep revision of some of the crucial concepts expressed by von Hayek since the early 1960s and which would be easy to show were *not* contained in his previous works—such as *The Constitution of Liberty.*[1]

In order to be more concise, I shall summarize my main critical thesis about von Hayek's ideas in two points. Of course, I shall have to express them in quite a crude way, without the required distinctions and nuances. Therefore my disagreement will appear greater than perhaps it really is.

No reasonably good definition of (social) "spontaneous order" is given by Hayek. This is a quite surprising but hardly deniable point. In all Hayek's works, the concept of spontaneous order is presented as if it were an almost self-evident idea, the full treatment of which can be found in the Scottish moralists of the Eighteenth century. Of course, it would be impossible to deny the importance of works by such giants as Adam Smith or Adam Ferguson, but it is equally difficult to accept that their ideas can be considered unquestionably true, and—more to the point—that they can be integrally and directly applied to our social and economic ("spontaneous") orders.

In the "Epilogue" of the third volume of *Law, Legislation and Liberty*, Hayek tried to link the concept of spontaneous (social) order to the more recent concept of self-organization in Prigogine's sense.[2] This is likely to be a promising research program. However as far as I know, we are far from having a theory of the so-called self-organizing physical systems which could be considered 1) a reasonably good foundation for *a* social and economic order,[3] and 2) a reasonably good foundation for von Hayek's primary (and perhaps *only*) example of spontaneous order, namely the *market* order. Of course, this second point is by far the most important for the purpose of our discussion, and it is also the most problematic for Hayek. It is worthwhile stressing that in both cases we cannot limit ourselves to the establishment of *analogical* patterns. Researches in a physical (or biological) field *may* have a heuristic value for the social theory, but they can never represent *per se* a "true" theory (or a theory at all) of social phenomena (including the economic phenomena). This would really be an example of scientism in the sense of Hayek.

Hayek does not produce good arguments in favor of the evolutionary superiority of the spontaneous order. He does not explain why the spontaneous order *had* to emerge from the evolutionary process. The fact that it emerged is merely taken as proof that it *is* the best kind of order. Of course, one could always answer that there is no need to give any justification for the superiority (or greater rationality, if one prefers) of the spontaneous order beyond the fact that it has emerged from the evolutionary process. However, this is a very unsatisfactory move, because it deprives *de jure* the concept of spontaneous order of any independent content. *Everything* which emerges from the evolutionary process would become, by definition, a spontaneous (and "superior" or "more rational") order. For example, if we accept this position, then the following remarks by James Buchanan becomes a devastating criticism of Hayek's theses: "Failure to understand the principle (of spontaneous order) has led, and will lead, to many ill-conceived and damaging interferences through the intrusion of political, governmental controls. But are not these intrusions themselves a part of general social evolution?"[4]

The example of market order can be considered a demonstration of my thesis. Of course, the "rationality" of market order (or, rather, its superiority over the other economic systems) can be argued in many different ways;[5] but there is no viable argument in Hayek which shows why this feature of the market does represent an *evolutionary* superiority over, say, planned economy. In many passages of his "recent" works Hayek affirms that it was the market order (and more generally, the spontaneous abstract social order) which made (and makes) possible the survival of the large numbers of individuals we know.[6] The increase in the size (or the absolute size?) of the group is exactly what Hayek considers an evolutionary success. But it is obvious that this fails to justify the evolutionary superiority (or greater rationality) of the market, given that other economic (and social) orders (Chinese communism, for example) *have* been by far more successful as far as the propagation of the group is concerned.

This is hardly surprising. The market is arguably the most efficient way of producing *and* allocating the goods and services people *want:* but this has nothing to do with the fact that the goods and services people want are good enough for the survival and the propagation of the group (or for satisfying any other criterion). If the aggregate preferences of the individuals are such as to let them prefer, say, diamonds and books on philosophy to food and steel, the market is the best way for satisfying their preferences: but it is likely that the probability of survival and propagation of this group will be lower than that of a group under a planned economy aimed at the production of food and steel.

The same criticism applies to Hayek's conception of the law. The system of abstract ("negative") rules of just conduct is arguably the best we can conceive in order to guarantee individual freedom *and* the working of the market. But there is no reason to expect that this system is also preferable from the evolutionary point of view. There is an indefinite number of situations in which it is conceivable that the group will survive (and propagate) and which will obey some non-abstract rules. There is absolutely no need to think (as Hayek does, it seems) that this will happen only under certain conditions (wars, natural catastrophes, etc.).

An important consequence of these points is that it is not possible to find a justification of the evolutionary superiority of *liberty*. Liberty *may* represent (under some well-specified "ecological" conditions) an evolutionary superiority for the group which practices it;[7] but we have absolutely no reason to expect that this holds under any *realistic* conditions. The fact that liberty (as well as the rule of law) is *de facto* such a rare (and precious) good (whose presence is manifestly not required at all for the biological survival and propagation of a population) can illustrate the point quite well.

Another important (even if trivial) consequence is that it is not possible to argue in favor of the validity of an economic, legal or social institution in the *future* on the basis of any description of its *origins*. Even if one could demonstrate the past evolutionary superiority of an institution (according to a given criterion) this would give no arguments in favor of its acceptance. To assume that the environment will be constant is obvi-

ously by far too unsatisfactory. Therefore, to argue in favor to the market
economy one must show that, under a reasonably wide range of possible
alternative environments, it will be the order which will better secure
"success." The *history* of the market economy will tell us nothing at all
about this point. Even if one could show that market economy prevailed
over another kind of economy, this would give us no logical *or* evolutionary reason in its favor as far as the future is concerned. Under new circumstances, the "old" economy could turn out to be more successful.

Of course, we have many good reasons for judging that a market
economy is the best instrument humans have to face a wide range of
possible changes in the environment (*e.g.,* lack of commodities or of energy). But all these arguments refer to the *structure* of the market order, not
to its origins or to its past achievements.

This point has in turn an important consequence as far as Hayek's
theses are concerned: his attempts to show that the market economy and
the law are the results of a process of cultural evolution have no interest at
all as far as their present and future validity is concerned. For example, in
trying to establish the superiority of law as a body of spontaneous evolved
rules over law as an act of will by the legislator, all Hayek's attempts to
show, *e.g.,* that "what we know about pre-human and primitive human
societies suggests a different origin and determination of law from that
assumed by theories which trace it to the will of a legislator,"[8] as well as to
show that even amongst some animals (as robins) some rules of conduct
hold which share many features with the rules of law, are irrelevant. The
great *historical* interest of such theses cannot be considered to be of theoretical value.

The problem of *property rights*—whose importance for the extended
order is stressed by Radnitzky—shows very well the difference between an
evolutionary and a theoretical approach. The contemporary most presti-
gious school of property rights[9] does not represent at all an attempt to find
some evolutionary features of the property rights. The theory is clearly
not historical. It is grounded on a theory of rational behavior—exactly
what Gary Becker's theory of human behavior is.[10] History is of interest as
long as it gives *examples* of relevant situations, but the historical/
evolutionary (social or economic) *process* as a whole has no importance in
producing a *theory* of property rights.

Radnitzky's analyses are undoubtedly fully informed of all these
difficulties of Hayek's positions. However, I am afraid that his attempts
to eliminate them are not in agreement with Hayek's evolutionary
principles.

One of Radnitzky's main departures is his strong acceptance of the
dichotomy between facts and values. "No amount of empirical knowledge
can decide a moral issue," and traditions and institutions, no matter what

their origins, can be evaluated on the basis of particular value systems. Once a value is given, we can formulate "hypothetical imperatives" on the basis of our empirical knowledge.[11]

According to Radnitzky, "Hayek's social and political philosophy has posited the *priority of liberty,* the autonomy, of the individual. Once the priority of liberty has been posited, the rest of the system can be derived with the help of empirical theories." I am very doubtful that this really happens. For the author of *Law, Legislation and Liberty* (but *not* for the author of *The Constitution of Liberty*) freedom is not a value which emerged from a deliberate attempt to implement it through institutional, legal or economic arrangements; it is an *unintended result* of those rules of conduct which made the group which had adopted them prevail. Once Hayek's theses about the rules of conduct and their evolutionary function have been posited, this becomes an inescapable conclusion. Independent of any question about theoretical validity, to assume that some rules of conduct have been deliberately adopted *because* the group knew that they would produce a free order would be contrary to the position often expressed by Hayek on this matter. We never "posit" any value, and we never *choose* the institutions that have to realize it. It is not a fortuitous case that Hayek seems not to accept, at the *social* level, the relevance of the "big divide"— facts/values.

To sum up, I think that Radnitzky's paper is more a restatement than an analysis of Hayek's ideas about spontaneous order. His rejection of the size of the group as a criterion for evaluating the success of a system of rules, his acceptance of the fundamental importance of *external* criticism related to genuine value standpoints, as well as his refusal to attribute optimality to the norms and institutions spontaneously evolved, deprives Hayek's social evolutionism of its main (and in my opinion, wrong) content. The consequences for the crucial problem of the *improvement* of a (social or economic) spontaneous order, and of the role for institutional reform, are not too far from those which follow from James Buchanan's criticism of Hayek's evolutionism. In another paper, I tried to defend Hayek's positions against Buchanan's criticism, but I am afraid that the reinterpretation I have given of the concept of spontaneous order is far from being acceptable to the author of *Law, Legislation and Liberty.* This reinterpretation implies that the spontaneous order in not a *fact,* but a kind of *Idealtypus.* Then, all Hayek's theses about, e.g., the (im)possibility of improving spontaneous orders should not be intended as referring to existing *real* "spontaneous" systems, but to the concept of spontaneous order. *If* a real order were a spontaneous order, *then* it would be true that it could not be improved by "interfering" in it. But this does not say anything about the possibility of *rationality* (*i.e.,* according to a recognizable and established rule or set of rules) improving an order which is only an approximation of the *Idealtypus* "spontaneous order." In order to be able to determine if an interference would destroy or improve (*e.g.*, in the sense of an higher efficiency) a given order, one should produce an *empirical* evaluation of the situation under examination. The answer cannot come as a theoretical (or "logical") consequence of the concept of spontaneous order.[12]

If I am right, it is very important to draw a sharp distinction between von Hayek's ideas about the evolution and the evolutionary value of spontaneous order from one side, and the content of his ideas about the *structure* of spontaneous order on the other. As I tried to point out, there is no necessary link between them. In particular, if we take the market order as a sort of "implicit definition" of what is meant for "spontaneous order," then none of the arguments in favor of the superiority of spontaneous order over other orders has to be linked to any evolutionary thesis—including the very dubious, semi-historical theses on the rising of the market order contained in his most recent masterpiece, which can perhaps be useful for producing a nice *als ob* story, but which are by far too general and aprioristic for having any significant historical/descriptive relevance.

NOTES

1. Hayek, *The Constitution of Liberty* (Chicago: The University of Chicago Press, 1960).

2. Hayek, *Law, Legislation and Liberty,* 3 vols. (London and Henley: Routledge & Kegan Paul, 1973, 1976, 1979), vol. III, pp. 158–159, and p. 200, note 33. An attempt to develop the analogy between Hayek's spontaneous order and the theories of self-organizing physical and biological systems has been provided by W. Weimer, in his 1983 ICUS paper "Spontaneously Ordered Complex Phenomena and the Unity of the Moral Sciences." Weimer's paper also contains a development of von Hayek's main epistemological theses about the nature (and the *limits*) of social sciences. I gave a criticism of these theses in my discussion paper "On 'Alleged Limitations and Constraints in the Unity of the Sciences.' Complex Phenomena and Simple Explanations." I think that Weimer's paper shows very well the deep difference between Hayek's conception of science and reason, and Popper's critical rationalism. To put it in a paradoxical way: if Popper tried to produce a *rational* theory of the tradition, von Hayek tries to produce a *traditional* theory of reason.

3. Even in a purely *prescriptive* sense.

4. Buchanan, "Law and the Invisible Hand," now in *Freedom and Constitutional Contract* (College Station, Texas: Texas A and M University Press, 1979, 25–39; p. 36). I discuss this point in my introduction to the Italian edition of *Law, Legislation and Liberty (Legge, legislazione e libertà)* (Milano: Il Saggiatore, 1986).

5. The two main contemporary defenses of the superiority of the market probably come from the neo-Austrian economics, and from the neo-Walrasian Arrow-Debreu general equilibrium theory. As it is well known, Hayek put forward a deep criticism of the whole general equilibrium theory approach. (On this topic see the interesting article by S. Littlechild, "Equilibrium and the Market Process," in I. Kirzner (ed.), *Method, Process, and Austrian Economics* (Lexington, Mass. and Toronto: Lexington Books, 1982, 75–102)). One of the main bases for his criticism was his view of the function of the market as a process of *discovery.* This function is also stressed by Radnitzky. However, it is important to note that we are faced here with a concept of discovery which is completely different from *scientific* discovery. Scientific discovery is the discovery of *laws;* the discovery in the market process is the discovery of *particular facts.* This difference has many important consequences. For example, even if one accepts the "Popperian" thesis of the impossibility of an algorithm for scientific discovery, this does not imply at all that an algorithm-like procedure is *de jure* impossible for discovering new particular facts in the market process. On this topic see A. Petroni and G. Scarampi, "On Herbert Simon's Logic of Discovery," forthcoming. For a criticism of Simon's theory of scientific discovery as far as the physical laws are concerned, see A. Petroni, *Dinamiche ed ellissi. Aspetti metodologici dell' "Astronomia Nova" di Giovanni Keplero* (Università di Pisa, tesi di laurea: 1982).

6. See for example F. von Hayek, *Law, Legislation and Liberty,* cit., vol. II, p. 147.

7. For example, because the individuals will follow a greater number of new patterns of behavior, and one of them could reveal itself to be extremely useful for the survival of the whole group.

8. Hayek, *Law, Legislation and Liberty,* vol. I, p. 73.

9. The names of Coase, Demsetz, Alchian, and Pejovich are among the best known.

10. See G. Becker, *The Economic Approach to Human Behavior* (Chicago: The University of Chicago Press, 1976).

11. I disagree with the justification Radnitzky gives of the dichotomy facts/values. According to Radnitzky, "Deducing a genuine (i.e. non-instrumental) value judgment from premises that have a purely descriptive function in the argument at hand is logically impossible, since ampliative inferences are not valid." I fail to see why there would be an "ampliative" inference. If it is true that "no amount of empirical knowledge can decide a moral issue," it is by far more true that no amount of moral knowledge can decide an empirical issue! Why it would not be equally "ampliative" an inference from an "ought" statement to an "is" statement? On the problem of "ought" statements and ampliative inferences see W. W. Bartley, III, "Logical Strength and Demarcation," in G. Andersson (ed.), *Rationality in Science and Politics* (Dordrecht: Reidel, 1984), 63–93, and my review-article of this volume in "Methodology and Science," 18:62–71 (1985).

12. See J. Buchanan's "Cultural Evolution and Institutional Reform," unpublished, and *The Limits of Liberty* (Chicago and London: The University of Chicago Press, 1975), chapter 10 (in particular p. 167); see also my "Introduzione." It is important to stress that even if it is impossible to attribute optimality to the institutions spontaneously evolved, this does not imply that Buchanan's theses about the possibility of rationally improving a spontaneous and complex order are true. Of

course, it is not difficult to produce examples of situations which can be made more efficient by changes in their ("institutional") structure. (Buchanan considers the case of a littered beach; cf. his "Law and the Invisible Hand"). But Buchanan does not give any demonstration that these examples have any value as far as more complex orders are concerned. There is an enormous difference between the reform of the institutional structure of a simple situation such as the littering of a beach, and the reform of the institutional structure of a state. In the first case, we assume that it is possible to know all the relevant elements of the situation (including the *aims* of the individuals—*at least,* their aim of having a non-littered beach). But this is exactly what does *not* happen (*de facto,* even if not *de jure,* as Hayek suggests) when we consider spontaneous ("complex") orders such as the market order or the legal order. Therefore, even if we have good reasons in favor of the non-optimality of such real orders, this does not imply that it is possible to undertake a rational modification of the institutional structure aimed at improving, e.g., its efficiency. Of course, this does not mean that a successful "reform" cannot *de facto* be realized. But the crucial point is that we have no rational (or "scientific," if one prefers) criteria for recognizing *a parte ante* those reforms which will be successful—or which are more likely to be successful. Under these hypotheses, the success will be due to chance, not to knowledge.

12

Self-Organization and Technological Change in the Economic System

ROBERT U. AYRES

1. INTRODUCTION

The second law of thermodynamics has been causing confusion and consternation since it was first formulated by Clausius in 1847. Once it was clearly recognized that processes are of two distinct kinds—reversible and irreversible—and that entropy is unchanged in the former but increases in the latter, an evolutionary principle or law of sorts was evident for the physical universe. This follows from the fact that *isolated* thermodynamic systems not at equilibrium (but near it) *must approach equilibrium irreversibly*, since equilibrium is characterized—in fact, defined—by maximum entropy. Moreover, since entropy in an isolated system never decreases (according to the second law), no such system can depart further from equilibrium than it is to start with. However many irreversible processes, being irreversible, tend to push the system in the direction of thermodynamic equilibrium, unless acted upon by external forces.

The discouraging aspect of the situation is that thermodynamic equilibrium is a changeless state in which all matter is uniformly distributed and there are no temperature or concentration differences—hence no gradients and no structure or order.[1] If the universe continues to expand physically without limit, such an asymptotic limit might be envisioned: Nernst called it "heat death" (Warmetöd) of the universe. It is a state of absolute uniformity and maximum disorder or mixing.

Almost at the same time thermodynamics was being developed, Charles Darwin's theory of biological evolution by the mechanism of natural selection was also formulated. Notwithstanding some severe challenges from physicists (notably William Thompson, Lord Kelvin) during the 19th century.[2] Darwin's work in biology presented a clear and convincing story of evolution of living systems towards ever-increasing complexity and structure/organization, at least on the Earth's surface, culminating in the development of the human brain. Given the fossil record and other evidence, this trend towards increasing organization appears indisputable. It can be argued that order is not necessarily the same as organization though the concepts are clearly related. But, for a long time, it was very hard to reconcile Darwin's theory with the second law of thermodynamics. On the other hand, there has been no convincing evidence of any absolute contradiction between biological evolution and thermodynamics.

New developments in mathematics and in non-equilibrium, non-linear thermodynamics in the past three decades have created the basis for such a reconciliation. In particular, Glandsdorff, Nicolis and Prigogine (1971, 1977) have constructed models of simple chemical systems that exhibit stable, coherent "self-organizing" behavior, yet are far from thermodynamic equilibrium. Eigen (1971) has even convincingly shown how complex macromolecules can reproduce themselves from simple "building blocks" via stable "hypercycles," but can also evolve by random mutation (copying errors) and selection according to an optimization principle that is definable in molecular terms.

Modern physicists are beginning to use the term *essergy*[3] which will be adopted hereafter. Lotka 1945 suggested that the direction of evolution could be explained in terms of ability to capture and utilize energy from the environment. Unfortunately the term *energy* in this context is clearly inappropriate since it is only the component that is available to do "work" that matters. Intuitively, this hypothesis helps explain at least two observable aspects of biological evolution.

- Organisms that use essergy (food) most efficiently will tend to compete most effectively, *ceteris paribus,* within a given niche.
- Organisms will evolve to utilize any and all available sources of essergy, including wastes. This implies ever-increasing diversity: the development of specialized scavengers and parasites, as well as a hierarchy of predators.

However, it is still unclear whether Lotka's maximum principle (or its equivalent expressed in terms of essergy) is equivalent truly to Darwin's principle of natural selection on the basis of "survival of the fittest." Nor is it clear that Lotka's principle could be explained by Eigen's micro optimization principle. That question also lies outside the scope of this paper.

2. ORDER, ENTROPY AND INFORMATION

As noted previously, there is a critical distinction between two usages of
the term "order." The first, which we retain, is order-in-
(thermodynamic)-equilibrium. It is exemplified by the formation of a
crystalline solid such as a snowflake. The second kind of order occurs in
systems that are stable in some sense but far from thermodynamic equilibrium, maintained so by a continuous renewable flow of essergy from
outside the system. Examples range from relatively simple chemical systems such as the "Brusselator" (Nicolis and Prigogine 1977) or the "Ore-
gonator" (Field 1985) to living cells (Schrödinger 1945). A rotating "top"
maintaining its dynamic equilibrium against the force of gravity offers a
mechanical example of the same kind of phenomenon.

For most chemical systems—and some physical systems, as it
happens—the concept of thermodynamic equilibrium is well-defined and
characterized by a minimum value of G, the Gibbs free energy.[4] The
forces driving the system toward equilibrium in a chemical system are
also well-defined and, in simple cases, can be expressed quantitatively as
a function of "distance" (ΔG) from equilibrium. In general, the governing relationships are non-linear. It has been shown that, for open systems
far from equilibrium, non-linear equations can have multiple solutions,
only one of which reduces to the solution of the linearized equation that
describes the situation near equilibrium. (Glansdorff and Prigogine 1971,
Nicolis and Prigogine 1977).

Far from equilibrium there are solutions corresponding to situations
where G is at a local, but not global, minimum. Such a state may characterize a non-isolated system at finite temperatures and entropy (because
of the negative term TS in the free energy function) but it depends on a
continuous inflow of essergy from the environment. Such stable states
tend to involve "coherent" behavior, which is equivalent to long-range
order in phase space. The term "dissipative structure" has been applied
to such systems by Nicolis and Prigogine (1977). Transitions from the
disordered state to a coherent (ordered) state of a system can occur suddenly. Such transitions, between two solutions of a non-linear equation,
have been classified topologically and termed "catastrophes" by the mathematician Thom (1972).

Unfortunately, in most complex open systems equilibrium conditions cannot be specified in explicit terms and in highly organized/
structured biological systems, for instance, the notion of long-range
correlation seems inappropriate. Indeed, thermodynamic variables may
not be definable at all. It is simply assumed that in such cases, "forces"
driving the system toward equilibrium are zero at equilibrium and increase, in general, with "distance." Again the (unknown) equation governing reaction rates is likely to be non-linear, with multiple solutions,

only one of which corresponds to the linear near-equilibrium case. However, detailed quantitative examples of such behavior are still scarce.

As noted above, the notions of order in the two situations are very different. Boltzmann's famous "order principle"—relating order to entropy—is not universally valid and, in any case, applies only in the near-equilibrium case (termed the "thermodynamic branch" by Glansdorff and Prigogine). Away from equilibrium, however, entropy can still be defined in terms of Boltzmann's rule

$$S = k \ln W$$

where W is a measure of the number of "complexions" or the inherent probability of an eigenstate of the system and k is the so-called Boltzmann constant. However, order may have to be defined independently of entropy for a dissipative structure. Intuitively, the orderliness of a structure such as DNA molecule is a function of its complexity or, equivalently, *the amount of information needed to describe it.* This is a perfectly well-defined concept, applicable in principle to any system, including physical, chemical, biological, social and even technological systems. It even offers a bridge between the various disciplines.

Information, like energy, is a primitive. It cannot really be defined in terms of anything more fundamental, notwithstanding Shannon's characterization of information as "reduction of uncertainty." Information is what communications channels transmit and what computers process. It is absolutely required for purposes of decision-making and control. It is conventionally measured in "bits" and both channel capacity and computer power are measured in bits/s.

The existence of a close relationship between information and entropy has been suspected since the 19th century debates on irreversibility and "Maxwell's demon." There is strong assertion of equivalence, due to Brillouin (1953), based in part on an earlier paper by Szilard (1929). Assume a Maxwell demon operating a valve between two chambers and shunting fast ("hot") molecules into one chamber and retaining slow ("cold") molecules in the other chamber. In time, a finite temperature gradient would be observable and the total entropy of the system would decrease. But, to select "hot" and "cold" molecules the demon requires information about the state of each approaching molecule in order to decide on the correct control valve setting. Acquisition of this information—first called "negentropy" by Brillouin (1951)—in turn, results in an entropic increase within the closed system at least as big as the decrease achieved by the activity of the "valve demon."

In modern information theory, developed principally by Claude Shannon (1948), a measure of inherent uncertainty with regard to the (information) content of a message was introduced.[5] This measure closely resembles the Boltzmann statistical definition of entropy above. It was so named at the suggestion of John von Neumann (Tribus and McIrvine, 1971), although the identity was originally based on the mathematical form alone. However, Jaynes (1957) soon rederived the basic theorems of statistical mechanics from information theory by an entropy maximization principle, and Tribus (1961) showed that the laws of thermodynamics can also be derived from information theory in this way. Thus, the identity of information and negentropy is now widely regarded by physicists as real, not formal—not withstanding the contrary assertion by Georgescu-Roegen, among others who continue to insist on a distinction between living organisms and "mechanisms."

The physical identification of information with negentropy suggests the possibility that "stocks" of information—in particular, technological information—can be regarded in some sense as reserves or storehouses of negative entropy that can be utilized to *increase the autonomy of dissipative systems*. This perspective will be further examined later.

3. INFORMATION AND ORGANIZATION

Three new notions are suggested by the identification of information stocks with negative entropy: first, a dissipative·structure far from equilibrium may conceivably "store" negative entropy for future use in the form of organization or structure. Second, *intelligence* can be tentatively defined as the ability of a dissipative system to capture and store (or embody) negentropy in structure. By this definition, all living organisms are intelligent to some degree, but intelligence need not be restricted to biological organisms. The third new idea is that intelligence as defined above is the argument of Eigen's maximization principle (1971). From this point on, incidentally, I will generally be talking about very complex systems which are self-evidently dissipative, but for which no straightforward quantitative relationship between reaction rate and "distance from equilibrium" can be defined. Biological organisms, ecosystems, human societies and techno-economic systems all fall under this heading.

That organisms capture disembodied information from the environment and "store" it in physical structures is obvious on reflection. The gene itself is nothing more or less than a packet of information in molecular form (Schrödinger, 1945). It contains both morphological and functional information needed by the organism. The information embodied in genes tells cells how and when to divide, how and when to differentiate and how to manufacture various enzymes, hormones, etc. It also tells the organism as a whole how to react to various stimuli, what food to eat, when and how to mate, where to lay eggs, etc. This information store is the result of a long evolutionary learning process, described by Darwin as natural selection and by Eigen as "value maximization." The cumulative nature of the process is evident from the fact that the higher organisms, arriving later on the evolutionary scene, carry far more genetic information than the simplest, earliest organisms (Figure 12-1). The ability of the higher organisms to reproduce this information can be regarded as evidence of increasing intelligence in the sense defined above.

As to the use of "stored negentropy-as-structure" to cut down on the need for a continuous flux of essergy, Polgar (1961) has identified four mechanisms—viz. persistence, replication, environmental modification and social evolution. On deeper reflection Polgar's classification is unsatisfactory, since self-replication and environmental modification are merely two mechanisms for extending the life of a system. In this sense "self modification" must surely be considered as another one.

At the molecular (i.e. genetic) level, Schrodinger (1945) showed that persistence, as reflected by the low rate of natural mutation, can be explained in terms of quantum mechanics—in particular, the non-continuity or continuity of possible states. At the level of chemical systems—recently applied to order-disorder phenomena in physics—Glansdorff, Nicolis, Prigogine et al. (1971, 1977) have given an explanation of persistence in terms of non-equilibrium thermodynamics.

Replication is, of course, one of nature's basic long term survival (and growth) mechanisms. A detailed understanding of replication at the cellular level may still be years away, but the famous discovery of the double helix structure of DNA and the so-called genetic code, provided a very useful starting point (Crick 1962). The other important natural means whereby living systems ensure their own long-term survival are by self-modification and environmental modification. The former has been explained, at the macro-level, by Darwin's theory of natural selection, and at the micro-level of Eigen (1971) and Dyson (1982) and need not be discussed here at length.

By comparison, environmental modification has received much less attention, though it is enormously important. Living organisms have modified the atmosphere and the ocean enormously over the past 2 billion years (Oparin 1953). The earth's primordial atmosphere was mostly carbon dioxide (CO_2) and water (H_2O) plus methane (CH_4) and ammonia (NH_3) with *no* free oxygen or nitrogen, while the primitive oceans were much smaller and saltier. Life as we know it today could not survive in such an environment.[6] Environmental modification in some form is still practiced today at the micro-level by viruses (upon their host cells), by wasps that paralyze their prey and lay eggs in them, by every nest-building species, and on the meso-level by some animals such as beavers. On a larger scale, tropical forests create their own macro-environment. (Deforestation in the tropics commonly leads to desertification). Coral reefs are the undersea analog. Of course, human activities such as agriculture and fossil fuel consumption have enormous environmental impact, which we need not consider here at length.

Another way in which negentropy-as-structure in the biosphere operates to cut down on the essergy flux per unit of biomass (and thus to retard the rate of global entropy increase) is by means of species diversity and specialization. Most of the biomass on the earth (by weight) is vegetation that extracts essergy directly from sunlight by photosynthesis. Assume a population of efficient specialized plants of one species. Each such community would, in principle, reach some stable natural level of total biomass depending on the availability of some limiting factor—usually water or a mineral nutrient. The critical role of limiting factors—notably trace nutrients—in agriculture was first pointed out by Leibig in 1876 (Lotka 1950). At this point, photosynthetic production would automatically adjust itself to satisfy replacement needs only. If water were the limiting factor, new plants could only grow after old ones had released their soluble mineral contents back into the environment.[7] This is exactly the situation in the Amazon basin today.

How does species diversity alter the situation? The key is that there must be relationships between function and structure. For instance, a second species of plant having a different function (i.e. a different niche) will have a different *structure*—hence a different microcomposition. The second plant can be expected to require a somewhat different combination of inputs from the first, so that the limiting factor will be different. Thus the total biomass of two species combined can generally be larger than that of either alone. A third species, with a different specialization, can add still more to the total biomass without exhausting the available resources.

The remarkable fact is that a hierarchy of animals can live off the plant kingdom (and each other) without depleting the resource base because continuous harvesting actually increases the photosynthetic activity level of the plants. In fact, every homeowner knows that grass grows faster immediately after it has been cut. Commercial logging is similarly predicated on the fact that young trees grow faster than mature ones. Agriculture is based on the same phenomenon: it is a general law of ecology that young plant communities are the most photosynthetically productive. The role of animals and decay organisms, then, is to maximize the overall productivity level of the photosynthesizers by efficiently recycling minerals (and where it is scarce, water). Deliberate fertilization and irrigation by humans is a straightforward extension of this natural phenomenon.

The lowest trophic level of animals obtain their food mainly as carbohydrates or cellulose, directly from photosynthetic plants. Higher animals, in turn, are able to exploit lower animals and obtain their food mainly as proteins and fats which are more useful and easier to digest. The top predators are therefore able to eat and digest much less bulk than they otherwise would have to by consuming foods more similar to their own tissues and more easily broken down to sugars and amino acids for reassembly. This enables active carnivores to consume more food (essergy) but spend much less time eating and digesting than the herbivores they prey on.

Significantly, the amount of genetic information required to reproduce an organism tends to increase with its trophic level in the predator-prey hierarchy. So, in general, does the information processing capacity of the organism itself: the processing capacity of its brain and central nervous system increase with trophic level (Figure 12-1). For higher mam-

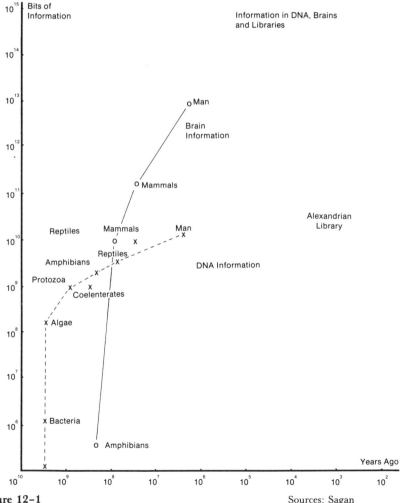

Figure 12-1

Sources: Sagan
Dragons of Eden

mals, the storage capacity of the brain vastly exceeds the storage capacity of the genetic material.

The situation sketched above is comparable for animal and human social systems and for the economic system. Humans are not the first organisms in nature to transmit non-genetic information from generation to generation. Most mammals and birds teach their young to some degree at least. Humans are, however, the first species to store non-genetic information in external repositories (e.g. libraries) that are maintained by the society as a whole.[8] Moreover, in recent centuries, this kind of intergenerational information accumulation and transfer has quantitatively approached, if not surpassed, the genetic transfer process, as indicated in Figure 12-2.

In the case of a human society, the systematic use of stored information to simplify the food gathering and production process need hardly be elaborated. Knowledge about plant reproduction, animal behavior,

Figure 12-2: Computers vs. Living Systems

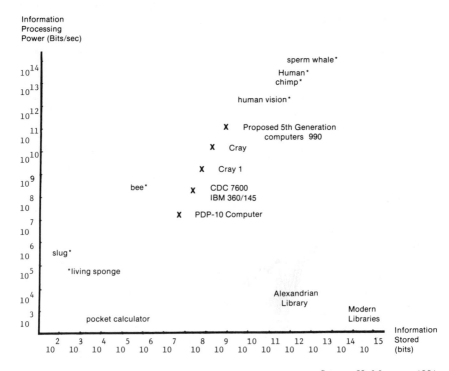

Source: H. Moravec, 1981

weather, climate, geography and even astronomy[9] had an immediate pay-off in terms of increasing the ability of a human population to support itself and prosper in prehistoric times. At first, much of this knowledge was acquired by accident. More recently, the application of knowledge to increase production has become increasingly systematic and intentional. The process of learning about nature and applying that knowledge for the benefit of man is now institutionalized, as will be discussed later.

The notion of "pure" technological information as an effective sub-stitute for resource inputs is suggested by the notion of using embodied information (knowledge) to increase the efficiency of capture of "natural" information in the form of essergy. The equivalence is neatly summarized by the proverb: "Give a man a fish and he can feed his family for a day. Teach him how to fish and he can feed his family forever." Ancient man obtained copper, silver, iron and other metals from nearly pure nuggets. Modern man has learned how to obtain these metals (and others) from low grade ones. As one resource is exhausted, typically, another is ex-ploited. Thus charcoal gave way to coke, and whale oil was replaced by kerosene. As the demand for motor gasoline grew rapidly in the early twentieth century, means of increasing the gasoline and octane output from each barrel of crude oil were actively sought. Using sophisticated modern refinery technology, and anti-knock additives, the gasoline recov-ery fraction has risen from 15 percent to as much as 60 percent of each barrel, while average octane levels have almost doubled from about 50 (for natural gasoline) to over 90 in the late 1960's. This, in turn permits higher engine compression ratios and correspondingly higher levels of thermal efficiency. Thus technological knowledge has enormously in-creased the amount of useful transportation work that can be extracted from crude oil.[10] It is not unreasonable to characterize this enhancement as embodied knowledge (intelligence) added by the techno-economic system.[11]

A final observation is relevant: the vast storehouse of fossil fuels in the earth's crust that humans are currently exploiting (and using up) is an accumulation of "surplus" natural negentropy left over from incompletely decayed living organisms in earlier geological periods. It is stored (from a molecular perspective) as chemical structure, i.e. energy-rich hydrocar-bon molecules that are quite stable at ambient temperatures, but which combine exothermically with oxygen above ignition temperature. Obvi-ously, humans will have to find other energy sources to replace hydrocar-bons within a century, more or less. It is already clear that several alternative possibilities exist,[12] though all of them will require large capital (i.e. stored information) investments, not to mention technologies more advanced than is currently available. In any case, some surplus negen-tropy in the form of capital will have to be set aside from the existing fossil fuel store to "finance" the eventual changeover.

4. THE ECONOMIC SYSTEM AS A DISSIPATIVE STRUCTURE

Economists do not normally think of economic activities and relationships in thermodynamic terms. When economists talk about equilibrium they refer to a balance between supply and demand, or (looking at it another way) between prices, wages and profits. Neo-classical economic models consider labor, capital goods and services to be abstractions. The exception is resource/environmental economics where some physical properties (e.g. mass, toxicity) cannot be neglected.

The proof of the existence of a static equilibrium (conjectured by Walras in 1877 finally proved by Arrow and Debreu in 1951) was one of the great achievements of neo-classical economics because it seems to provide a theoretical explanation for Adam Smith's price-setting "invisible hand." There can be no question that the operation of a money-based free competitive market generates a kind of coherence, or long-range order, in contrast to the unstable price/wage anarchy that prevails in a barter society, for instance.[13] The static competitive free-market based economic system described in textbooks does reflect a kind of order very similar to cooperative phenomena in physics. It has also been proved that an idealized market-based system tends to a so-called Pareto-optimum—a situation where nobody can be better off without making somebody else worse off—although it does not necessarily allocate resources equitably. (Equity is, of course, a moral concept.) Finally, the market system is, in theory, self-regulating and capable of recovering from a perturbation in demand, for instance.

Even the abstract model of the economic system depends on resource *inputs,* although in a closed Walrasian model resources are assumed to be generated by labor and capital. Thus the neoclassical system is, in effect, a perpetual motion machine.[14] In reality, these resource *inputs* are physical: they include air, water, sunlight and material substances, fuels, food and fiber crops, all of which embody thermodynamically available work (essergy). *Outputs,* on the other hand, are "final goods" that are ultimately used up and thrown away or, in rare cases, recycled. Available work is expended at every state, viz. extraction, refining, manufacturing, construction and even final consumption (Ayres 1978). Though total energy is always conserved, essergy is not. Energy inputs such as fossil fuels are rich in essergy, while energy outputs are mostly in the form of low temperature waste heat, oxidation products, or degraded materials. Thus, the economic system, in reality, is absolutely dependent on a continuing flow of essergy from the environment. In pre-industrial times, it was the sun that provided almost all essergy in the form of wood, food, crops, animals, water power or windpower. Today, the major source, by far, is fossil fuels: petroleum, natural gas and coal from earth's crust. These resources are exhaustible, of course.

Evidently the real economic system looks somewhat like a "dissipative structure" in Prigogine's sense: it is dependent on a continuous flow of essergy (the sun, or fossil fuels) as well as information in more familiar form—not instantly recognized as essergy—and it exhibits coherent orderly behavior. In fact, it is self-evidently capable of growth. Economic growth can be of two distinct kinds. First, an economic system can (in principle) expand like a balloon without technological or structural change. It simply gets bigger, as capital and labor inputs increase proportionally. This kind of quasi-static growth can lead to increased final consumption per capita while maintaining its equilibrium, but only by producing more of everything, in fixed ratios. (This is only possible if there are no economies or diseconomies of scale, which is an unrealistic but common economic assumption.) The second kind of growth also involves evolutionary changes in structure. These changes are driven by innovations—new products, new processes—resulting not only in quantitative increases in per capita consumption, but also in qualitative changes in the mix of goods and services generated by the economy. In general this kind of growth results in increased complexity and organization.

Quasi-static growth of the first kind can be modeled theoretically as an optimal control model with aggregate consumption (or welfare) as the objective function. The control variable is the rate of savings diverted from immediate consumption to replace depreciated capital and add new capital to support a higher level of future consumption.[15] The rate of growth in this simple model is directly proportioned to the rate of savings which, in turn, depends on the assumed depreciation rate and an assumed temporal discount rate to compare present versus future benefits. Note that assumptions about the operation of the market play almost no role in this type of growth model. Savings, in this model, can be enforced or voluntary by the government.

It is noteworthy (and unfortunate) that most economic development programs in the Third World are based on the generalized Harrod-Domar model assuming a primary role for aggregate capital investment and depending on central planners to maintain balance between the capital needs of various sectors.[16] Empirical research carried out as early as the 1950's established quite clearly that economic growth in the U.S. *cannot* be accounted for primarily in terms of increased capital inputs (Abramovitz 1956, Fabricant 1954, Solow 1957). In fact, the linked notion of increasing factor productivity as a reflection of technological progress was introduced into economics at this time (Kendrick 1956). The relatively poor performance of most centrally planned economic development programs is probably due in part to their focus on investment *per se,* to the detriment of structural adjustment and innovation.

Dynamic growth of the second, evolutionary, kind is less dependent on savings and/or capital investment. However, it cannot occur *without* capital investment since new production technologies, in particular, are largely embodied in capital equipment. Technological innovation is the driver of this kind of dynamic growth, as will be discussed later. There is ample evidence, incidentally, that technological progress is not an autonomous (i.e. self-organizing) process. On the contrary, knowledge and inventions are purposefully created by individuals and institutions in response to incentives and signals generated within and propagated by the larger socioeconomic system. The techno-system is discussed next.

5. THE TECHNOSYSTEM

The technosystem is, by definition, the creator of new techniques, new products and new applications. Its activities can and do enable an economy to grow beyond the limits set by any given level of technology by finding more efficient methods to exploit existing resources, discovering new sources, or finding viable substitutes, and discovering new products and processes. The technosystem operates within the larger economic framework, however.[17] In particular, it is the macro-system that determines both the demand for technology and its supply. The impressions of certain social critics to the contrary, technology is not an autonomous or self-acting force outside its economic context.

A debate has raged for many decades over the extent to which technology is created in response to exogenously determined demand, *vis a vis* the extent to which supply, in this case, may sometimes create its own demand—a variant of Say's law in economics. Extensive empirical work by economists and sociologists of science tends toward the view that perceived demand is by far the dominant factor. That is to say, most successful inventors/innovations and most industrial R & D establishments have responded to a clearly articulated need by consumers, government or industry itself. On the other hand, it could be argued that occasionally a spectacular technological opportunity comes along before there is any immediate need for it. The laser, invented in the early 1960's, seems to be one example. Genetic engineering may be another. But, in both cases, major future applications were immediately obvious—to the point of stimulating continuing R & D expenditures.

Quite apart from the question of primacy of demand versus supply, however, it is clear that the economic (and political) framework determines the pattern of prices (including wages) and profits that actually govern the existing allocation of societal resources to, and within, the technosystem.

The pattern of prices, wages and profits constitute a set of signals, transmitted by society as a whole (i.e., consumers, government and industry) that constitute a guide for individual decisions, through established market mechanisms. For example, enrollment in engineering schools, which compete with liberal arts schools, directly reflects engineering salaries and job prospects in different fields. Similarly, investment moves out of stagnant or unprofitable sectors and into profitable growing sectors.

Signals are sometimes confused, as when government interference or private collusion distort the operations of the competitive market. In addition, there are pervasive market imperfections. Some of these can only be compensated for by government action. One of these imperfections is the inherent difficulty of protecting technological information, which makes it relatively easy for imitators and "free riders" and inhibits the development of an effective market for exchanging technological knowledge in pure form (i.e. not embodied in a product). This, in turn, makes it impossible for those who invest in new knowledge to capture more than a small fraction of the benefits, in most cases. The consequence is to discourage such investment by the private sector. Since the private sector tends to underinvest in R & D, the public sector must make up the gap—particularly in those areas where the private incentives are most lacking.[18]

6. THE ECONOMIC MECHANISM DRIVING TECHNOLOGICAL PROGRESS

It is axiomatic that technological progress is dependent on the knowledge base, and that the knowledge base can be increased, at the margin, by deliberate investment in R & D. The question of interest is: Why should individuals or enterprises invest in R & D? This is tantamount to asking: How and why does an R & D investment pay off in economic terms? The general outlines of an answer to this question have been clear for some time. Many detailed outlines of an answer to this question have been clear for some time. Many detailed issues, however, still remain to be cleared up. However, in contrast to the case of "quasi-static" economic growth, which is driven by savings and does not depend on market structure, there is reason to believe that market structure plays a significant role in the process of technology creation. Joseph Schumpeter, in 1912, first pinpointed the driving force underlying dynamic economic growth as technological innovation by entrepreneurs seeking "supernormal" profits. Such profits arise from a temporary monopoly position conferred by each innovation until successful imitators are able to enter the market.

This simple conception seems to solve the main problem of neoclassical economics at a stroke by providing at once a qualitative explanation of several phenomena: the existence of supernormal profits, capital accumulation from profits, technological obsolescence and "technological progress." Schumpeter regarded formal R & D as a vital mechanism for corporations—especially large ones—to develop a stream of new and innovative products to maintain a level of profits higher than could be achieved in a quasi-static free competitive market (where competition drives profits toward zero). Unfortunately, Schumpeter occupied himself in later years primarily with questions of business cycle theory and political economy (and, for a time, government) and did not work out the full range of implications of his idea. Schumpeter's simple conceptual model also, unfortunately, left a number of key questions unanswered.

Modern theorists tend to associate Schumpeter with two specific hypotheses, (e.g. Kamien and Schwartz, 1982)

1. There is a positive correlation between innovation and supernormal monopoly-profits.
2. Large firms tend to be proportionately more innovative than small firms, *ceteris paribus*. (This notion was more fully discussed later by Galbraith 1952).

The first Schumpeterian hypothesis involves two possible causal relations between innovation and monopoly. On the one hand innovation may facilitate achieving monopoly power and profits as originally postulated. But, on the other hand, monopoly power may make it easier to innovate, as he suggested. The second relationship is more controversial. Under various assumptions, monopoly power may either encourage or discourage further innovation. Positive correlation may arise from technological spinoffs, brand-name identity, product "bundling," common channels of distribution, or the ability to respond quickly to a rival innovation. Another cause may be an enhanced ability to finance innovations internally. On the other hand, a firm enjoying supernormal monopoly profits (and expecting them to continue indefinitely) might in some cases have less inherent incentive to take risks to increase them than a firm with normal profits only. In effect, firms may be characterized by declining marginal utility of profits (e.g. Arrow 1962, Usher 1964).

Ultimately, the validity of the Schumpeterian hypotheses must be resolved by empirical study. Unfortunately, there are enormous difficulties in defining innovations and measuring R & D inputs, firm size and/or degree of monopoly power, not to mention problems of interpretation. A large number of statistical studies have been carried out, using many different data sets and surrogate measures. (See Kamien and Schwartz 1982, pp. 49–104.) The empirical data tend to confirm that relationships do exist among these variables, but the nature of the underlying pattern remains far from clear. What is fairly clear is that the simple relationship between innovator and firm size is not generally true (except possibly in the chemical industry). A somewhat modified hypothesis has been suggested (e.g. by Scherer 1967, Scott 1984): that innovation is optimized by a market structure intermediate between perfect competition and monopoly. But in many ways, this modification raises more questions than it answers. One is tempted to question whether, in fact, monopoly (or market structure) is the critical factor at all. In all probability other factors play an important role.

7. THERMODYNAMIC CONSTRAINTS ON ECONOMIC GROWTH?

Several themes from the prior discussion can now be summarized, in terms of their implications for economic growth. First, since the economy is, by assumption, a dissipative structure, it depends on continuous energy (essergy) and material flow from (and back to) the environment. Such links are precluded by closed neoclassical general equilibrium models, either static or quasi-static. Second, the energy and physical materials inputs to the economy have shifted, over the past two centuries, from mainly renewable resources to mainly non-renewable resources. Third, dynamic economic growth is driven by technological change (generated, in turn, by economic forces) which also results in continuous structural change[19] in the economic system. It follows, incidentally, that a long-term survival path must sooner or later reverse the historical shift away from renewable resources. This will only be feasible if human technological capabilities continue to rise to levels much higher than current ones. But, since technological capability is endogenous, it will continue to increase only if the pace of deliberate investment in R & D is continued or even increased. In short, the role of knowledge-generating activity in retarding the global entropic increase seems to be growing in importance.

Looking at it in another way, external resource constraints in themselves may not constitute an ultimate "limit to growth," since technological improvements and substitutions appear to offer a possible way out. This has always been the basis on which most scientists and economists have criticized the "limits" thesis of the Club of Rome and others. But the critique itself has tended to assume that new technology always appears (essentially) without cost in response to any perceived scarcity or need. This is not the case in reality. Large scale future substitutions, such as the eventual replacement of motor gasoline by methanol or ethanol, will necessarily entail massive R & D investments (mainly for scaling up from pilot plants to full-scale production) not to mention even more massive capital outlays. But, because of market failures, the private incentives to invest in this kind of research may be inadequate while the (U.S.) government may neglect it for short term political reasons (e.g., "industry should do it," need to reduce the budget deficit, etc.). The "system" is not working as well as it should.

NOTES

I am indebted to Professor Georgescu-Roegen for pointing out several inaccuracies in my earlier draft. He is in no way responsible for any errors that may remain.

1. Order is unavoidably a somewhat anthropomorphic concept. However, in normal usage, it implies sorting or separation, as opposed to mixing. A more general definition relates order to long-range spatial (or momentum) correlations. It is important to emphasize that the term "order" is often used improperly (e.g. by Schrodinger, 1945) and that disorder is not necessarily equivalent to entropy, as suggested by Boltzmann. Disorder corresponds with entropy only in three very special (and unrepresentative) cases: the perfect gas, a crystal at low temperature, and isotopic mixing (McGlashan 1966).

2. The objection raised by Thomson had to do with the geological age of the earth. Lacking any inkling of the true source of the sun's heat or the earth's interior heat (nuclear reactions), physicists calculated a maximum age for the earth to be on the order of 25 million years or less—far too little for Darwin's theory of slow natural selection to accommodate.

3. Essergy (from "essence of energy") is formally defined as a general measure of departure from thermodynamic equilibrium and is, in fact, the most general such measure (see Tribus and McIrvine 1971). It actually reduces to other measures such as the Helmholtz free energy, the Gibbs free energy, and Keenan's index of availability under appropriate constraints.

4. By definition, $G = U + PV - TS$. The Gibbs free energy is the correct measure of departure from equilibrium only for processes that take place at constant temperature and pressure, whence $\Delta G = \Delta U + P\Delta V - T\Delta S$.

5. More recently, so-called algorithmic information theory has been developed to estimate the amount of information (in bits) required to describe an object or, equivalently, the number of instructions needed by a general-purpose computer to reproduce that object. The two kinds of information theory are essentially equivalent.

6. By the same token, the present oxygen-rich environment is quite unsuitable to the spontaneous formation of organic molecules by known mechanisms (e.g. Miller and Orgell 1974).

7. Needless to say, decay organisms facilitate this recycling.

8. The development of spoken and, later, written languages were obviously critical steps.

9. Astronomy evolved historically as means of predicting dates of annual spring runoff in the Nile Valley, where seasonal changes at lower latitudes are very slight.

10. The remainder of the barrel of crude oil is used for a variety of other purposes (from chemicals to asphalt) but most of it is used for process heat, space heating or electricity generation.

11. Some of the negentropy in question is obviously embodied directly in capital equipment. However, some of it, like computer software, is quite portable. Moreover, the portable component appears to be increasing in relative importance.

12. Including fission, fusion and photovoltaic cells on the earth or in space.

13. Central planning attempts to introduce order of another kind.

14. This fact was emphatically pointed out by the Nobel-price winning chemist F. Soddy in 1922 (see Daley 1980). Soddy was ignored or ridiculed by virtually all economists of his time. Among the first economists to stress the dissipative nature of the economic system was Georgescu-Roegen (1971). The relevance of mass-energy conservation to environmental/resource economics was particularly emphasized by Keese, Ayres and d'Arge (1971).

15. Aggregative models have been studied by Harrod (1936) and Domar (1956). Sectoral growth models have been studied by von Neumann (1945), Leontief (1953), and Sraffa (1960).

16. Harrod called this balancing process "walking on the razor's edge." However, it was later shown that the H-D model's extreme sensitivity to balancing is an artifact of its particular choice of production function (Solow 1956).

17. Similarly, the economic system functions in a social framework, which in turn functions in an ecological-biological framework. The latter in turn, functions within climatic geochemical and astrophysical frameworks. The fundamental laws of physics (e.g. mechanics and thermodynamics) operate directly or indirectly at all levels of the hierarchy including the highest. Basic biological laws also govern social behavior, and so on. On the other hand, higher level laws are irrelevant at lower levels of the hierarchy.

18. One cogent example of such an area is the development of technical means for controlling pollutant emissions. Pollution is, in itself, a market imperfection, and there is very little profit motive in this field. Other areas of minimal private incentive are the natural public sector monopolies—e.g., defense, public health and public safety.

19. For instance, so-called Leontief input-output coefficients do not remain constant.

REFERENCES

Abramovitz, Moses. 1956. "Resources and Output Trends in the United States Since 1870," *American Economic Review* 46 (May).

Allred, J. C. 1977. *Application Of Entropy Concepts To National Energy Problems*, Entropy Economics Symposium, Houston, TX. (November 2) [Note: Unpublished].

Ayres, Robert U. 1978. *Resources, Environment & Economics: Applications Of The Materials/ Energy Balance Principle*, New York: Wiley.

———. 1987. *Manufacturing As An Information Process*. Institute for Applied Systems Analysis, Laxenburg, Austria (July). [NOTE: Forthcoming IIASA Research Report.]

———. 1987. *Human Labor As An Information Process: Some Implications Of Error-Proneness*. Carnegie-Mellon University and IIASA, USA and Austria (July). [NOTE: Forthcoming IISA Research Report.]

————. 1987. *The Industry-Technology Life Cycle: An Integrating Meta-Model?*, Research
Report (RR–87–3), IIASA, Laxenburg, Austria (March).

Blum, H. F. 1955. *Time's Arrow And Evolution*. Princeton, NJ: Princeton University
Press.

Boulding, Kenneth E. 1966. "Environmental Quality in a Growing Economy," in:
Essays from the Sixth RFF Forum, Baltimore, Johns Hopkins Univ. Press.

Breder, C. 1942. "A Consideration of Evolutionary Hypotheses in Reference to the
Origin of Life," *Zoologica* 27:132–143.

Brillouin, Leon. 1949. "Life, Thermodynamics and Cybernetics," *American Scientist*
37:554–568.

————. 1951. "Physical Entropy and Information," of *J. of Applied Physics* 22(3):338–
43.

————. 1962. *Science And Information Theory*, Orlando, FL: Academic Press. 2nd edition.

Burmeister, E. and A. R. Dobell, 1970. *Mathematical Theories Of Economic Growth*,
London: MacMillan.

Cherry, Colin. 1978. *On Human Communications*. Cambridge, MA: MIT Press. 3rd
edition.

Crick, Francis H. C. 1962. "The Genetic Code," *Scientific American* (October).

Daly, Herman E. 1980. "The Economic Thought of Frederick Soddy," College Station, NC: Duke University Press.

Domar, E. D. 1956. "Capital Expansion, Rate of Growth and Employment," *Econo-
metrica* 14:137–147.

Dyson, Freeman J. 1982. "Origin of Life," *Journal of Molecular Evolution* 18:344–355.

Eigen, Manfred. 1971. "Self-organization of Matter and the Evolution of Biological
Macromolecules," *Naturwiss* 58, October).

Enos, J. L. 1962. *Petroleum Progress And Profits: A History of Process Innovation*, Cambridge, MA, MIT Press.

Fabricant, Solomon. 1954. "Economic Progress and Economic Change," in *34th Annual Report*, New York: National Bureau of Economic Research.

Field, R. J. 1985. "Chemical Organization in Time and Space," *American Scientist*
73:142–149 (March-April).

Gaffron, H. 1965. "The Role of Light in Evolution: The Transition From a One
Quantum to a Two Quantum Mechanism," in S. W. Fox [ed], *The Origins of
Prebiological Systems and of their Molecular Matrices:* New York: Academic Press.

Georgescu-Roegen, Nicholas. 1971. *The Entropy Law and the Economic Process*, Cambridge, MA, Harvard University Press.

Glandsdorff, P. & Ilya Prigogine. *Thermodynamic Theory Of Structure, Stability And Fluctuations*, New York: Wiley-Interscience.

Graham, R. and H. Haken. 1970. *Zeitschrift fur Physik* 237(31).

Harrod, Roy F. 1936. *The Trade Cycle*, New York: Oxford Univ. Press.

Hartley, R. V. L. 1928. "Transmission of Information," *Bell System Technical Journal* 7.

Huxley, J. S. 1956. "Evolution, Cultural and Biological," in W. I. Thomas, ed.,
*Current Anthropology:*3–25, Chicago: University of Chicago Press.

Jaynes, Edwin T. 1957. "Information Theory and Statistical Mechanics," I, *Physical Review* 106:620.

———. 1957. "Information Theory and Statistical Mechanics," II, *Physical Review* 108:171.

Jensen, R. V. 1987. "Classical Chaos," *American Scientist* 75:168–181, (March-April).

Johnstone, James. 1921. *The Mechanism Of Life in Relation to Modern Physical Theory,* London: Longmans.

Kendrick, John W. 1956. "Productivity Trends: Capital and Labor," *Review of Economics and Statistics* (August).

Khinchin, A. I. 1957. *Mathematical Foundations Of Information Theory,* New York: Dover.

Kneese, A. V., R. U. Ayres, and R. C. d"Arge. 1970. *Aspects Of Environmental Economics: A Materials Balance-General Equilibrium Approach,* Baltimore, MD: John Hopkins University Press. [NOTE: Japanese Edition, 1974.]

Lotka, Alfred J. 1945. "The Law of Evolution as a Maximal Principle," *Human Biology* 17(3):167–194.

———. 1950. *Elements Of Physical Biology,* New York: Dover Editions. First published 1925.

May, R. M. 1976. "Simple Mathematical Models with Very Complicated Dynamics," *Nature* 261:459.

McGlashan, M. L. 1966. "The Use and Misuse of the Laws of Thermodynamics," *Journal of Chemical Education* 43(5):226–232.

Miller, James G. 1978. *Living Systems* 5, New York: McGraw-Hill.

Miller, J. G. 1987. *Keynote Lecture At Iiasa Workshop, On "Life Cycles and Long Cycles",* Montpellier, France, July 8 (Unpublished).

Miller, S. & L. Orgell. 1974. *The Origins Of Life On The Earth,* Englewood Cliffs, NJ, Prentice-Hall.

Moravec, Hans. 1981. *Unknown* (Unpublished).

———. 1985. *Life, The Universe And Everything,* Pittsburgh, PA: Carnegie-Mellon University, Robotics Institute (Unpublished).

Needham, Joseph. 1943. *The The Refreshing River,* London: Allen & Unwin.

Nicolis, Gregoire & Ilya Prigogine. 1977. *Self-Organization In Non-Equilibrium Systems,* New York: Wiley-Interscience.

Oparin, A. I. 1953. *Origin Of Life,* New York: Dover Publications.

Ott, Edward. 1981. "Strange Attractors and Chaotic Motions of Dynamical Systems," *Rev. Mod. Physics* 53:655.

Polgar, Steven. 1961. "Evolution and the Thermodynamic Imperative," *Human Biology* 33(2):99–109.

Prigogine, I., G. Nicolis, and A. Babloyantz. 1972. "Thermodynamics of Evolution," *Physics Today* 23(11/12):23–28 (November); 38–44 (December).

Sagan, Carl. 1977. *Dragons Of Eden: Speculations On The Evolution Of Human Intelligence,* New York: Random House.

Schrodinger, Erwin. 1945. *What Is Life? The Physical Aspects Of The Living Cell,* London: Cambridge University Press.

Schumpeter, Joseph A. 1912. *Theorie Der Wirtschaftlichen Entwicklungen,* Leipzig: Duncker & Humboldt.

———. 1962. *The Theory Of Economic Development,* New York: Oxford University Press. (American Edition, 1961). [NOTE: English translation from the 1911 German Edition]

Shannon, Claude E. 1948. "A Mathematical Theory of Communication," *Bell System Technical Journal* 27.

Shannon, Claude E. & Warren Weaver. 1949. *The Mathematical Theory Of Communication,* Urbana, IL: University of Illinois Press.

Solow, Robert M. 1956. "A Contribution to the Theory of Economic Growth," *Quarterly Journal of Economics* 70:65–94.

Solow, Robert M. 1957. "Technical Change and the Aggregate Production Function," *Review of Economics and Statistics* (August).

Thom, R. 1972. *Structural Stability And Morphogenesis: General Theory Of Models,* Reading, MA: Addison-Wesley.

Tribus, Myron. 1961. "Information Theory as the Basis for Thermostatics and Thermodynamics," *J. Applied Mechanics* 28:1–8 (March).

———. 1961. *Thermostatics And Thermodynamics,* New York: Van Nostrand.

———. and Edward C. McIrvine. 1971. "Energy and Information," *Scientific American* 225(3):179–188 (September).

Velarde, Manuel and Christiane Normand. 1980. "Convection," *Scientific American* 243 (July).

Von Neumann, John. 1945. "A Model of General Economic Equilibrium," *Rev. Econ. Studies* 13:1–9.

Wald, George. 1955. *The Origin Of Life In The Physics And Chemistry Of Life,* New York: Simon & Schuster.

13

Thermodynamics, Economics and Information

NICHOLAS GEORGESCU-ROEGEN

Professor Ayres's chapter in this volume deals with one of the most baffling issues, perhaps the most baffling of all. Is evolution a real phenomenon? And if it is, what are its sustaining factors? Numerous ideas have been set forth about this problem ever since the "obscure" Heraclitus, but the most salient of them belong to the past fifty years or so.

The task of Professor Ayres was truly arduous, all the more so since economic life transgresses not only the inorganic but also the organic domain. Humans are not just biological creatures seeking only to feed, defend, and perpetuate themselves. True, the life of any human, like that of any other living creature, is entropic in all its material fibers: we, too, "suck"—as Erwin Schrödinger explained—low entropy from the environment and discharge high entropy into it. But without taking into account the specific faculties of our species that have given rise to the unique form of human culture, we are not in the true economic domain. For humanity is not just a Carnot cycle. What is missing from Professor Ayres's paper is any consideration of a human as an agent, especially as an economic agent. For humans are not just price-takers, but as Adam Smith repeatedly noted, every individual continuously seek to better his or her own economic position, a struggle that is responsible for most articulations of the social evolution of *homo sapiens*. As a social animal, every human is a complex—in the words of Thorstein Veblen—of "instinctive proclivities and tropismatic aptitudes" that is spurred by instincts, such as that of workmanship and idle curiosity. The specific human culture is dominated by Veblenian institutions—prevalent "ways of acting, feeling, and thinking," as A. L. Kroeber later explained again. By now there is hardly any doubt that a strong interplay exists between the institutional aspects and the mode by which people satisfy their wants by tapping and transforming environmental resources.

It would have been interesting if Professor Ayres had devoted some attention to this interplay. Instead, he has spun his presentation only from a purely thermodynamic viewpoint, which is, no doubt, an interesting one. This epistemological temper, it is true, has become the fashion ever since ideas from several directions converged on the entropic nature of the biological processes. As a result, the main points—historical and analytical—are by now familiar knowledge to others besides those who have a special interest in this crossroad of biology, thermodynamics and the so-called information theory. Be this as it may, Professor Ayres's review contains a few inadvertences that deserve to be pointed out.

A word should first be said about the substitution of "essergy" for "energy," or even for "food." The terminological innovation is far from being innocuous. For "exergy," which is the preferred form, has been introduced by several European scholars to denote the *amount* of available energy supplied by a thermodynamic system in relation to its specific environment. But the element measured by exergy is just energy, as is the case for other thermodynamic measures, say, enthalpy and Helmholtz's or Gibbs's free energy.[1]

There was indeed a scientific crisis that grew out of Rudolf Clausius' studies. But that crisis (which is still unresolved and which is, in my judgment, deeper even than that caused by Einstein's relativity of time) did not turn upon the difference between the concepts of reversible processes (moving at an infinitesimally slow pace) and the irreversible ones (with a finite speed). It turned upon the antinomy between the behavior of heat and the laws of Newtonian mechanics. We should not forget that Clausius's first (and still the most transparent) formulation of the second law is that "Heat always passes *by itself* from the warmer to the colder body, never in reverse." More snags appeared as one solution after another claimed to reduce that famous antinomy. But on close examination even the most sophisticated ones boil down to a deft *petitio principii*.

More subject to objection is the definition of thermodynamic equilibrium as "a changeless state in which *all matter is uniformly distributed* and there are no temperature or concentration differences" (italics mine). This definition describes a Chaos, not a "Heat Death." If a brick, for example, has the same temperature as the water into which it is immersed, the whole ensemble is a case of heat death, but not of chaos.

Thermodynamics has never been concerned with the dissipation of matter. The famous contribution of Ilya Prigogine and his school did extend the domain of classical thermodynamics (confined to closed systems) to open systems as well. But we should not fail to realize that in Prigogine's framework, matter plays a restricted role—not as matter per se, but only as carrier of energy. To wit, the classical formula involving only transfer of heat, dQ, and work, pdV,

$$dE = dQ - pdV,$$

was replaced by

$$dE = d\Phi - pdV,$$

where dΦ represents the flow of energy "due to heat transfer and exchange of matter" (Prigogine, 1961, p. 11).[2] But as strange as it may seem, neither the Bruxelles school nor any other thermodynamicist asked what happens to matter when it serves as an effective support of a material process—say, the pistons and the cylinders in a motor or the graphite of a writing pencil. Friction, which is the main factor that degrades matter entropically, is mentioned in the thermodynamic literature solely as the cause of loss of available energy, very likely because friction is a most baffling phenomenon. Yet matter matters too.[3] We would greatly err to ignore this truth in seeking a conformable representation of material processes.

It was apposite for Professor Ayres in his chapter in this volume to mention in his review the connection between entropy and "order": most everybody nowadays defines entropy as the measure of disorder. But his brief notice about order leaves the impression that, after all is said and done, the concept is not plagued by the immense difficulties exposed by renowned scholars—by Percy Bridgman (a physicist), Henri Bergson (a philosopher), Jacques Hadamard (a mathematician), as well as by Schrödinger. The familiar proposition that the disorder of a macrostate is proportional to the number of its possible microstates is a pure dictionary definition, not an elucidating one. The same is true of McGlashan's proposal endorsed by Professor Ayres. We speak quite sensibly of order and disorder, but only with ad hoc meanings associated with some purpose. A stack of book invoices may be in perfect order for the bookkeeper but in great disorder for the cataloguer. A highly edifying proof of the insubstantiality of the concept of order occurred at a 1981 international colloquium on the bearings of thermodynamics as Jacques Tonnelat displayed three pictures to illustrate the change from order to disorder. Almost everyone in the rather initiated audience thought that the gradient of order was the opposite of that intended by Tonnelat.[4]

For the description of thermodynamics *vis-a-vis* biology, Professor Ayres follows the view that permeates most of the accretive literature on the issue, which is to take many things for granted, as is the case with the concepts of complexity, structure, organism and organization. Here, one should not fail to consider F. A. Hayek's enlightening criticism of these concepts, concepts that have usually formed the subject of a plethora of wordy, inconclusive performances. Hayek defined the concept of order as *"a state of affairs in which a multiplicity of elements of various kinds are so related to each other that* we may learn from our acquaintance with some spatial or temporal part of the whole to form correct expectations concerning the rest, or at least expectations which have a good chance of proving correct" (Hayek 1973, p. 36).[5] The extraordinary merit of this definition is that, in addition to its clear expression, it focuses on a fundamental epistemological element—the organically ordered structure that must map any proper system. The quintessence of this structure is portrayed in mathematics by the analytical function, that is, by a function whose values over its entire range can be deduced from the knowledge of its values over any interval however small (Kein, 1972, p. 643). It is because of this singular property of the functions ordinarily used in quantitative disciplines that we can extrapolate the corresponding laws beyond the limits of actual observations (Georgescu-Roegen 1966). As we may have expected, Hayek's conception of analytical structure has a tradition of service outside mathematics before it was naturalized in that realm by A. L. Cauchy and K. Weierstrass. The most salient illustration is the famous achievement of Baron Georges Cuvier. Guided by his perception that the body of any animal must have a harmonious—viz. analytical—structure, Cuvier succeeded in reconstructing the skeleton of many an extinct vertebrate "from just one vertebra," as the feat has been sung in praise (Coleman, 1964). Interestingly, Hayek went on to observe that in the sciences concerned with life we can never determine all the factors that promote a process, but—as Darwinism supplies a glaring proof—the ubiquity of the ordered system in those domains makes it possible for us to advance nonetheless.

Professor Ayres is right in recalling that there is no "evidence of any absolute contradiction" between thermodynamics and the life of an organism. (This, not biological evolution, is the proper opposite.) But nor has anyone been able to show, except by modeling with pencil on paper, how thermodynamics may actually account for numerous puzzling biological phenomena. It is not an accidental trivia that illustrious physicists have expressed definite reservations on the equivalence of an organism with a thermodynamic system. Lord Kelvin, one of the architects of thermodynamics, enunciated (in 1851) the second law for inanimate systems alone, and forty years later (1892) still clung to that restriction. About the same time Hermann von Helmholtz, who made memorable contributions to medicine, biology, psychology and the theory of music, and who set the first law on a solid foundation, also thought that "the delicate structures of the organic living tissues" could elude the second law. A fantastic mental experiment related by G. N. Lewis reveals as no other that I know the relevance of life in actual processes: some aimlessly running mice crowded in a corner of a box hinged down on its center ultimately disperse themselves so that the box is kept in horizontal equilibrium.[6] Undoubtedly, the same could not be brought about if the rats were replaced even by some billiard balls.

Of course, there was Clerk Maxwell with his demon.[7] The voluminous literature on Maxwell's fable is commensurate only with its great popularity. Widespread also is the belief that the paradox of the possibility of converting high into low entropy in an isolated system has been disposed of by Leo Szilard.[8] But now that an English translation of Szilard's paper is available, even the Anglophones who do not read German may see for themselves that Szilard's argument is based on "an inanimate device" and that his conclusion is that *such* a device would create an amount of low entropy just equal to that used up in observing and measuring. By any kind of logic, therefore, Szilard did not "exorcise" (as the claim goes) the demon.

But a paradox cannot be shattered by invoking the very principle(s) challenged by it, as Szilard did in his proof. Bertrand Russell, for instance, replaced the old principles of classes by a new theory of types so as to do away with the paradox of the class of all classes. It is indeed easier, as Norbert Wiener observed, to dismiss the puzzle as a paradox than to answer it. Suggestions for disposing of Maxwell's paradox have not been lacking. Georg Hirth set forth the idea taken over by F. Auerbach (1910) that in nature there is also an *ektropy* tendency opposed to entropy. Even a physicist of Sir Arthur Eddington's caliber argued that besides randomness, on which the modern theory of thermodynamics rests, an opposite factor, the anti-chance, must be at work in nature. Something thus must be added to physicochemical laws—as Werner Heisenberg argued—in order to account for the phenomena peculiar to life. There are some renowned physicists, however, such as E. Wigner, who do not share this belief. But as Manfred Eigen pointed out in his admirable essay, Wigner took for granted that any known organism can be assembled by a random process. Eigen (on whom Professor Ayres markedly relies) disagreed on this and pointed out that proteins, in particular, cannot reproduce themselves. Whether a *new* physics may explain directly how the intelligent human evolved from the single cell is still a typically moot question.

It is because, in his general discussion of life phenomena, Professor Ayres seems to accept the numerous formal equivalences about those phenomena as explanations valid on the workbench that I deemed it necessary to insert the ideas of the foregoing sections.

Eigen's basic diagram (1971, p. 466), for example, serves only as a simile of the input-output in a self-reproducing cell, but it is not an explanation of how things go exactly where they have to be. The simulation presented by Zeleny and Pierre in a sequence of twelve diagrams is also only a simile of a particular feature.

And not to forget, an old theorem of John von Neumann stated that some Turing universal *machine* could reproduce itself if left floating in a medium together with plenty of its elementary parts. On paper, such a machine may be a simile of a protein, but only if we have the protein to start with (the troublesome issue that arrested Eigen's attention). And interestingly, a negation of Neumann's theorem is H. von Foerster's equally formal proof that "There are no such things as self-organizing systems!"

As is the fashion now for writers about complex structures, Professor Ayres mentions the results concerning the nonequilibrium structures obtained by the Bruxelles school. The crux of that endeavor, the concept of dissipative structure, is a landmark in modern science thought up by Prigogine (1967, chap. viii), who described it only by verbal, yet illuminating, considerations. Moreover, Prigogine was not then as self-assured of the general bearings of that concept as he became later. On the basis of a few processes—the transition of a liquid to solid, a hydrodynamic convection and some chemical reactions proposed by A. M. Turing, for example—Prigogine concluded that "Dissipative processes *may* therefore also lead to an increase of organization."[9] There, we are also told that through dissipative processes homogeneous turns into heterogeneous, an idea which in his subsequent writings Prigogine elevated to a universal law of nature.[10] The paradoxical face value of this tenet enchanted legions of writers who, following the very suggestions of Prigogine," snatched [it up] to justify all manners of social, psychological, [and] political "phenomena" (*New York Times,* 2 June 1979).

What led to this quandary is certainly the improper use of "homogeneous," a fact manifest from Prigogine's most transparent illustration of the tenet (1980, p. 89), the process by which a highly organized pattern of convection cells forms in heated water. But the initial situation being composed of a heat bath and some unheated water is not a *homogeneous* structure. An initial homogeneous structure would contradict Eigen's reservation mentioned earlier. Nothing has yet occurred to prove that from a true homogenous structure a heterogeneous one could develop. According to the ideas that have cropped up in recent years, the origin of the universe was not Chaos. But Chaos will very probably be its fate.

I find myself in even sharper disagreement with Professor Ayres on his use of *information* and *negentropy.* True, the so-called theory of information is in a muddle for the simple reason that information has been defined only implicitly, that is, as a vocable for negative (low) entropy (Georgescu-Roegen 1976). The meaning of the early idea of G. N. Lewis (1930) that "gain in entropy always means loss of information" was clear: the player no longer knows where a card is in a shuffled deck. But Lewis's addition "and nothing else" set the stage for some otiose developments. For, if entropy is nothing but a mental event, then an engineer, for instance, would have to say that the entropy of an engine is just his degree of ignorance.

Claude Shannon was justified in defining "information" as the measure of the capacity of a code to represent different messages, whether meaningful or not. That the formula for this measure coincides with that of Boltzmann's for entropy is a pure accident. So, to say that the Boltzmann-Shannon formula measures the information of, say, an income distribution or the structure of a cell, is a vacuous statement as long as "information" is defined only implicitly by Leon Brillouin's equation

$$\text{Information} = \text{Negentropy}.$$

Brillouin did not supply a "famous proof of [this] equivalence," as Professor Ayres asserts;[11] he only shows the *algebraic* identity of Boltzmann's and Shannon's formulae.

However, in his writings Brillouin often substituted "knowledge" for "information," as he rightly argued that any gain of knowledge is necessarily paid for by an increase in entropy (a loss of negentropy) of the total system. This shift led to even greater exercises of verbalism. For example, we find "stocks of information" (such as a telephone directory?) regarded as "storehouses of negative entropy" (such as a coal mine?). Moreover, "the ability of a dissipative system to capture (or embody) negentropy in structure" is *intelligence;* even an amoeba is thus intelligent. Yet a few lines further, embodied information is equated with "knowledge" and "natural" information with essergy.

Concerning the discussion of technological progress in relation to the growing scarcity of fossil fuels and even of uranium ores, Professor Ayres is confident that some of the familiar "alternative resources" will become operative. Whether or not this will happen is a matter of crystal ball gazing. What is certain, but we ignore, is that any viable exchange between mankind and the material environment must necessarily generate a surplus as well. There have been only three such processes: agriculture, the mastery of fire, and the transformation of thermal energy (heat) into work by the heat engine. Any one hoped for must also be capable of yielding a surplus.

Turning to the sections on economics, I must first point out two inexactitudes in Professor Aires's paper. Leon Walras's argument that his system has a solution because the number of equations in it is equal to that of the unknowns is of no avail. The proof of the existence of a solution under very restricted conditions was given by K. J. Arrow and G. Debreu only in 1951. Also, Ayres is inexact in asserting that Vilfredo Pareto proved that a market economy "maximizes total welfare." The market economy only tends to a Pareto optimum, a situation in which nobody may become better off without someone else becoming worse off.[12]

Finally, there is the theory of economic development of Joseph A. Schumpeter, which, far from being a "simple conceptual model" as Professor Ayres claims, represents a vision not only unique in the history of economic thought but a novel understanding of the nature of evolution. Schumpeter's basic idea was that evolution is the result of qualitative novelties, which in economics have their roots in the continuous product of our minds: inventions. These, in turn, led to economic innovations, which, according to Schumpeter were not limited to the technological domain. We owe to Schumpeter the essential (albeit nowadays overlooked) distinction between growth (mere accretion) and development (in economics or in biology). His splendid aphorism, "Add successively as many mail coaches as you please, you will never get a railway thereby," tells a lot about what evolution means.

Professor Ayres fails to mention these ideas as well as another, still more decisive thought. An important point in Schumpeter's system is that only great (substantial) innovations affect the economic conditions. And he took great pains to explain the difference between small and great innovations in a way that was certainly dialectic and which he also adopted in clarifying the quality of entrepreneurship.

The reason why I consider Schumpeter's theory one of the highest marks of economic thought is that his idea about evolution was independently thought up some thirty years later by a renowned biologist, R. Goldschmidt (1940). Against the prevailing neo-Darwinian view that speciation results from the accumulation of small, imperceptible modifications, Goldschmidt maintained that species derive from the emergence of "successful monsters." By analogy a railway engine is a successful monster in comparison with a mail coach.

To gauge the depth of Schumpeter's vision we should note that the explanation of speciation by successful monsters has recently been revived by one of the greatest minds in contemporary biology, Stephen Jay Gould (1977). Interestingly, Gould (1980), too, recognizes the strict relation of dialectics with his new interpretation of speciation.

Professor Ayres is the author of many valuable contributions, in particular, he co-authored a volume (1970) that dealt with resources at a time when their problem was side-stepped. Therefore, I feel ill at ease to have found so many ideas in his paper with which I could not agree.

NOTES

1. In the usual literature the concept of exergy is found under the transparent term "available energy," an original notion used by both Lord Kelvin and Walter Nernst in preference in entropy. For the more recent formula of availability, see K. Denbigh, *The Principles of Chemical Equilibrium,* Cambridge University Press, 1973). But for this concept, hence for exergy as well, there are two distinct formu-

lae, one for closed, another for open systems (W. H. Giedt, *Thermophysics,* New York: Van Nostrand, 1971).

2. A. Katchalsky and P. Curran, *Nonequilibrium Thermodynamics in Biophysics* (Cambridge: Harvard University Press, 1965), are more precise: $d\Phi$ represents "all the energy transported into the (open system) including that resulting from the transfer of matter."

3. To argue on the basis of Einsteinian equivalence between energy and mass, $E = mc^2$, that matter is just a form of energy would not do. It would negate the difference between closed and open systems, and, implicitly, would deny all importance to Prigogine's contribution. But that argument also overlooks the important fact that thermodynamics is a science of macrosystems, of matter-energy in bulk.

4. The curious reader may look up the 1982 special issue of *Entropie,* pp. 68 and 72.

5. In the original, the entire definition is in italics; for my own emphasis, I have changed part of it into roman type.

6. "The Symmetry of Time in Physics," *Science,* June 6, 1930. Curiously though, by that article Lewis purported to refute the idea that life displays some special features.

7. In fact it was J. Loschmidt who imagined that demon long before Maxwell.

8. Professor Ayres is inexact in attributing the introduction of "negentropy" to Szilard. Schrodinger introduced the troublesome term "negative entropy" in 1944, but it was L. Brillouin who coined "negentropy" (abbreviation of negative entropy) in 1950. Another inaccuracy appears in his note 8. It was in Egypt that astronomy served to predict the flooding of the Nile in time for the agricultural works, not in Mesopotamia whose slow rivers calmly descended only 30 feet over a length of 500 miles (Ronan 1982, pp. 18, 31.)

9. The verb italicized by me appears almost regularly in that particular argument. And even later, Prigogine (1976), relies on some illustrations to explain the "concepts of dissipative structure and order through fluctuations."

10. Prigogine (1980), attributed the tenet to Herbert Spencer. Indeed, Spencer spelled it out in 1847 and traced it back to two earlier embryologists, K. Wolff and E. von Baer, who refuted the old belief that the embryo contained the whole organism in miniature.

11. Professor Ayres's reference to Brillouin (1953) is not exact.

12. This concept is rather tricky so that even P. Samuelson in the eleventh edition of his *Economics,* p. 435, slipped over it.

REFERENCES

Auerbach, F. 1910. *Ektropismus oder die physikalische Theorie des Lebens.* Leipzig: Engelmann.

Brillouin, L. 1950. "Thermodynamics and Information Theory." *American Scientist*, 38:594–9.

Coleman, W. 1964. *Georges Cuvier Zoologist*. Cambridge: Harvard University Press.

Eddington, A. 1959. *New Pathways in Science*. Ann Arbor: University of Michigan Press.

Eigen, M. 1971. "Self-Organization of Matter and the Evolution of Biological Macromolecules." *Naturwissenschaften* 58:465–523.

Georgescu-Roegen, N. 1966. *Analytical Economics: Issues and Problems*. Harvard University Press.

————. 1976. "The Measure of Information: A Critique." *Proceedings of the Third International Conference on Cybernetics and Systems*. Edited by J. Rose and C. Bilciu. Volume I. New York: Springer Verlag.

Goldschmidt, R. 1940. *The Material Basis of Evolution*. New Haven: Yale University Press.

Gould, S. J. 1977. "The Return of Hopeful Monsters." *Natural History* 86:22–30.

————. 1980. *The Panda's Thumb*. New York: Norton.

Hayek. F. A. 1973. *Rules and Order*. Chicago: University of Chicago Press.

Helmholtz, H. von, 1882. *Wissenschaftliche Abhandlung*. Volume II. Leipzig: Barth.

Jantsch, E. and Waddington, C., editors. 1976. *Evolution and Consciousness: Human Systems in Transition*. Reading: Addison-Wesley.

Kline, M. 1972. *Mathematical Thought from Ancient to Modern Times*. New York: Oxford University Press.

Kneese, A. *et al.* 1970. *Economics and the Environment*. Baltimore: John Hopkins Press.

Kroeber, A. 1952. *The Nature of Culture*. Chicago: University of Chicago Press.

Lotka, A. 1945. "The Law of Evolution as a Maximal Principle." *Human Biology* 17:167–194.

Nagel, E. 1961. *The Structure of Science*. New York: Harcourt, Brace and World.

Prigogine, I. 1961. *Introduction to Thermodynamics of Irreversible Processes*. New York: Interscience.

Ronan, C. 1982. *Science: Its History and Development Among the World's Cultures*. New York: Facts on File.

Schumpeter, J. 1934. *The Theory of Economic Development*. Harvard University Press. (German original published in 1912).

Spencer, H. 1901. *Essays: Scientific, Political, and Speculative*. Volume I. London: Williams and Norgate.

Szilard, L. 1972. *Collected Works*. New York: MIT Press.

Thompson, Lord W. 1894. Popular Lectures and Addresses. Two volumes. London: Macmillan.

Wiener, N. 1961. *Cybernetics*. Second Edition. New York: MIT Press.

IV

GENERAL CONSIDERATIONS

14

Integrative Concepts in the Physical Sciences

MAX JAMMER

Exactly fifty years ago Garrett Birkhoff and John von Neumann tried to discover "what logical structure one may hope to find in physical theories which, like quantum mechanics, do not conform to classical logic."[1] Since then the question whether modern physics admits or suggests or even requires a logic deviant from the traditional Aristotelian Logic has been the subject of lively discussions among physicists and philosophers of science.

The present paper is not designed to be a contribution to this controversy. Its thesis can be maintained independently of whether or not modern physics has the logical structure of a propositional calculus with an orthocomplemented modular lattice, or whether or not it has the syntactical structure of a multi-valued logic.

This paper discusses not the structure of logic, but rather, the mode of its use as conditioned by the results of modern physics. Its principal aim is merely to draw attention to the possibility of a new mode of conceptualization in physical thought, namely the possibility of an integrative (or integrationist) approach, as opposed to, and in addition to, the reductive (or reductionist) approach to concept formation.

Since the beginning of the seventeenth century when Francis Bacon, in his *Novum Organon* of 1620, declared that "malius autem est naturam secare quam abstrahere" ("that it is better to dissect nature than to abstract") and that "nisi facta mundi dissectione atque anatomia diligentissima" ("without dissecting and anatomizing the world most diligently") no real knowledge of nature can be obtained, progress in scientific research has generally been thought to require a methodology which proceeds in the direction from the larger to the smaller, from system to subsystem, from a higher level to a lower level of organization. Descartes' "Second Rule of Investigation" and Galileo's "Metodo Resolutivo" canonized this trend towards fragmentation as the only admissible method of scientific analysis. In fact, the very term "analysis," derived from the Greek λύελι, meaning "to dissolve" and etymologically related to the English word "loosen," indicates this conceptual procedure towards increasing diminuition. Probably the most appropriate term to characterize this methodological mode of thinking would be "disintegration"; but since the term presupposes an understanding of "integration" or "integrativeness," notions not easy to define, and since it lacks general currency, I shall abstain from using terms like "disintegrationism" and, instead, shall speak of the "reductionist" mode of thinking.

Strictly speaking, to use the term "reductionism" in the sense mentioned above is an abuse of language. For the Latin "re-ducere" means only "to lead back" without carrying any connotation as to a decreasing order of size. The very fact that "reduction" is generally understood in the sense of a transition from a system to its subsystems and never in the opposite direction is, of course, a result of the Baconian-Cartesian-Galilean influence and its apparent legitimation by the mechanical world-picture of the seventeenth and eighteen centuries.

Reductionism is based on the following three principles.

(1) The *Principle of Epistemological Reductionism* which asserts that to understand the whole it suffices to understand its parts.

Principle (1) expresses the belief in an inverse relation between intelligibility and size, assuming that "complexity" is an "additive" property.

(2) The *Principle of Nomological Reductionism* which asserts that the laws pertaining to the whole are logical consequences of the laws pertaining individually to its parts. It differs from Principle (1) by asserting an objective state of affairs, whereas Principle (1) asserts a subjective feature.

(3) The *Principle of Ontological Reductionism* which asserts that the whole has no reality beyond and above the reality of its parts. It obviously assumes some kind of realistic interpretation of physics, in contrast to the two former Principles which may be valid also in a purely structuralistic philosophy of nature.

This reductionist approach can be recognized already in the atomistic doctrines of the ancient Greeks. It reemerged in modern times as a product of the anti-Aristotelianism of the sixteenth and seventeenth centuries. Guided by the development of classical mechanics, these anti-Aristotelians rejected the teleological thesis that a *causa finalis* is operative in every process in nature. True, with the discovery of the so-called integral principles of dynamics, based on the principle of least action (Lagrange, Hamilton, Gauss etc.), there were some physicists who thought it necessary to reintroduce teleological arguments into physics. But it was soon understood that these integral principles are merely reformulations of differential equations of the usual type employed in mechanics.

Early theories of science were not reductionist. In fact, Aristotle, perhaps the first systematic student of scientific methodology, stressed the priority of the whole over its parts when he wrote in *De Partibus Animalium*: "Just as in discussing a house, it is the whole figure and form of the house which should attract our attention, not merely the bricks and mortar and timber; so in natural science, it is the composite thing, the thing as a whole, which is our primary concern . . ." In *De Caelo* Aristotle declared that the behavior of a particular element, such as earth, "must not be considered in isolation, but only as a part of the cosmos with its universal laws." These statements clearly show that the three Principles of Reductionism do not hold in the Aristotelian philosophy of science.

An even more radical anti-reductionist attitude characterizes the physics of the Stoics. According to the Stoics the cosmos is filled with an all-pervasive substratum, which they called the "pneuma"; it is subjected to a kind of elastic tension of "tonos" (τόνος) that makes the universe into a single cohesive unit. The "tonos," in turn, gives rise to a "hexis" (ἕξις) which characterizes the physical state of a body in its coexistence and interdependence with the totality of all other bodies. Consequently, the seat or carrier of physical properties (ποιότητες) is, strictly speaking, no longer the individual physical object as such but rather its "interlacing and coalescent union (συμφυὴς πρὸς ἀλληλας ἕνωσις) with all other existents."[2] This mutual interdependence is often referred to as "sympathy" (συμπαθείη); an example is the relation between the moon and the tides, as Poseidonius pointed out, the earliest attempt of a physical explanation of a phenomenon on a cosmic scale.

The integrative character of physical reality applies, according to the Stoics, to cosmologically large dimensions just as well as to microscopically small dimensions, even though they form conceptually different layers of reality. "The Stoics distinguish," wrote Simplicius,[3] "between qualities of lower structures (ποιά) produced by cooperating effects . . . and physical properties which are immanent in the unified structure . . . and are related by one law." The Stoics may be credited with having anticipated the concept of a physical "field," a typically integrative notion as we shall see in due course.

With the development of Newtonian and post-Newtonian physics, based as it was on a dualistic foundational scheme of particles and fields, a phenomenon like that of the moon-tides effect, which for the Stoics constituted an inseparable unity, had to be "analyzed" into separate ingredients; a source of gravitational force, a mechanism of the propagation of this force through space and time, and an object affected by the force. Such an analysis was made possible only through the introduction of certain theoretical terms like ether, gravitational force, etc. In fact, the formation of most, if not all, of the so-called "theoretical concepts," widely discussed by modern philosophers of science, resulted from such processes of fragmentation of the phenomena into independent constitutive elements, a strategem fully akin to the spirit of Bacon's "dissection of nature."

The very fact that the reductionist approach—especially as employed in microphysics where it undoubtedly scored its greatest success—implied the introduction of theoretical concepts and "unobservables in principle" may be viewed as this methodological procedure's weak point.

It will have been noticed that in the preceding historical introduction certain notions have been employed without being provided with rigorous definitions. This applies in the first place, of course, to the notions of "integrative concepts" and "integrative principles." Although frequently used by biologists and occasionally also by physicists, these notions have never—to the best of my knowledge—been given a strict definition. Even in Henry Margenau's valuable monograph on "Integrative Principles of Modern Thought"[4] one looks in vain for such a definition.

To prepare the ground for such a definition let us start with a mathematical paradigm, familiar to every physicist, and translate it subsequently into the language of logic and methodology. True, from a semantical point of view, mathematics presupposes logic even if it may be questioned that the relation of logic to mathematics is that of "theory priority" in the strong sense as understood by Alonzo Church.[5] However, from the methodological point of view mathematics preceded logic since it motivated the development of logic and does so still today. Especially if one is interested in a new classificatory category of concepts, as we are in our case, it may prove useful to search for analogies in mathematics.

Contrary to what may be expected, especially in view of the etymological proximity, it is not the mathematical notion of the "integral" (whether in the sense of Darboux, Riemann or Lebesque) which can serve as a characteristic model for the definition of "integrativeness"; for after all mathematical integration is but a set-theoretical procedure of summation and lacks therefore precisely that feature which distinguishes integrativeness from summary comprehensiveness, namely the emergence of a new property which distinguishes the whole from the sum of its parts. The notion of an affine connection, however, as employed in the theory of differential manifolds, does just this. As will be recalled, the first step in the establishment of a geometrical theory of differential manifolds consists in the construction of tangent vectors and tangent planes at each of the points of the manifold. But this does not suffice to define parallelism even between two infinitesimally near tangent vectors. For each tangent plane is an isolated geometrical system devoid of any relation to other such systems. But by defining arbitrarily certain functions of the coordinates at each point of the manifold (the well-known $\Gamma_{\beta\gamma}$) an affine connection is constructed which, so to say, at one strike, transforms the ensemble of previously unrelated tangent spaces into a new system of interrelated entities, the "affine manifold."

Following this model, we propose the following definition of "integrative concepts" and "integrative principles," or "integrative constructs" collectively. Let there be given a (class, set or) system "s" of (subsets or) subsystems s_k, where k is an index running over a given finite or infinite, discrete or continuous indexical range, and let each s_k be described by a description or theory T_k. A concept A is an integrative concept (with respect to the system "s") if and only if it makes it possible to extend all the T_k to a single (new) description or theory T', the referent being s'. In this case s' will be called the (integrative) supersystem of the systems s_k.

In our geometrical model each s_k was a point of the manifold and T_k the geometry of the tangent space belonging to that point. The "new" property, generated by the integrative concept A, is the "affine connection" which extends all the individual T_k into a single (new) geometry T' the referent of which is s', the affine manifold, which is a supersystem of the systems s_k. There are many such supersystems, for by choosing different connections one obtains different T' and corresponding different supersystems s'. Additional constraints may, of course, restrict this dimension of freedom. In fact, if in our geometrical example the manifold is a metric Riemannian space, the connection is uniquely determined by the components of the metric tensor and only one single supersystem results. As the example also shows, the integrative concept need not be explicitly definable; it suffices to define it as the generator of a property by virtue of which all the T_k can be extended to a single T. The s_k are usually referred to as systems of a lower level (than the level of s') and, conversely, s' is referred to as a system of a higher level (than the level of the s_k).

The definition clearly shows that the properties of the supersystem cannot all be described or explained by the properties of the subsystems. The integrationist expresses this fact by saying that the whole is not just the sum of its parts.

Obviously, this integrative process can be iterated: the supersystems, now denoted by s'_k, may be regarded as the components of a system of still higher order which, due to the integrative process, forms a supersystem of order 2 or what may be called a "super-supersystem, denoted by s''. Thus a hierarchial order of integrative supersystems can be constructed with corresponding descriptions or theories of increasing order.

Although rarely encountered in physics, explicit formulations of such integrative processes are frequently mentioned in biology. Certain statements made by Claude Bernard[6] and by many modern biologists agree very well with our definition. The famous Nobel laureate François Jacob in his history of heredity even coined a special term in this connection. "At each level," he wrote, "units of relatively well defined size and almost identical structure associate to form a unit of the level above. Each of these units formed by the integration of sub-units may be given the general name 'integron.' An integron is formed by assembling integrons of the level below it; it takes part in the construction of the integron of the level above."[7]

Examples of such hierarchies in physics are well known: atoms, molecules, crystals is one example, stars, galaxies, clusters, super-clusters is another. That, as mentioned above, to each level corresponds a description or theory $T^{(n)}$ of its own is illustrated by the fact that we distinguish between "atomic physics," "molecular physics" and "solid state physics," for example. That in the physical sciences, perhaps in contrast to biology, the hierarchial order of integrons, to use the term coined by Jacob, need not be limited is exemplified by the cosmological hypotheses of J. H. Lambert or, more recently, of C. V. L. Charlier who postulated an unending hierarchial order of stellar systems to avoid Olber's well-known paradox in its optical or gravitational version.

Turning now to the specific use of integrative principles in physics proper, I wish to defend the following theses: the application of integrative principles is a necessary condition for the possibility of physics as a science.

In order to prove this thesis in its generality we have first to clarify the notion of symmetry and invariance and to understand the relation of these notions to integrativeness. As is well known, symmetry is a widespread property in nature and human artifacts. Already in antiquity it has been used, for example by Anaximander, Plato and Archimedes, as an argument for the logical derivation of certain assertions in the physical sciences. But what is symmetry? Look at a snow flake! If you rotate it around its center by $60°$ or any multiple thereof, the rotated shape will coincide with the original shape: the shape remains invariant. Symmetry, in other words, is the invariance of certain aspects under a group of transformations. Recalling our definition of integrativeness, we may say that the set of different rotated shapes of the snowflake corresponds to the set of the different s_k, their equality of appearance corresponds to the property which makes it possible to extend the various T_k, the description of the s_k, to a single description T the referent of which is s' (the corresponding equivalence class). We conclude that symmetry is an integrative concept! In fact, every invariance under a given set of transformations gives rise to a symmetry and hence to an integrative process. Now, every physical law expresses a relation between phenomena, whether it is the relation between cause and effect or merely that of a functional correlation is in our context irrelevant. What matters is the fact that a statement in physics is a physical law only if the relation it expresses holds always and everywhere under the same initial conditions. In other words, a phys-

ical law is an assertion of an invariance under certain spatial and temporal transformations. It incorporates a symmetry and hence an integrative
principle.

Professor Wigner once wrote: "The statement, that absolute time
and position are never essential initial conditions, is the first and perhaps
the most important theorem of invariance in physics. If it were not for it,
it might have been impossible for us to discover laws of nature."[8]

Paraphrasing Wigner I assert that "if it were not for integrative
constructs, it might have been impossible for us to formulate laws of
nature."

But I dare to say even more. A law in physics not only presupposes
an integrative principle as we just saw; it represents itself an integrative
principle.

In order to substantiate this claim I wish to quote a second statement made by Wigner—but this time a statement with which I disagree.
Wigner once observed that ". . . if we had a complete knowledge of all
events in the world, everywhere and at all times, there would be no use
for the laws of physics."[9] In the sequel Professor Wigner slightly qualified
his assertion by pointing out that "If we knew the position of the planet at
all times, the mathematical relation between these positions which the
planetary laws furnish would not be useful but might still be interesting.
It might give us a certain pleasure and perhaps amazement to contem-
plate, even if it did not furnish us new information.[10]

It seems to me, in contrast to these statements, that a formalized law
conveys information beyond and above that supplied by all the individual
cases subsumed by it. The so-called Calculatores at Merton College in
Oxford or at the University of Paris emphasized already in the fourteenth
century, especially in their writings "De Latitudinibus," that the overall
shape of a graphical representation of a functional relation has an inform-
ative value for itself—today we would call it its "Gestalt." Indeed, the fact
that such a relation is linear or quadratic or otherwise, a fact not expressed nor expressable by any of the individual cases may turn out to be
an important piece of information. Moreover, meta-scientific statements
are often statements about laws and could hardly be made if a law were
merely the list of correlated measurement results. It is precisely because
of this surplus information that a physical law embodies an integrative
principle.

The necessity of integrative principles for the possibility of physics is
also shown by the fact that the most fundamental concepts of physics owe
their existence to such principles. Take for example the notion of "time"
as understood in modern physics. It would lead us too far astray to discuss
the development of this notion. Let me only point out that in classical
physics two (spatially separated) events were simultaneous if they occurred at the same time; in modern physics "time" is an ordered class of

simultaneities, or more technically expressed, of spacelike hypersurfaces in a Minkowski manifold. The problem of "time" became therefore essentially that of how to define (intrasystemic) simultaneity of spatially separated events and was solved by Einstein in the first section of his monumental essay on the special relativity theory. There Einstein declared: "We have so far defined only an 'A-time' (namely the reading of a clock located at the position A) and a 'B-time' (namely the reading of a similar clock located at the position B). We have not defined a common 'time' for A and B. This latter time can now be defined if we *establish by definition* that the 'time' required by light to travel from A to B equals the 'time' it requires to travel from B to A."[11] And in the sequel Einstein described his famous method of standard synchronization by means of a light signal, emitted from A and reflected from B back to A, the details of which are well known and need not be recounted. On the basis of his definition of simultaneity Einstein was able to derive the Lorentz transformations and thereby all the theorems of relativistic kinematics. It is clear that Einstein's definition of time (via simultaneity) constitutes essentially an application of an integrative principle. In fact, one may look upon it as a translation of the geometrical paradigm, mentioned above, into the language of temporal expressions, the notion of "A-time" and "B-time" corresponding to different tangent planes of the manifold. Clearly, "time" in modern physics is an integrative concept.

The special theory of relativity incorporates integrative principles in an even two-fold sense. Being based, as explained, on the notion of time it inherits, so to say, integrativeness through the notion of time; but it is itself a theory of invariants under the Lorentz or Poincaré group of transformations; in other words, it is a theory of symmetries and therefore based again on integrative principles.

This result can be generalized to the following conclusion. Whenever a physical theory incorporates a conceptual or operational principle of indiscriminacy, it incorporates an integrative principle. Typical examples are Pauli's Exclusion Principle or, more generally, the Fermi-Dirac statistics in quantum mechanics, based on the physical indiscriminacy of the so-called "identical" particles.

The question naturally arises whether there are physical concepts that are integrative without being rooted in symmetry considerations. That such concepts are logically possible follows from the fact that in our definition of integrative constructs the various T_k, describing the s_k, were not assumed to be necessarily identical with each other—as it happens in the case of integrative concepts based on symmetry. The only condition imposed upon them was the possibility to extend them to a common T, the description or theory of the supersystem or integron of the next higher order.

That symmetry is a sufficient but not necessary precondition for the occurrence or formation of integrative constructs is best shown by an example. Consider the notion of a "field" in classical or, for that matter also, in quantum physics. A field of forces, say, of gravitational or electromagnetic forces, is not merely the sum total of all the force vectors in space; it has properties of its own, such as solenoidality (irrotationality), divergences and so on. Likewise, the concept of "potential" is not merely a scalar function the negative gradient of which equals the field quantity at the point under discussion; it has additional features to offer such as those exhibited by the Bohm-Aharonov effect. Similarly, the Lagrangian and the Hamiltonian function of a dynamical system are based on integrative principles and so are, consequently, the conservation theorems which they imply *via* the well-known Noether theorem. That these conservation theorems are again expressions of certain symmetries is an additional feature and, in the present context, a circumstantial feature since not all Lagrangian or Hamiltonian functions satisfy the conditions of Noether's theorem. An integrative principle, *par exellence,* is of course the action principle (or principle of least action) with its remarkably wide domain of applicability both in classical and in modern physics.

Recent results in modern physics seem to indicate that there exists a special category of integrative concepts which have their origin not in symmetry features but owe their existence to the holistic character of the theory. It has been said that quantum mechanics is the first—and so far perhaps the only—holistic theory in physics that has been formalized. In any case, it is in quantum mechanics that we find a number of holistic-integrative concepts of great importance.

It is probably no exaggeration to say that the still ongoing controversy concerning the interpretation of quantum mechanics involves— perhaps to a critical extent—the question of whether to recognize or to reject the legitimacy of holistic-integrative constructs. The clash of opinion between the proponents of realistic interpretations, such as Einstein, Popper or the authors of hidden variable theories, on the one hand, and proponents of more orthodox interpretations, such as Bohr or Heisenberg, seems to have its ultimate origin in this question. Ultimately, it may well be just the conflict between reductionists and integrationists.

Consider, for example, the famous reality criterion proposed by Einstein, Podolsky and Rosen (EPR), in their celebrated paper of 1935: "If, without in any way disturbing a system, we can predict with certainty (i.e., with probability unity) the value of a physical quantity, then there exists an element of physical reality corresponding to this physical quantity."[12] Bohr challenged the EPR criterion of physical reality by claiming that "the conditions which define the possible types of predictions regarding the future behavior of the system . . . constitute an inherent element of the description of any phenomena to which the term 'physical reality' can be properly attached."[13] Only by an appeal to the integrativeness of the notions of quantum state and its disturbance could Bohr defend the completeness of quantum mechanics. In the last analysis, the conflict between Bohr and EPR is the same as the difference between Poseidonius and Newton with regard to their respective conceptions of the moon-tides phenomenon.

Before turning to the question which naturally arises at this point, whether the definition of integrative constructs mentioned above applies also to such holistic-integrative notions, it will prove useful to consider in greater detail one of the most important holistic-integrative concepts in modern physics, that of "non-separability."

Consider a sequence of N of spin-$1/2$ particles, each pair being in a singlet state ($S = 0$). Assume further that the members of each pair, labeled by an index j ($j = 1, 2, \ldots N$), separate from each other, one of them moving toward a Stern-Gerlach type analyzer A and the other member to a similar analyzer B in the opposite direction. The principal direction of A can make an angle α_1 or α_2 with the direction of the electron's motion and B can make an angle β_1 or β_2 with that direction. The result of measuring the spin of the first member of the j-th pair at A, when A's position is in α_m (m = 1 or 2) and B's position is in β_n (n = 1 or 2) will be denoted by a_{jmn}. Analogously, the result of measuring the spin of the second member of the j-th pair at B, when B's position is in β_n and A's position is in α_m will be denoted by b_{jnm}.

In units of $n/2$ these results are either $+1$ or -1 as is well known. We shall now show that each pair of such particles possesses a property above and beyond that of simply being "a set of two particles": each pair will exhibit a holistic coherence in the sense that no matter how far the two members may be separated, what happens with the one affects the other, even though no direct interaction between them can be operative. The possibility of such a holistic feature has been taken already into consideration by the use of the two indices m and n, in addition to the index j for each measurement result. For a_{j12}, for example, has the following meaning: the spin of the particle (belonging to the j-th pair) which was measured by the apparatus A, when A was in position α_1 while the position of apparatus B was β_2, was $+1$ (or "spin-up"). In the absence of "non-separability," that is if separability prevails, the third index would be irrelevant and we would have

$$a_{jmn} = a_{jm} \text{ and } b_{jnm} = b_{jn}. \tag{1}$$

We shall now show[14] that the omission of this third index or, equivalently, the assumption of separability, leads to consequences which conflict with empirical evidence.

To this end we define the correlation function

$$c_{mn} = \sum_{j=1}^{N} a_{jm} b_{jn} \qquad (2)$$

This definition obviously implies that $c_{mn} \leq 1$. $\qquad (3)$
According to quantum mechanics (See Appendix)

$$c_{mn} = -\cos (\beta_n - \alpha_m) \qquad (4)$$

We further define

$$c_j = a_{j1}b_{j1} + a_{j1}b_{j2} + a_{j2}b_{j1} - a_{j2}b_{j2} \qquad (5)$$

and finally

$$c = \frac{1}{N} \sum_{j=1}^{N} c_j = c_{11} - c_{12} + c_{21} - c_{22} \qquad (6)$$

where

$$c_{mn} = \frac{1}{N} \sum_{j=1}^{N} a_{jm} b_{jn} \qquad (7)$$

Now, since

$$c_j = a_{j1}(b_{j1} + b_{j2}) + a_{j2}(b_{j1} - b_{j2}) \qquad (8)$$

it follows that if sign b_{j1} = sign b_{j2} then

$$c_j = a_{j1}(b_{j1} + b_{j2}) = 2(\text{sign } b_{j1})a_{j1} = \pm 2 \qquad (9)$$

and, alternatively, if sign b_{j1} = $-$sign b_{j2} then

$$c_j = a_{j2}(b_{j1} - b_{j2}) = 2(\text{sign } b_{j1})a_{j2} = \pm \qquad (10)$$

so that in any case, in view of (6),

$$|c| = |c_{11} + c_{22} + c_{21} - c_{22}| \leq 2 \qquad (11)$$

We shall now show that the conclusion (11) derived from the assumption of separability is contradicted by the statistical predictions of quantum mechanics. To this end we choose

$$\alpha_1 = 0° \quad \alpha_2 = 90° \quad \beta_1 = 45° \quad \text{and } \beta_2 = -45° \qquad (8\text{-}12)$$

and apply formula (4). A simple calculation yields the following results:

$$c_{11} = -\frac{1}{2}\sqrt{2} \qquad c_{12} = -\frac{1}{2}\sqrt{2} \qquad c_{21} = -\frac{1}{2}\sqrt{2} \qquad c_{22} = \frac{1}{2}\sqrt{2}$$

so that

$$|c| = |c_{11} + c_{12} + c_{21} - c_{22}| = |-2\sqrt{2}| = 2\sqrt{2} > 2 \qquad (8\text{-}13)$$

in contradiction to (8-11). Since the statistical predictions of quantum mechanics seem to agree very well with experience we are forced to conclude: the result of a measurement carried out at A on one member of a pair depends on the result of the measurement carried out at B on the other member of the pair. It seems as if the two particles are connected by some invisible linkage; this linkage, as recent experiments performed by Aspect and others demonstrate, cannot be conceived of as a dynamical interaction.[15] It is the manifestation of a holistic-integrative principle at action and reveals the insufficiency of Bacon's advice of "dissecare naturam"; for no matter how closely the behavior of either of the two particles, forming a pair, may individually be examined, the effect of that invisible linkage, and hence its very existence, could not be discovered.

A critical examination of the reasoning that led us to this conclusion will, however, reveal the following difficulty. In (8-5) we defined for every j, that is for every pair of particles, the quantity cj in terms of the four measurements results a_{j1}, a_{j2}, b_{j1} and b_{j2}. But only two out of these four numbers can empirically be obtained since for a given j apparatus A can have only one orientation and apparatus B can have only one orientation. Assume, for example, that their orientations were α_1 and β_2, respectively. If it were then certain that, had α_2 been chosen instead of α_1, a *definite* measurement result a_{j2} would have been obtained, the use of a_{j2}, even though not *de facto* determined, could have been admitted for the statistical calculation as performed. But what assurance is there that in this counterfactual case a *definite* value of a_{j2} exists at all? Perhaps it is false, or at least meaningless, to posit a_{j2} if a_{j1} is actually being measured, just as it may be false, or at least meaningless, according to the orthodox interpretation of quantum mechanics, to assume that the momentum of a particle has a definite value if its position is being measured. We are facing here what has been called the problem of counterfactual definiteness.

Moreover, none of the four additive terms $a_{jm}b_{jn}$ on the right-hand side of equation (8-5), which represent results of measurements performed in spacelike separated regions, is a product of numbers both of which can appear in the consciousness of any single observer during the process of measurement. The specification of c in (8-6) thus requires some additional information transfer which may seriously complicate the whole argument and may lead to profound difficulties especially within the context of the many-worlds interpretation of quantum mechanics. Although these problems may still await their resolution they hardly seem to call in question our conclusion concerning the existence of holistic-integrative concepts and principles in quantum mechanics.

Having shown that, if the statistical predictions of quantum mechanics are correct, "non-separability" is a basic feature of modern physics, we now turn to the question of whether this undoubtedly holistic notion is also integrative in the sense defined by the above-mentioned definition of integrativeness. The answer is provided by the very formalism of quantum mechanics itself!

For the j-th particle-pair let $s_1 = s_{ja}$ denote that member which is subjected to the measurement process performed at A ; let ψ_{ja}^+ be its state function if the measurement result is $+1$ (spin-up) and ψ_{ja}^- if it is -1 (spin-down). Analogously, let $s_2 = s_{jb}$ denote the member which is subjected to the measurement process performed at B ; let ψ_{jb}^+ be its state function if the measurement result is $+1$ (spin-up) and ψ_{jb}^- if it is -1 (spin-down). For each index j we have therefore for s_1 the description $T_1 = \psi_{ja}^+ \vee \psi_{ja}^-$ and for s_2 the description $T_2 = \psi_{jb}^+ \vee \psi_{jb}^-$, where "$\vee$" denotes a logical disjunction ("or"). Now, according to quantum mechanics the description of the set s of the two particles is given by an element T' of the tensor product of the Hilbert spaces belonging to s_1 and s_2. The most famous example is the case where s happens to be in singlet state (S = O) so that $T' = (1/\sqrt{2})(\psi_{ja}^+\psi_{jb}^- - \psi_{ja}^-\psi_{jb}^+)$. In this case the preceding statistics are additionally conditioned by the EPR correlations.

Our use of the notion of "extension" cannot be criticized as being excessively liberal since our definition of integrative constructs does not impose any restrictions upon the mathematical and/or logical structure of this extension. It should be noted, however, that due to the presence of the connective "$\vee$" this extension is not carried out in the object-language but rather in the meta-language of the formalism. It may well be that this switch of language is typical for all holistic-integrative constructs in theoretical physics. In any case, it has been shown that also "non-separability," probably the most general of all holistic notions in physics, is an integrative concept in accordance with our definition.

The use of the notion of "extension" made in our definitions of integrative conceptions allows us also to clarify the relation between properties described by integrative concepts and so-called *emergent properties*. The latter play an important role in the general system analysis and especially in Hermann Haken's synergetics. To bring the notion of emergent properties within the context of our analysis I shall define them as properties of a system s' which are due to interactions among the subsystems s_k of s' without being reducible to them. This definition includes the possibility of describing them, as is so often done, as having their origin in non-linear interactions combined, perhaps, with acausal fluctuation at that sublevel, but always with the proviso of not being reducible to the properties of that sublevel or the properties of the systems s_k.

The problem of emergent properties manifests itself most prominently, of course, in the controversy between physicalism and vitalism in biology. As Professor Bulent Atalay has shown in his paper on "The Origin of Life," all attempts so far of explaining the emergence of organized self-replicating molecular systems take refuge to certain physico-chemical processes the probabilities of which to occur are extremely minute. No wonder that Professor Ady Mann, in his commentary to this paper, raised the question: "Is it indeed reasonable to suppose that biology is ultimately a branch of physics, in the sense in which chemistry is now known to be, in principle, a branch of physics?" Let me remind you that the reduction of chemistry to physics is itself still an issue far from being completely settled.

The irreducibility, at least for the time being, of the emergent properties of life to the properties of physico-chemical agents as viewed in the perspective of our present approach, has been emphasized by Samuel Alexander when he wrote: "Material things have certain motions of their own which carry the quality of materials . . . Physical and chemical processes of a certain complexity have the quality of life . . . The higher quality emerges from the lower level and has its roots therein, but it emerges therefrom, and it does not belong to that lower level, but constitutes its possessor a new order of existent with its special laws of behaviour. The existence of emerging qualities thus described is something to be noted, as some would say, under the compulsion of brute empirical fact, or, as I should prefer to say in less harsh terms, to be accepted with the 'natural piety' of the investigator. It admits no explanation."

It seems, indeed, highly questionable whether a theory of the origin of life, which is based, as most monophylectic theories are, on the assumption of a chance event, does really offer an explanation. Whether or not we accept the Hempel-Oppenheim model of explanation, I think the biochemist Christian Schwabe is right when he wrote in the periodical *Origins of Life*: "It is worse yet to do research that is irrelevant to an existing hypothesis because the hypothesis itself (chance event) is untestable! A scientific hypothesis must be testable in principle and thereby give rise to experiments and the kind of intellectual exchanges on scientific grounds that make for the enrichment of the human venture called science."

Let us study the logical consequences of the assumptions that there exists such an explanation tantamount to a reduction of life to physico-chemical processes, an assumption which then would deny the occurrence of emergent properties and with them of integrative conceptions. Let us, for the sake of the argument, also generalize Alexander's account by taking into consideration properties at the level of mind or consciousness in addition to the properties at the level of living organisms. Finally, let us denote the properties at the level of physico-chemical processes p_1, p_2, . . . or briefly p, those of living organisms p' and those at the level of consciousness p ". If p' were reducible to p, then p would be, expressed in the language of logic, a sufficient condition for p'; and if, analogously, p " were reducible to p', then p' would be a sufficient condition for p ". But the relation of "being a sufficient condition for" is a transitive relation: if A is a sufficient condition of B, and B is a sufficient condition of C, then also A is a sufficient condition of C. Logic also teaches us that in this case C is a *necessary* condition of A. If we apply this inference to the generalization of Alexander's reasoning we must conclude that properties of consciousness, or consciousness in short, is a necessary condition for physico-chemical properties or, in agreement with reductionism, for quantum mechanics. The assumption of a complete explanation, or equivalently the denial of an essential irreducibility of what are called "emergent properties" would thus lead us to conclusions, such as the London-Bauer theory of observation in quantum mechanics, which take consciousness as an integral—not integrative!—factor for the occurrence of physical phenomena. A realistic interpretation of physics, as we see, must affirm emergence and integrativeness to be *sui generis* characteristics.

Let us now, in conclusion ask whether physics itself, without transcending into the realm of life or consciousness, arrives at the same conclusion. To this end we will study the emergence of turbulence in hydrodynamic systems or fluids in general.

Consider a system s composed of molecules s_k constituting an ideal gas. The theory T_k of each s_k comprises essentially only the conservation laws of energy and momentum of Newtonian mechanics. But statistical considerations make it possible to describe s by a theory T for a given volume V and a given temperature of the gas. If we assume that V has the form of a tube (or capillary) of length large compared to its diameter and if we apply a small pressure difference $\Delta p = p_1 - p_2$ to the ends of the tube, we obtain a constant laminar flow of the gas, provided quantities of gas are supplied at the one end and withdrawn at the other at an appropriate rate. To calculate the latter, the viscosity η of the gas has to be taken into consideration. The viscosity η is given by a formula discovered experimentally by Hagen in 1839 and independently by Poiseuille in 1840 which reads

$$\eta = \pi r^4 (p_1 - p_2) t / 8LV$$

where L is the length of the capillary tube and t is the time of the flow of the gas through the tube of radius r. It is important to recall that this relation can be established on the basis of the theory T for it can be derived by an integration of Newton's friction law. Moreover, the kinetic theory of gases, that is essentially again T, shows that η is (approximately) proportional to the square of the absolute temperature of the gas. Viscosity, we conclude, is *not* an emergent property and no integrative conceptions are involved.

The situation, however, changes radically as soon as p increases beyond a certain value characterized by what is called Reynolds number R which itself can still be accounted for on the basis of T. Once the limit defined by R is surpassed the laminar motion becomes unstable and a state of "irregular" eddying motion or *turbulence* emerges. Turbulence, now, defies theoretical description in the sense that it is subject to a theory T' which cannot be reduced to T, although it constitutes an "extension" of it. It is an "extension" of T because the laws of T do not lose their validity even in the case of turbulence but are not sufficient to explain this new phenomenon, just as the laws of physics remain valid for living organisms without having that the properties of the latter can be fully explained by those laws. Turbulence, in other words, is an emergent property and its definition requires integrative conceptions.

APPENDIX

The statistical prediction (4) can be derived from the fundamentals of quantum mechanics as follows.

Using the Pauli spin matrices

$$\sigma_x = \begin{pmatrix} 0 & 1 \\ 1 & 0 \end{pmatrix} \quad \sigma_y = \begin{pmatrix} 0 & -i \\ i & 0 \end{pmatrix} \quad \sigma_z = \begin{pmatrix} 1 & 0 \\ 0 & -1 \end{pmatrix}$$

we obtain for a spin in the direction

$$n = (\sin\theta \, \cos\varphi, \, \sin\theta \, \sin\varphi, \, \cos\varphi)$$

the matrix

$$\sigma_n = \sigma n = \begin{pmatrix} \cos\theta & e^{-i\varphi}\sin\theta \\ e^{i\varphi}\sin\theta & -\cos\theta \end{pmatrix}$$

The eigenvalues of σ_n are $+1$ and -1 and the eigenvectors, correspondingly, are

$$\varphi_n^+ = \begin{pmatrix} \cos\theta/2 \\ e^{i\varphi}\sin\theta/2 \end{pmatrix} \quad \text{and} \quad \varphi_n^- = \begin{pmatrix} -e^{-i\varphi}\sin\theta/2 \\ \cos\theta/2 \end{pmatrix}$$

From $\psi_n^+ = \cos\theta/2\binom{1}{0} + e^{i\phi}\sin\theta/2\binom{0}{1}$ it follows that if the particle is in the state $\binom{1}{0}$, i.e. spin-up in the z-direction, the probability of obtaining $+1$ in direction n is given by $\cos^{2\theta}$ where θ is the angle between the direction of the z^2-axis and the direction of n.

For a singlet state (S = 0) of the two spins $\sigma(1)$ and $\sigma(2)$ we have $\sigma(1) + \sigma(2) = 0$. To find the expectation value $\sigma_{\alpha\beta} = \,<\sigma(1)\alpha \ \sigma(2)\beta>$ we assume the spin of particle (1) to be the z-direction and to make an angle $\theta = \beta - \alpha$ with the direction of the spin of particle (2). It then follows from the above that

$$c_{\alpha\beta} = (+1)\cos^2\frac{1}{2}(180° - \theta) + (-1)\cos^2\frac{\theta}{2} = -\cos\theta \text{ or}$$

$$c_{\alpha\beta} = -\cos(\beta - \alpha)$$

as stated in equation (4).

NOTES

1. Birkhoff, G. and Neumann, J.von, 1936. "The logic of quantum mechanics," *Annals of Mathematics 37*: 823.

2. Simplicius, 1907. *In Aristotelis Categorias Commentarium*, edited by Kalbfleisch, C., Georg Reimer, Berlin: p. 214.

3. *Ibid.*

4. Margenau, H. ed., 1972. *Integrative Principles in Modern Thought* (Gordon and Breach, New York).

5. Nagel, E. et al., editors, 1962. *Logic, Methodology and Philosophy of Science*, Stanford University Press, Stanford.

6. Bernard, C., 1878. *Lecons sur les Phenomenes de la Vie* (Paris, vol. I, p. 50 et seq.

7. Jacob, F., 1970. *La Logique du Vivant*, (Gallimard, Paris: and *The Logic of Living Systems*. (Allen Lane, London: 1974): p. 302.

8. Wigner, E., 1949. "Invariance in physical theory," *Proceedings of the American Philosophical Society 93.*

9. E. P. Wigner, 1964. "Symmetry and conservation laws," *Physics Today 17* (n.3), 35.

10. *Ibid.* p. 35

11. Einstein, A., 1905. "Zur Elektrodynamik bewegter Körper", *Annalen* der Physik 17: 891.

12. Einstein, A., et al. 1935, "Can quantum mechanical description of physical reality be considered complete?" *Physical Review 47*: 777.

13. Bohr, N., 1935. "Can quantum mechanical description of physical reality be considered complete?" *Physical Review 48*: 696.

14. 1977 Cf. the derivation of the Clauser-Horne-Shimony-Holt inequality and its application to the polarization of photons in Eberhard, P. "Bell's inequality without hidden variables." *Nuovo Cimento 38 B*: 75.

15. Aspect, A., et al., 1982. "Experimental test of Bell's inequality using time-varying analyzers," *Physical Review Letters 49*: 1804.

15

Self-Organization and Evolution Through Fluctuations and Instabilities

MANUEL G. VELARDE

1. INTRODUCTION

How did life originate and evolve on Earth? This is one of the fascinating questions to which modern science, in the present century, has provided partial though definite answers—answers that no longer reflect a specific ideology but, rather, are the products of carefully controlled experiments and detailed model studies. There are, however, lots of unanswered questions about morphogenesis and other important details and thus we cannot claim having obtained a homogeneous body of knowledge comparable to Newtonian physics. We are in fact, in a period of transition, a period of fertile, albeit fragmentary and occasionally contradictory, scientific development. But we begin to see the emergence of a new paradigm that tends to replace the Newtonian one. Now we also see as a *matter of fact* a new approach to science that incorporates man, and so a science that embraces in a natural way man and nature, thus embracing all disciplines from physics, chemistry and biology to economy, sociology, etc.

Nowadays, the study of prebiotic or biological evolution is not merely related to the study of evolution of inanimate matter (magnets, fluids, fluid flows, turbulence, lasers etc). It is in fact quite related to the study of human (individual or societal) behavior, economic behavior, and the humanities at large.

How has this come about? What are the conceptual building blocks of this new approach to nature and man?

There has been, on the one hand, the extraordinary development of the statistical mechanics of cooperative (critical) phenomena and equilibrium phase transitions (melting, crystallization, vaporization, ferromagnetism, etc.) that culminated in the work of K. G. Wilson (winner of the 1982 Nobel Prize in Physics). On the other hand, there has also been an extraordinary development of the methods in nonlinear mathematics applied to non-equilibrium thermodynamic systems. A wealth of knowledge has accumulated since the pioneering and seminal work of L. Onsager (winner of the 1968 Nobel Prize in Chemistry) and I. Prigogine (winner of the 1977 Nobel Prize in Chemistry). And there has also been extraordinary progress in our experimental and theoretical study of non-equilibrium cooperative, synergetic phenomena like Bénard convection, laser action and the evolution of chemical and biochemical processes (like the Belousov-Zhabotinskii reaction: the oxidation of malonic acid or other acids in the presence of Cerium or other catalyzers). H. Haken has had an enormous influence on these developments. Altogether these three lines of research have led to new unifying concepts whose usefulness goes far beyond the original contexts.

2. EXAMPLES IN THE NATURAL SCIENCES AND A BIT OF VOCABULARY

Consider the case of a horizontal liquid layer heated from below and either open to the ambient air or enclosed between, say, two copper plates. For low enough values of the temperature difference between the bottom and the top the actual state for the system is the state of rest with a steady nonequilibrium linear vertical temperature profile. Yet for each value of the rate of heating (or energy transfer) the liquid explores not only this motionless state but many other possible states including numerous convective modes and turbulence. The actual state is, however, that of rest for it is the only stable one. If we increase the rate of heating we observe that past a certain *threshold* value the system evolves to steady cellular convection (Bénard convection). Which pattern of convection (rolls, polygonal cells, etc.) develops is determined by boundary conditions, i.e., it depends on the constraints at the boundaries, or on the specific kind of fluid dynamics involved. However, it is universally found both from theory and experiment that the system fluctuates through as many states as possible in order to finally establish itself in a particular one. This actual state, reached just beyond a certain threshold value of the temperature difference across the layer, is the state *bifurcated* from the state of rest. Moreover, in terms of a suitably chosen (dimensionless) quantity or control parameter, the critical (threshold) value is universal, i.e., it does not depend on the liquid for a given geometry (set-up) or on some of the aspects of the geometry for a chosen liquid.

The bifurcation from rest to cellular convection or to more complex behavior is a form of non-equilibrium *phase transition*. The new state is a specific *dissipative structure*. This bifurcation can be continuous, soft and direct, or else it can be discontinous, hard and inverted with metastability and hysteretic phenomena. The terminology is straightforward, though not always fully justified taken *verbatim* from the terminology invented by L. D. Landau (winner of the 1962 Nobel Prize in Physics) for equilibrium thermodynamics and statistical mechanics. Here, the system is not at equilibrium but rather it is in one of its available non-equilibrium dynamic states along its "evolution."

Cellular convection is just one of the possible and actual states of the liquid layer heated from below. Another possibility is oscillatory convection, i.e., a state of time-periodic variation of the velocity and temperature, or other measurable quantities. Other oscillatory periodic motions are the pulsed behavior typical of T. Maiman's 1960 ruby laser (the first to be operated) or of a laser with an intracavity absorber. Generally, oscillatory states arise when there is competition between two or more agents, two or more constraints or two or more largely separate time scales in a way such that a recurring relaxation process develops.

Another possible and, on occasion, actual state of a system driven away from equilibrium is *turbulence* or, in a more restricted situation, *deterministic chaos*. These cases occur when all time (or space and time) correlations in the system decay as time proceeds (as time approaches infinity) or in more technical language, when the power spectrum of all time signals in the system shows broad band noise (well above instrumental noise). Note that the power spectrum of steady cellular convection is a spike centered at the origin (a time-independent signal has an "infinite" period and thus it corresponds to a zero frequency motion). On the other hand a periodic (or nearly periodic) state always has a power spectrum with a discrete (finite or infinite) set of spikes well above the noise level.

At present, there is tremendous impetus in the study of deterministic chaos, i.e., turbulence generated not by stochastic elements but rather as a consequence of the deterministic complexity (sophistication) of the system (feedback loops, autocatalysis, nonlinear evolution laws, high enough dissipation, etc., or non-integrability in a conservative system). Deterministic chaos is generally linked to time-dependent albeit aperiodic states lying on "volumes" of *fractal* (non-integer) dimensionality, i.e., on "space" that almost, but not quite, fills a volume and as a matter of fact has zero volume. B. Mandelbrot has played a key role in the dissemination of these ideas. A system evolving towards such a state, called, in the jargon, a *strange attractor*, shows extraordinary *sensitivity* to the values given at the *initial time* in its evolution towards the attractor. Moreover, although the laws of the system may be purely deterministic, there is no possibility of predictability in the sense of Newton's paradigm. This lack of predictability of the behavior of a system is well known by meteorologists. E. N. Lorenz has been a pioneer in this field.

Finally, another possibility for complexity in a system is to have a multiplicity of possible steady or oscillatory states for one and the same value of the constraints at any given time. The actual state to be attained among the possible ones depends strongly on fluctuations and external noise or forces, and eventually on aspects of its history; for some complex systems, initial conditions may never be forgotten at all. This contrasts with simple classical systems where the past is generally irrelevant for the future.

3. FUTURE OUTLOOK: FROM PHYSICS TO OTHER DISCIPLINES

The more the ideas of the preceding sections penetrate into other disciplines and become part of the culture of our colleagues in the soft sciences, the more it becomes apparent how useful they are. Consider, for instance, the evolution of climate on Earth. It has recently been shown that glaciations and related climatic phenomena have an apparently chaotic evolution; the same appears to be true for stock market data (time periodic states are also known in economics). What about the propagation of fashion, or the spread of a rumor or of a disease? What about political revolutions and the evolution of human behavior before and near election days? These are fascinating questions in the realm of the social sciences that are similar to questions asked about the behavior of inanimate matter.

I do not know if transdisciplinary concepts defined in physics will prove really useful in other sciences in the near future. But I do believe that we are facing the downfall of the almighty and deeply-rooted Newtonian paradigm that has for several centuries—with great success— explicitly or implicity supported all science, hard (natural) or soft (humanities including economy).

REFERENCES

Haken, H. 1981. *Erfolgsgeheimnisse der Natur.* Deutsche Verlag Stuttgart: (*The Science of Structure-Synergetics.* New York: Van Nostrand.)

Haken, H. 1983. *Synergetics,* Third Edition. Berlin: Springer-Verlag; *Advanced Synergetics.* Berlin: Springer-Verlag.

Mandelbrot, B. 1982. *The Fractal Geometry of Nature.* San Francisco: Freeman.

Nicolis, G. and Prigogine, I. 1977. *Self-Organization in Non-equilibrium Systems.* New York: J. Wiley.

Prigogine, I. and Stengers, I. 1984. *La Nouvelle Alliance.* Paris: Gallimard. (*Order out of Chaos: Man's New Dialogue with Nature.* New York: Bantam Books.)

Velarde, M. G. and Normand, C. 1980. "Convection." *Scientific American,* 243:92–108.

Velarde, M. G.,1982. *Dissipative Structures and Oscillations in Reaction-Diffusion Models with or without Time-delay in Stability of Thermodynamic Systems.* J. Casas and G. G. Lebon, editors. Berlin: Springer-Verlag.

Velarde, M. G., editor, 1984. *Non-Equilibrium Cooperative Phenomena in Physics and Related Fields.* New York: Plenum Press.

Verlade, M. G., editor, 1988, *Synergetics, Order, and Chaos,* London; World Scientific.

Verlade, M. G., editor, 1988, *Physicochemical Hydrodynamics: Interfacial Phenomena,* New York: Plenum Press.

Verlade, M. G. and Chu X. L., *Interfacial Instabilities,* London: World Scientific (in preparation).

16

Order Out of Chaos Through Fluctuations and Instabilities

CARL RAU

1. TOWARDS THE UNITY OF SCIENCES

In the past few decades, there has been enormous progress in our understanding of the behavior of matter under equilibrium and nonequilibrium conditions. By studying the self-organizing features of matter through fluctuations and instabilities, many scientific breakthroughs have been achieved. In particular, it has been found that fluctuations and instabilities can take a system away from an equilibrium state towards new steady states characterized by periodic or turbulent behavior.

By introducing *synergetic behavior* as a key feature in understanding and describing many systems, H. Haken has played a dominant role. He explains how unordered or disordered structures organize themselves and become spontaneously ordered. The new structures that appear are drastically different from those predicted by classical (equilibrium) thermodynamics.

These macroscopically ordered structures are created through the amplification of appropriate fluctuations. To characterize them, G. Nicolis and I. Prigogine introduce the term *dissipative structures*. On a macroscopic scale, these structures are stable under far-from-equilibrium conditions and can only be maintained and survive with a sufficient flow of energy and matter. Enormous progress has also been achieved in relating the formation of these macroscopic structures to the underlying microscopic mechanisms.

The most successfully applied tool in the study of the emergence of ordered structures was the mathematical theory of bifurcations. This theory describes the branching or bifurcation of solutions of nonlinear equations for certain critical values of a parameter or for certain boundary conditions imposed on a system. New types of solutions to nonlinear equations appear at the critical or bifurcation (branching) points. Using these methods, one can easily understand the emergence of ordering, of self-organization, of cooperative behavior or of chaotic behavior in various systems.

At present, it seems that these new concepts from the natural sciences can be successfully transferred to other sciences such as economics, sociology or political sciences. If carefully applied, they can provide important clues even for the understanding of nature and human culture, thus leading to the unity of the sciences.

2. DEFINITIONS AND ANALOGIES

Contrary to the situation prevailing in the past, in the present, our understanding of the origin and evolution of life on earth is no longer dependent on a specific ideology. Through carefully controlled experiments and detailed model studies, we are now capable of developing a deeper comprehension of the origin and evolution of life. We are now also in a period of transition. The new approaches towards arriving at a unified scientific picture of the universe involve man and nature and include all disciplines: physics, chemistry, biology, economics, psychology, sociology, etc.

For further discussion of these many new ideas and models, we refer the reader to the papers of Haken, Nicolis and Prigogine. The purpose of this article is not to review all these new models and ideas, but rather introduce a wider community of readers to a basic understanding of some specifically selected phenomena and guide them from the natural sciences to other sciences where the parameters than can be used to characterize the system, are often less well-defined and characterized.

In the following, using analogies, we discuss the possible meaning of well-established physical parameters in other sciences. Discussing such analogies, we create a new vocabulary which can guide us towards a unified picture of the world.

It is now generally accepted that the creation of ordered states in nature is a phenomenon related to the occurrence of large fluctuations and instabilities where one accidental fluctuation causes the breaking of symmetry in the system and enslaves other fluctuations thereby stabilizing the system towards ordered behavior. Or, in more common language: through the cooperation of the individual parts of a system, an *order parameter* is created. This order parameter *rules* the behavior of the individual parts, or, in the language of synergetics, we would say that the order parameter *enslaves* the individual parts which themselves create the order parameter by their cooperative behavior. For example, the members of a nation are enslaved by its language (order parameter).

Synergetics has been very successful in demonstrating that the creation of order out of chaos, or self-organized, collective behavior, is subject to fundamental laws and is independent of the specific system in which it is observed. We cite only a few fields where such general laws are found: magnetism, laser physics, cloud formation, the creation of a new fashion, the formation of public opinion.

In the past, theories of *ferromagnetism* (models of the creation of order out of chaos through collective behavior of atomic magnets) have been successfully applied to a variety of systems. A characteristic of ferromagnets is the occurrence of a phase transition (transition from disorder to order, or from order to disorder).

In the disordered, nonmagnetic state, the atomic magnets can be aligned in all directions (highly symmetric state), whereas in the ordered, magnetic state, the atomic magnets are aligned along one direction (state of low symmetry) and hence produce a macroscopic order (the so-called magnetization). Or, in more common language: order in the *microscopic* world produces strength (magnetization) in the *macroscopic* world. In the critical, disorder-order *transition region,* the system is dominated by large fluctuations and instabilities. The breaking of symmetry then occurs through an accidental fluctuation.

In a recent article, Callen and Shapero report on the occurrence of order in a variety of systems and discuss structural similarities. *Magnets* break symmetry in *groups:* they align parallel to each other. *Fish* break symmetry in *groups:* they also align parallel to each other. *People* break symmetry in *groups:* they become angry, they wear hair or skirts of the same length. Note that, although the causes of the orientation of atomic magnets, of fish or of people may be completely different, the statistical behavior of an ensemble of magnets, fish or people may show interesting similarities allowing a quantitative discussion of these phenomena within the framework of the theories of magnetism.

What quantity acts as the *order parameter* in the various systems mentioned above? In magnets, it is the angular orientation of the atomic magnets; in laser light, it is the electric field strength; in groups of fish, it is the alignment of the fish along a common direction; in groups of people, it is the length of hair or skirts; in groups of persons, it is the orientation of public opinion. What is the *important* (stochastic) variable in a specific system possessing a phase transition? In magnets, it is the temperature; in lasers, the analogous variable is the population inversion; in sociology, however, one may ask, what is a social temperature? At present, there is no answer to this question. Here, we point out that great care has to be taken in applying models originally developed for physical systems (and all the consequences following from them) to social or political systems. Nevertheless, we believe, that through the application of statistical methods, these attractive analogies will be made quantitative.

3. EXAMPLES IN THE NATURAL SCIENCES

In 1900, Bénard observed that the heat flow in a liquid can occur through a *macroscopic rolling motion* of the liquid (Bénard convection). Heating a liquid from the bottom and maintaining a *small* temperature gradient between the bottom and the top of the liquid, the heat flow occurs by heat conduction (microscopic laminar heat flow) and *no* macroscopic motion of the liquid can be observed. For these conditions, there exists a steady, non-equilibrium, linear, vertical temperature profile. When the temperature difference between the bottom and the top is increased above a critical value (characterized by a given Reynolds number), turbulence (chaos) begins to occur with the onset of a *macroscopic* motion in the liquid. The system becomes unstable through the creation of large fluctuations (convection instability) and a collective macroscopic motion sets in. It is observed that hot drops in the liquid perform a rolling motion in an ordered manner. It is also observed that a *minor* fluctuation initiates a collective type of motion which becomes a macroscopic rolling motion of the liquid. In the language of synergetics, we would say that one accidental fluctuation enslaves the others and stabilizes the system. The breaking of symmetry occurs through the accidental selection of a clockwise or anticlockwise direction of the rolling motion. This is an example of evolution of a system towards a macroscopic motion in *one* direction.

The laser, a well-known powerful light source in use for several decades, is another most interesting example of self-organization in a physical system.

The experimental arrangement of a laser system is comparable to a gas discharge tube possessing mirrors at its ends. The mirrors help to increase the residence time of the light waves in the tube. In general, one mirror is slightly transparent. This then allows for the emission of light from the tube. Gas atoms in the tube radiate through spontaneous (random, accidental) and stimulated emission of light waves. Stimulated emission can be induced by a light wave forcing an atom to radiate *in phase* with the light wave. This effect helps to increase the intensity of that specific light wave. In a laser, single waves compete with each other to achieve stimulated emission of light from other atoms. The mirrors help to keep axial waves within the tube for a long time. Accidentally, the intensity of a wave which fits perfectly between the mirrors can be increased by stimulated emission of light from other atoms. This light wave, which can act as an order parameter, becomes more and more dominant in the system and enslaves other waves, forcing the other atoms to radiate in phase. At some point, the system exhibits self-organization and one observes sudden macroscopic ordering (as in magnetism) resulting in the *coherent* (single phase) emission of light waves from the system. We observe then the emission of sudden, intense light flashes. The transition from ordinary light emission to laser light emission occurs at a critical point where the electric current in the tube is large enough to provide a balance between the energy loss caused by waves leaving the system and by the energy gain due to stimulated emission. Therefore, lasers represent open systems far from thermal equilibrium, in contrast to magnetic systems, which are closed systems in thermal equilibrium. However, in the critical region, they both can successfully be described by theories of phase transitions.

4. FROM PHYSICS TO OTHER SCIENCES

At present, there exists no complete and unified theory of self-organization that can be applied to all systems occurring in nature. Important progress, however, has recently been achieved by applying physical theories, especially theories of magnetism, to sciences other than physics. In 1971, Weidlich applied physical models (the famous Ising model of ferromagnetism), after appropriate redefinition and reinterpretation of the fundamental concepts, to sociological phenomena. He discussed the structural similarity between an ensemble of interacting atomic magnets in thermal equilibrium, and a group of human individuals interacting in a society. He gave a sociological interpretation of the Ising model, reinterpreted it to make it applicable to sociological groups, and then described polarization phenomena in social groups which, he claims, allow a quantitative comparison between the model and reality. Using the predominant public opinion as the order parameter, he asked: are revolutions predictable, or, can people be influenced, or, how can a change of public opinion take place? The answer to these challenging questions is that it is the fluctuations (opinions of a small group of people) that can become decisive and can cause the formation of a new and ordered political structure in a nation. Near a transition from order to disorder (or disorder to order), where large fluctuations exist, the response of a system to an external stimulus is very large. Therefore, it pays to influence the political opinion in that region. This can be done by using a small group of polarized people to flip (in a crisis) large groups of people towards a newly oriented (ordered) structure.

Further interesting examples of ordered systems, where theories on magnetism can successfully be applied, are: midges fly stationary in clouds; ducks fly suddenly in one direction; fish break symmetry and align in schools; insects fire light flashes collectively and synchronously; humans follow collectively the dictates of fashion (group thinking); millions of people become collectively and simultaneously impressed with one delusion (military glory, religious scruples, new political directions, etc.).

From the above, it is clear that a unified description of a large number of very different systems occurring in nature can be directly achieved by applying theories of phase transitions. The picture of ordering (alignment, polarization) of atomic magnets is transferred to the ordering of fish, insects, human beings, social groups, societies and nations.

We are still left with many questions. To name a few: what causes the orientation of atomic magnets? Is it the interaction between neighboring atomic magnets? Or: what causes the orientation of the public opinion? Is it the interaction of the individual with his or her neighbors?

Despite the lack of this knowledge on a *microscopic* scale (behavior of an individual: fish, insect, human being, etc.), we are able to make qualitative and quantitative predictions about the behavior of a system (group of fish, insects, society, nation,) on a *macroscopic* scale.

In many examples, we discussed the creation of order out of chaos. What about the creation of chaotic behavior in a system? Is chaos in synergetics (the theory of cooperation) a contradiction? Here the answer is that a synergetic system can often be governed by many order parameters which cooperate. During the course of evolution, the order parameters can also *compete* with each other. For a certain period of time, one order parameter *enslaves* the others, then another order parameter dominates. It is this change in domination that is totally irregular (chaotic).

REFERENCES

Bénard, H. 1900. *Rev. Gen. Sci. Pures. Appl.,* 12:1261.

Callen, E. and Shapero, D. 1974. "A theory of social imitation." *Physics Today,* 27:7.

DeGiorgio, V. and Scully, M. 1970. *Physical Review A,* 2:1170.

Haken, H. 1981. *Erfolgsgeheimnisse der Natur.* (Stuttgart: Deutsche Verlags-Anstalt), and 1983, *Synergetics.* (Berlin: Springer).

Morrow, J. 1948. *Quarterly Review of Biology.* 23:27.

Nicolis, G. and Prigogine, I. 1977. *Self-Organization in Nonequilibrium Systems.* (New York: Wiley).

Prigogine, I. 1984. *Order out of Chaos.* (New York: Bantam Books).

Weidlich, W. 1971. *British Journal of Mathematics and Statistical Psychology.* 24:251.

Contributors

Marcelo Alonso is President of Technoconsult; formerly Executive Director of Florida Institute of Technology Research and Engineering, Inc., Melbourne, Florida.

Bulent Atalay is Professor of Physics, Mary Washington College, Fredericksburg, Virginia.

Robert U. Ayres is at the Department of Engineering and Public Policy, Carnegie-Mellon University, Pittsburgh, Pennsylvania.

Jacob D. Bekenstein is at the Department of Physics, Ben-Gurion University, Beersheva, Israel.

Harald Fritzsch is Professor of Theoretical Physics, University of Munich and Max Planck Institute of Physics, Munich, West Germany.

Nicholas Georgescu-Roegen is Distinguished Professor of Economics Emeritus, Vanderbilt University, Nashville, Tennessee.

Max Jammer is a professor with the Association for Advancement of Science, Jerusalem, Israel.

Percy Löwenhard is Associate Professor of Psychology, Psychology Institute, University of Goteborg, Goteborg, Sweden.

Angelo M. Petroni is a member of the Instituto di Metodologia, Torino, Italy.

Guido Pincheira is Professor of Genetics, Faculty of Sciences, University of Chile, Santiago, Chile.

Gerard Radnitzky is Professor of Philosophy of Science, University of Trier, Trier, West Germany.

Carl Rau is in the Department of Physics, Rice University, Houston, Texas.

Roman U. Sexl (deceased) was Professor of Physics, Institute of Theoretical Physics, University of Vienna, Vienna, Austria.

George Sussmann is Professor of Theoretical Physics, University of Munich, Munich, West Germany.

Manuel G. Velarde is at the Department of Physics, Universidad Nacional Educion Distancia, Madrid, Spain.

Claude A. Villee, Jr. is Andelot Professor of Biological Chemistry, Laboratory of Human Reproduction and Reproductive Biology, Harvard University Medical School, Boston, Massachusetts.

Index

and gravitation, 1–23
inflationary cosmology, 17
matter density, 62–64
order in, 18–20
see also Galaxies
Lattice. *See* Microtrabecular lattice
Lenticular galaxies, 5, 8
Leptons
family classifications, 46
unity of, 47–50
Liberal democracy vs. totalitarian
state, 182
Liberty, 198, 200
Life
complexity, 107–109
conditions for, 130
and consciousness, 138–139
functions, 129
see also origin of life
Lifshitz's calculation of gravitational
radiation, 2–3
Liquid layers, 256–257
Living systems
basic characteristics, 92–93
chance occurrence, 131
complexity, 107–109, 129–133
vs. computers, 212
emerging properties, 130
enzyme sites, 77
general aspects, 90–91
genetic program, 93
genome structure and dynamics,
90–93
homeostasis, 110
information transfer, 133–137
mind and reality, 126–154
Monod's model, 92
self-organization, 127, 129–133
see also Eukaryotic cells
Logic, 237
Lysosomes, 119

Magnetism. *See* Ferromagnetism
Man
civilized against will, 177–178
rule-following model, 188n
see also Evolution

Market order, 169–170
institutional framework, 170–174
rationality of, 197–198
Markets
function of, 202n
impersonal, 168–169
real vs. free, 191n
Matter density in large structures,
62–64
Maximization, Eigen's principle,
208–209
Maxwell's demon, 207, 229
Medulla oblongata, evolutionary states,
142
Memory
brain states, 147–148
multi-level intricacy, 147
objects and events, 138, 143, 147
Messages, types of, 149
Microtrabecular lattice, 111
Microtubules and microfilaments,
119–120
Microwave background radiation,
2–3, 14
Miller-Urey hypothesis of chemical
evolution, 71–72
Mind
defined, 138
holistic phenomenon, 139
mapping, 126–154
and reality, 126–154
see also Brain
Misner's hypothesis of chaotic
universe, 16
Mitochondria, 119
Molecular chaos, 38
Molecular systems
Cairns-Smith model, 74–75
chemical evolution, 70–72
genetic takeover, 73–75
mathematical model, 76–83
polymerization, 72–73
self-replicating, 69–88
Monod's model of living systems, 92
Monomers
autocatalytic capability, 84–85
chemical evolution, 77–79